Abstracts of Account Books of Edward Dixon

Merchant of Port Royal, Virginia

Volume II: 1747-1752

Ruth and Sam Sparacio

The Antient Press Collection
from

Colonial Roots
Millsboro, Delaware
2016

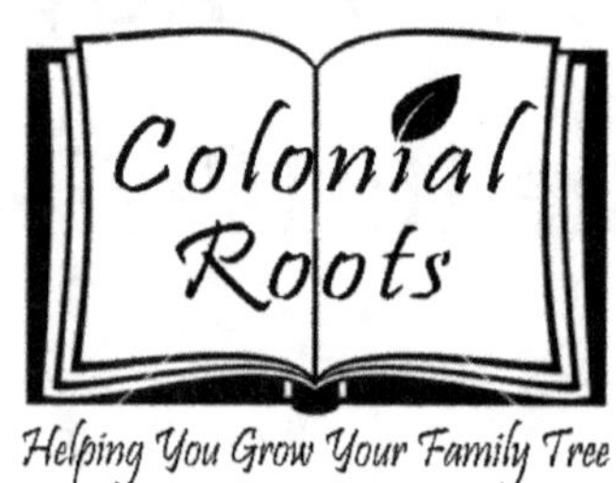

ISBN 978-1-68034-110-2

Printed February 2016

Originally printed 1991 by The Antient Press
Printed in the United States of America

CONTENTS

[this page intentionally blank]

The Paper of
EDWARD DIXON
Volume II

- (p. 1). July 30, 1747. The Debit Account of THOMAS APPERSON.(no purchases made, ballance brought forward from Ledger F. No Credits shown.

- (p. 1). July 30, 1747. The Debit Account of ISAAC ARNOLD SENR. Debit brought forward from Ledger F. (p. 229). 3 Sept. 1747: purchase of cloth. pr. shoe buckles, 2 bushells of Salt, a rusty pen knife, 1 m. 3d nails, a drinking glass; 23 November 1747: a Linen handkerchief, various materials and thread; 1/2 lb. Pepper; Sundrys from day book pr. yr: Wife; a dozen breast buttons, pr mens shoes, pr. hose buckles, To your rent for the year 1747 (7 shillings); 1748: Sundrys bought at RANKINS's Outcry; To Cr. of CLEMENT RICE; 2 barrells of Corn at the Mill & here at home; 2 barrells of do of Colo. LOMAX; pd. Capt. STROTHER 1 levy; several more kinds of materials, 3 felts, 50 20d. nails, a pr. of mens shoes; a fine lock; dozen pipes, a boys felt; Debit account ends 10th October 1748; Credit account: by 4 empty Hogshds., by 3 crop Notes, by 3 casks; By ballance carried forward p. 135).

- (p. 1). July 30, 1747. The Debt Account of WILLIAM ALLISON. To your Acct. from Ledger F, fol: (21); (This entry has been torn): To a Curry Comb & brush; 92 foot of 1 1/2 plank, 9 foot inch do; a pr. of slippers; (Credit Account torn.)

- (p. 2). July 30, 4747. The Debit Account of JOHN ALLAN. To your Acct. from Ledger F, fo: (34). Several purchases of material; an Ivory Comb; 1/2 lbs of powder and shott; To your Debt to Mr. KNIGHTON. The Credit accounts shows severall tobacco payments, in April 1751 payment by Mr. ROSE, by 2 months wages; By work done to this day (April 10, 1753); By work done to WM. MARSHALLs House.

- (p. 2). July 30, 1747. The Debit Account of MARGARET ARNOLD carried forward and paid.. The Debit Account of BENJAMIN ARNOLD carried forward, no Credit entries;

- (p. 2). July 30, 1747; The Debit Account of WEEDON ARNOLD carried forward from Ledger F, fo (105); September 26; To your Promissory Note for SAML. WHEELER; 16 October: To 2 packs Cards; To 1 Mattox Note; Purchases of Bohea and green Tea; 1949: pr. womens shoes; (The Contra Account is torn.)

- (p. 3). July 30, 1747; The Debit Account of JAMES ARNOLD carried forward from Ledger F fo: (147); purchased two shoe knives; several amounts of material; March 30, 1748: pd. JUDY JOHNSONs Levy; pd. JOHN ROACH; Debit account ends 8 Sept. 1749. The Credit Accounty 30th March 1748 payment of Hogshd. of tobacco and cask; July 15th 1749 paid by Capt. JOS: STROTHER; 5th December 1750 pd. by ISAAC ARNOLD JUNR. Account paid in full.

- (p. 3). July 30, 1747. The Debit Account of ISAAC ARNOLD JUNR. carried forward from Legder F, fol: (243); 19 October 500 6d nails; 30th November pd. Mrs. JONES; purchases of thread, cotton, pepper; pins, 1 1/2 bushells of salt and 250 6d nails. April 2, 1748, To sundrys purchased at RANKINS's Outcry; June 5, 2 felts; 30 August Cr. WM. WHITE pr. yr. Note; 25 October: To Cr. JOHN & JAMES RANKINS; (ballance of Debit Account torn). Credit Account shows payments by a number of empty hogsheads and a ballance carried forward to p. 144.

- (p. 4). July 30, 1747. The Debit Account of EDWARD ALMOND brought forward; no additional entries; no entries in the Credit account.

- (p. 4). July 30, 1747. The Debit Account of Mrs. MARY ASHTON brought forward with entry: 1 bushel Salt by Mr. SHROPSHIRE; 1 pr. of Gloves purchased in January. The Credit account shows payment in full; party by Cash of Mr. SHROPSHIRE.

- (p. 4). July 30, 1747. The Debit Account of JOHN ANDERSON at HOLDSWORTHs carried forward from Ledger F. fo. (47); an enry: To your Promise for Widow HACKLEY; No entries in the Credit Account.

- (p. 4). July 30, 1747. The Debit Account of Mr. CHARLES ASHTON carried forward from Ledger F (155). purchased 25 10d. nails. 23 December 1747: To Cr. JOHN JOHNSON pr. your Note; 4 bushels of Salt; 23d. March: To pd. ROBERT GILCHRIST; pd. PATRICK MITCHELL; to WM. WHITEs Order; to WM. WHITEs Ballance; 1748: To 1 pr. Womens Shoes by JAS. BERRYMAN; 100 8d. nails; 11 1/4 bushels of Salt. 1752; 1 gallon of Wine; A torn Credit Account shows two payments by Cash and a cash payment of JAMES BERRYMAN

- (p. 5). July 30, 1747. The Debit Account of THOMAS BARTLETT carried foreard from Ledger F (263); August 17: pd. WILLIAM MARSHALLs Judgmt. agt. you; levy for DAVID JONES; part of NORMANs Levy; Credit Capt. SKINKER; purchases of cloth, salt, nails &c., pd. JOSIAH FARGUSONs Clerks Fees; The Credit Account shows ballance carried forward; a payment by WM. COATON, and ballance carried forward to Fo. (123).

- (p. -5). July 30, 1747. The Debit Account of Capt. JOSEPH BERRY carried forward from Ledger F. fo. (235): purchases of paper, cloth, pr. Spectacles, thread; To Cr. DAVID ROBINSON pr. yr. Note; 1748: purchases 2 ruggs; side saddle & furniture; a snaffle bridle; cloth, mettle buttons; To your Assumpsit for yr. Son; BENJA.; nails, pr. mens shows; shoe buckles, hose, paper, cloth, drawing knife; The Credit Account shows payments by Crop Notes; pd yr. 5 Leases; by JOS: STEWARD; for Six days surveying; by JOS: BERRY JUNR. (Appears Account paid)

- (p. -6). July 30, 1747. Debit Account of JOHN BROWN carried forward from Ledger F fo: (54); several purchases of Cloth added; 1/2 bushell Salt yr. Brother, JERE: The Credit Account shows payaments by Mr. MOORE; by Cash; by SAML. SIMS, by Capt. EDWARD DIXON; account paid in full.

- (p. 6). November 14, 1747. Debit Account of BENJAMIN BERRY (Capt. BERRYs Son: Purchased a yd. of Irish, 5 yds. of white Duffle, 1/2 doz. Coat buttons; The Credit Account shows payment in full by Capt. JOS: BERRY.

- (p. 6.) July 30, 1747. Debit Account of NEWMAN BROWN carried forward from Ledger F. fo. (268). Additional purchases include a saddle & bridle; 1 boys castor; cloth, buttons, salt, powder & shott, nails; ivory comb; pd. Capt. STROTHERs 3 levys; The Credit Account shows payments by JAMES STIGLERs bond; by WM. DODGINS bond; by Mr. ALLENs Bond; by Mr. ROSE bond; by PATK. COUTTS.

- (p. 7). July 30, 1747. Debit Account of HENRY BERRY JUNR. carried forward from Ledger F fo. (79); purchases of cloth, a linen handkerchief, gunpowder added. The Credit Account shows a credit of his Account against me; (Capt. DIXON).

- (p. 7). May 25, 1748; The Debit Account of Mr. JAMES BOWIE shows purchase of 48 foot Inch Plank. No Credit Account entries.

- (p. 7). July 30, 1747. The Debit Account of CHRISTOPHER BELL carried forward from Ledger F, fo: (103), no additional purchases. Credit Account shows payment by RICHD. BERNARD in Tobo: in full of the Debit.

- (p. 7). July 30, 1747. The Debit Account of ANDREW BEARD carried forward from Ledger F, fo: (124); with additional entry for purchase of a bushel of Salt. The Credit Account shows a payment by Majr. WAGENER.

- (p. 7). July 30, 1747. The Debit Account of SAMUEL BROWN carried forward from Ledger F, fo: (126); no additional purchases; no entries in Credit Account.

- (p. 7). July 30, 1747. The Debit Account of Mr. JAMES BERRYMAN. In 1748 purchased 2 bushells of Salt; and a Credit to JOHN JAMES; in 1749 another 1 1/2 bushels Salt. The Credit Account shows a payment by cash (apparently for Account in full.)

- (p. 8). July 31, 1747. The Debit Account of Mr. JAMES BOWIE carried forward from Ledger F. fo: (110): among additional purchases; 31 gallons of Beer; 2 qts. Linseed Oyl; a mans hatt; To yr. Note Cr. to LAWR: SMITH for 16 panes Glass; 50 bushells of Salt; gallon of Wine; bushel salt to Capt. CAMPBELL; bushel do. to Negro Sarah; a considerable quantity of Beef; The Credit Account shows payments by WEEDON ARNOLD; by 30 lbs. Myrtle Wax; by Mr. MARMOCK; and credit for a number of articles returned.

- (p. 8). July 31, 1747. Debit Account of ELIZABETH BROWN carried forward from Ledger F, fo: (153; and additional purchase of 1/2 bushels of Salt, a pr. of womens shoes and 3 1/2 yds. of Linen. The Credit Account shows payments by ISAAC GREEN, by Capt. DIXON; account paid in full.

- (p. 8). A Debit Account of JAMES BOWIE dated in 1751 is faded and torn; no entries in the Credit Account.

- (p. 8). July 31, 1747. The Debit Account of JOHN BILLING (LOMAX's Overseer) carried forward from Ledger F, fo: (153); no additional entries; no entries in Credit Account

- (p. 9). July 10, 1747. The Debit Account of Mr. RICHARD BUCKNER carried forward from Ledger F, fo: (191); some additional entries shows cash paid at Caroline Court; protested Bill; interest on several Notes; to a Bond taken; and on 22 June 1752, 6 gallons & 3 pints of Wine. The Credit Account shows payment of 30 barrels of Corn; by 5 30 gallon barrels, by JAMES BOWIE, by WM. BOWLER. The Credit Account shows payment except the 1752 purchase of Wine.

- (p. 9). July 31,1747. The Debit Account of GEORGE BROWNE carried forward from Ledger F, fo. (133); some additional debits: powder and shott; cloth, breast buttons; salt, 1 felt., 750 10d nails.; The Credit Account shows payments by a Light hogd. tobo: & cask; 2 bushels of Beens, a Transfer Note; 2 cash payments; Debit still due brot: forward.

- (p. 9). September 22, 1748. The Debit Account of PRUE BENSON include a box iron, a linnen handkerchief, 2 empty hogsheads; The Credit Account shows a Cash payment (apparently in full of Account; Debit amount torn off).

- (p. 10). July 31, 1747. The Debit Account of JOHN BODDINGTON carried forward from Ledger F, fo: (148); additional purchases include Salt, 4 entries of powder & shott; cloth; 1/4 lb. Powder by WM. MARSHALL SENR., The Credit Account shows payment in full by one cash payment and by work done.

- (p. 10). July 31, 1747. The Debit Account of COSSUM BENNETT carried forward from Ledger F, fo: (155); with one additional Entry: To MASON FRENCHs Debt from Do. The Credit Account shows payment of account in full by Cash.

- (p. 10). July 9, 1748. The Debit Account of Mr. ENOCH BERRY shows one purchase of 2 broad hoes. The Credit Account shows a payment by GEO: WRINGLESBY for the account in full.

- (p. 10). July 31, 1747. The Debit Account of JOHN BRYAN at Mountains carried forward from Ledger F, fo: (154); no additional purchases entered; no entries in the Credit Account

- (p. 10). July 31, 1747. The Debit Account of WILLIAM BAILEY carried forward from Ledger F, fo: (29); no additional purchases entered; no entries in Credit Account.

- (p. 11). July 31, 1747. The Debit Account of EDWARD BALLANCE carried forward from Ledger F., fo: (173); some additiona purchases 1/2 bushel of Salt; a tin Quart pot; a dozen breast button, 1 yds. Tartan and part of a pr. of Scissors. No entries in the Credit Account

- (p. 11). August 15, 1748. Debit Account of Mrs. BERRYMAN at the MILL shows a purchase of a bushel of Salt; and a payment in the Credit Account May 26, 1752 by Mr. JAMES BERRYMAN the amount in full.

- (p. 11). July 31, 1747. The Debit Account of ROBERT BENSON carried forward from Ledger F. fo: (205); some additional purchases 1 felt; 500 10d nails; cloth, a bushell of Salt, thread, silk laces, 2 lbs. of Shott; a pr. of girls shoes; yarn hose, pd. WM. TURLANDs. Levy; The Credit Account shows several payments in Tobo: and a notation: "ballanced in Parish Book.)

- (p. 12). July 31, 1747. The Debit Account of FRANCIS BALTROP carried forward from Ledger F. fo: (251); some additional purchases, 3 horn combs; 30 gallons of Ale; to Cash; To Ballance in a Japan'd Mug; To paid your Note to GEO: HARRISON; 4 bushells of Salt. 1 bottle Stroughtons Drops; 2 glasses; purchases of cloth in 1750; The Credit Account shows payments by JOHN STROTHER (twice), by a lb. of Shoe Thread, by Cash in full; the 1750 purchases paid by 3 Transfer Notes and payment by WM. HARRISON

- (p. 12). July 31, 1747. The Debit Account of Mr. THOMAS BUNBERRY carried forward from Ledger F, fo: (27). April 17, 1748 made three purchases of Cloth. The Credit Account shows partial payment November 3, 1749 by Mr. HOOE and balance paid March 2, 1748/9.

- (p. 12). October 24, 1747. The Debit Account of WILLIAM BOWLING; To your ballance due from day book this day; purchases of Salt, a mealsifter, thread & cloth; in 1748, 2 yds. Irish, 1/2 m Pins, 1/2 lb. power, 2 lbs. shott.1/2 bushell salt; in December 1749 2 1/2 bushels of salt. The Credit Account shows several payments by tobacco and by one Note on BOYDS HOLE (the account appears to be paid, Debit account ballance torn off.)

- (p. 13). July 31, 1747. The Debit Account of GRACE BERRY Muddy Creek carried forward from Ledger F. fo: (56); The Credit Account shows payment in full in 1748 "by charged yr: Son, JAMES."

- (p. 13). July 31, 1747. The Debit Account of GRACE BERRY King George carried forward from Ledger F, fo: (69); The Credit Account shows payment in full 8 September 1747 "by cash by Capt. STROTHER."

- (p. 13); July 31, 1747. The Debit Account of Mr. WILLIAM BERRYMAN carried forward from Ledger F, fo: (28); with additional purchase of 1 bushell of salt in 1477 and a bushel of salt in April 1748; The Credit Account shows two cash payments in 1748 for the ballance in full.

- (p. 13). July 31, 1747. The Debit Account of EDWARD BURGE carried forward from Ledger F, fo: (196); shows additional purchases through 29 April 1749 of 1 m. 6d nails, 500 10d. nails, an ivory comb, a horn do; 1/2 lb. of pepper; 2 bushels of Salt powder and shott, a thimble, 500 8d. nails, 300 10d. nails; further purchases of nails salt and 11 3/4 yards of Drogheda. The Credit Account shows two payments by tobacco and by the cask (the account appears to be paid, Debit account ballance torn off).

- (p. 14). July 31, 1747. The Debit Account of JAMES BANKHEAD carried forward from Ledger F, fo: (127); with additional entries through 1752 of 1 Best Curb Bridle, 1 crupper; 6 gallons Madeira Wine; To your Account with ROBT. RANKINS for Vinegar; 5 gallons of Wine and three entries for cash lent; The Credit Account shows a payment by NEWMAN BROWN, a cash payment to settle the account.

- (p. 14). July 31, 1747. The Debit Account of WILLIAM BEDDEL Bricklayer, carried forward from Ledger F, fo: (141), not additional purchases. The Credit Account shows no entries.

- (p. 14). July 31, 1747. The Debit Account of JOHN BUTLER carried forward from Ledger F, fo: (256); with a number of purchases made through 22 December 1748 including 1 felt; 2 yds. bro: linnen; 1 m 8d. nails, 1 pr. womens shoes; 5 yds. Oznabrigs and other cloth; 1/2 m pins, a hammer, salt; The Credit Account shows partial payment by 1 hhd. of tobacco and by the cask.

- (p. 14). July 31, 1747; The Debit Account of GEORGE BEARD carried forward from Ledger F, fo: (77); no additional purchases; The Credit Account shows a payment by Majr; WAGGENER, in full of the account

- (p. 15). July 31, 1747. The Debit Account of JOSEPH BERRY, Capt. BERRYs Son; carried forward from Ledger F., fo: (160); with additional purchases through December 1750 which include a razor, cloth, thread, pr. mens shoes, 42 lbs. of Brown Sugar; "To your Father's ballance," "To pd. yr. ordr. to WM. PARKER," The Credit Account shows payment in full by 1750 by part of a cagg Cyder, by cash, by 30 barrels of Corn and by ROBT. GILCHRIST.

- (p. 15). July 31, 1747. The Debit Account of JOHN BOON carried forward from Ledger F, fo: (57); additional entries include 1 felt by ANN FURLONG; 5 yds. of Cotton by ANN FURLONG; a bushell of salt; to yr. bond of ye date; to interest; to paid Majr. MURDOCK; To ballance of yr. bond; to Cash. The Credit Account shows a payment by Bond the 10th August 1748 and a Transfer note. In both accounts the notation: By your Bond payable 25th Decr. next 1086. 12/6.

- (p. 15). July 31, 1747. The Debit Account of JOHN BEVERSHAM carried forward from Ledger F, fo: (86); additional purchases of cloth, a pr. of mens shoes, a linen handkerchief and a pr. of Yarn Hose. The Credit Account shows two cash payment for the debit in full.

- (p. 16). July 31, 1747. The Debit Account of JAMES BUTLER at Mrs. JONES's carried forward from Leger F, fo: (91); no additional entries; The Credit Account shows a payment by Mrs. JONES in Cash, account paid in full.

- (p. 16). July 31, 1747. The Debit Account of Colo. WILLIAM BEVERLEY for purchases through April 10, 1748 which include 1 pr. Girls Silver Laced Morrocco Shoes; carried forward from Ledger F, fo: (66); "Tocash at WMS:BURG last April," "To Cash recd. of the Treasurer," "To your Interest on a Bond to S. SKINKER," "To cash at Caroline Court," "To EDMOND PENDLETONs Order," "This Account Ballanced." The Credit Account shows by cash pd. BEVERLEY WHITING for Capt. Peirce and a cash payment; This account is ballanced.

- (p. 16). July 31, 1747. The Debit Account of PETER BELEN carried forward from Ledger F, fo: (79); with an additional purchase of 3 yds. Drogheda in October. The Credit Account shows one payment by tobacco.

- (p. 17). July 31, 1747. The Debit Account of Majr. JOHN CHAMPE carried forward from Ledger F, fo: (117); with a number of additiona entries including, To THOMAS ROSS Exchange; To forty pr. Cent on do; To sundry checks sent you a pr Acct. therewith; To 65 gallons of Ale; To 6 lbs. Hops; To Credit Mr. SAML. SKINKER fo: (82); To 314 foot Inch Plank p Note by DANL. McCOY; To Cash pd. Mr. BLACK; To Colo. NAT: GRAY; To Prince William Transfer Notes; To 2 Prince William Notes; To 3 lbs. Hyson Tea - Lent; To Mr. JOHN WASHINGTONs Order; To my order on Mr. CHAS: DICK; To 300 40d. Nails p NICHO: FRY; To paid JAMES STIGLER by yr: Note; To 58 Gallons Ale; To 11 hhds. tobo: at FALMOUTH; 10 hhds. at GIBSONS; 1 do at ROYs. 295 foot 1 1/4 Plank; To MORTONs Crop Note; To 2 loaves of refined Sugar; To 11 Crop Notes (Account through 23d July 1752); The Credit Account shows By cash paid Capt. HALLs for 63 lbs. Rope; By a Bale Drogheda Linnen; By cash; By HARRY TURNER cash; By JOHN STROTHERs Order; By JOHN TRIPLETT; By Cash 20 Pistoles; By 1 bag Corks 17 gross; By MARTHA HELLIER for Doctor ALLISON; By 100 bushels of Salt; By WM. LONGMIRE for Sugar; By LUKE BURFORD. "This Account settled in Colo. CHAMPEs Book March 9th 1750." By cash sent p Major SKINKER; By a FALMOUTH Note; By Cr. on acct. of OLIVER TOWLES; (no indication account paid in full.)

- (p. 17). May 18, 1748. The Debit Account of Revd. Mr. ARCHIBALD CAMPBELL; account through 17 December 1750 includes 5 gallons of Madira Wine; 2 bushells of Salt, 2 Stears, 30 gallons of Wine & cask, 3 bushels of Salt. The Credit Account shows two payments by cash, account paid in full.

- (p. 17). July 31, 1747. The Debit Account of HENRY COPE carried forward from Ledger F, fo: (64), no additional entries. The Debit account shows a payment by RICHD. FRY, account paid in full.

- (p. 18). July 31, 1747. The Debit Account of JOHN CAVE, Prince William, carried forward from Ledger F, fo: (76), no additional purchases; The Credit Account shows no entries.

- (p. 18). July 31, 1747. The Debit Account of ROBERT CALL carried forward from Ledger F, fo: (161), with the following additions: To Cash; To Cr. ROBERT MONDAY, To 1 hogd. tobo: for your Rent; To pd. Capt. JOS: STROTHER; To Cash; The Credit Account shows payment by a hogd. tobo. for cash; By Colo. ANDREW MONROE; By Capt. CAMPBELL for a Lamb; Then a Debit Account added for purchases in 1749 of a boys felt, 100 8d. nails and a bushel of Salt. On March 4, 1749/50; "balanced by a Lamb."

- (p. 18). July 31, 1747. The Debit Account of OWEN CAMPBELL carried forward from Ledger F, fo: (268); with additional purchases which include cloth, pr. of womens shoes, thread, salt. 2 felts, pr. womens worsted hose pr MOSES RANKINS; pr. womens Pumps, a comb, a bason; The Credit Account shows payment in full by yr. acct. of Smiths Work to this day, By WM. FURLONGs Order; By ROBT. JOHNSON; By EDWARD DONOHOEs Cr., By ballance charged fo. (140).

- (p. 18). October 11, 1748. The Debit Account of LUKE BURFORD includes 33 gallons of Cyder; 64 gallons Rum; 29 gallons of Wine; a barrell of Ale of 29 gallons; another purchase of Ale of same quantity; 4 lbs. of Chocolate; 5 gallons & 3 qts. of Molasses. The Credit Account shows four cash payments, a payment by WILLIAM JOHNSON and one by HENRY JOHNSON; Ballance carried to fo: (141).

- (p. 19). 1747. The Debt account of Mrs. MARTHA CATLETT carried forward from Ledger F, fo: (131) and additional entry of December 16, 1748 of a case of Knives & Forks pr. WM. HAMPTON. The Credit Account shows a payment by 6 bushels of Wheat and a payment on July 18, 1949 by Colo. SPOTSWOOD; account paid in full.

- (p. 19). January 13, 1747/8. The Debit Account of STEPHEN CASH, ROBT. WALKERs Overseer. To 1/2 m Pins yr. Wife; 1/8 whitd. thread, 4 laces, 2 pr. sleeve buttons; 1 1/2 yds of Check; 2 1/2 yds Drogheda. The Credit Account shows a payment by ROBT. WALKER his Note, payment in full.

- (p. 19). July 31, 1747. The Debit Account of Mrs. MARY CATLETT carried forward from Ledger F, fo: (145); with one other entry: To yr: Debt to H: TURNER. The Credit Account shows a payment by JAMES BOWIE in Cash; account paid in full.

- (p. 19). July 31, 1747. The Debit Account of WILLIAM COCKRILL carried forward from Ledger F, fo: (177). No additional entries and no entries in Credit Account.

- (p. 20) July 31, 1747. The Debit Account of THOMAS CARVER carried forward from Ledger F, fo: (205). No additional entries. The Credit Account shows a payment by tobacco and two cash payments, account paid in full.

- (.20). July 31, 1747. The Debit Account of JOSEPH CLIFT carried forward from Ledger F, fo: (168). On July 14, 1748 purchased 5 yds. of Check; 1/4 lb. Brown thread; pr. mens worsd. hose; 1 knife & fork; on 28th April 1750 To a Lawyers fee & tobo: cost. The Credit Account shows three cash payments the last two 28th April 1750, account paid in full.

- (p. 20). July 31, 1747. The Debit Account of JOHN CHILTON in MATTOX carried forward from Ledger F, fo: (210); No additional entries. The Credit Account shows a payment by ROBT. GILCHRIST (appears account paid in full, Debit ballance torn off.)

- (p. 21). July 31, 1747; The Debit Account of Mr. SAMUEL COLEMAN carried forward from Ledger F., fo: (114); Additional entries for 1748 and 1749 include Dr: Colo. GAWIN CORBIN; To 2 horn combs & 4 butcher knives; 150 8d. nails, 2 bushells of Salt; a set of Shoemakers Tools, 15 lbs. of Chocolate; 100 10d. nails; To pd. ROBT. WALKER part of his Smiths Account; The Credit Account shows two payments by Cash; by Cash reced of Mr. GILCHRIST; By 7 hhds. of tobacco; by Colo. CHAMPE; account paid in full

- (p. 21). July 31, 1747. The Debit Account of CHARLES CARTER Esqr. carried forward from Ledger F, fo: (62). Additional entries include To 200 8d. nails pr. MACHEN; To your Assumpsit for HENRY MACHEN; To a Mahogany Board; To 2 bushells of Pease deliv'd CHAS. BENSON (retd.) (Account through November 2, 1750). The Credit Account shows By FRAN: WATS for ten bushells of Salt for my ELK RUN QTR., By Colo. ANDREW MONROE, By 2 bushels of pease retd., By CHAS. BENSON for 7 bushels Salt; By H. TURNER 16 bushels of Salt, By 1 qtr. Beef; (Accounts not totalled or ballanced)

- (p. 21). July 31, 1747. The Debit of ROBERT COLEMAN carried forward from Ledger F., fo: (121); No additional entries. The Credit Account shows "By Cash reced," account paid in full.

- (p. 22). July 31, 1747. The Debit Account of Mr. FRANCIS CONWAY carried forward from Ledger F, fo: (37). No additional entries. The Credit Account shows Credit brot. forward from Ledger F. fo: (37).

- (p. 22). July 31, 1747. The Debit Account of Mr. JOHN CORBIN, Portobago, carried forward from Ledger F., fo: 34). No additional entries. The Credit Accunt shows By yr: Exchange on JAS. BUCHANNON, By 35 p. cent on do; By Cash; account paid in full.

- (p. 22). July 31, 1747. The Debit Account of JOHN CLIFT carried forward from Ledger F, fo: (26); with additional entries, To 1 Caro: Hat by yr. Brother, ROBERT; 2 pr. of shoe buckles; an ivory comb; a Clasp knife, 2 tin pans; 4 bushels of Salt, To Lawyers Fee 7/6 cost of suit in tobo: 70. The Credit Account shows payment in cash and a payment by THOS: CARVER, account paid in full.

- (p. 23). July 31, 1747. The Debit Account of JOHN DOGINS carried forward from Ledger F, fo: (82). No additional entries. No entries in the Credit Account.

- (p. 23). July 31, 1747. the Debit Account of EDMOND DONOHOE carried forward from Ledger F, fo: (267). A number of entries through 20th of Aprill 1748 include many purchases of various kinds of cloth, thread, To 2 lbs. dble. refined Sugar by JNO: BROWN, To Cr. old JOHN KENDALL; 2 1/2 dozens coat buttons; nails, salt, ribbon, 1 snaffle bridle, pr. plaid hose; pr. mens shoes; linen handkerchief; ivory comb; pr large scissors; To Cr. OWIN CAMBLE; powder & shot; to 3 levies; To pd. Capt. FRANS: THORNTON on Acct. of H. TURNER There is no Credit account.

- (p. 23). July 31, 1747. The Debit Account of JOSEPH DODD carried forward from Ledger F, fo: (162); with additional entries through May 27, 1748 which include salt, cloth, powder and one best felt hat. The Credit Account shows a payment by DANL. WHITE, a payment by Cash; account paid in full.

- (p. 24). July 31, 1747. The Debit Account of SAMUEL DINGLE carried forward from Ledger F, fo: (192). No additional entries. The Credit Account of Aprill 18, 1748 shows "By your Acct. Taylors Work to this day." (Debit amount remains)

- (p. 24). April 18, 1748. The Debit Account of Mr. HENRY DRAKE shows three entries in 1748; To 6 1/2 gallons Madeira Wine @ 5/6; To a Pipe of Madeira Wine; To a cask Rum 72 gallons, 1 do 60. In 1750 two entries: To 111 galls Rum @ 3/10; To 30 galls. Wine & cask. The Credit Account shows 8 cash payments; By 2 gross bottles, By HARRY TURNER; by 1 1/2 gross bottles. Account paid in full.

- (p. 24). July 31, 1747. The Debit Account of Mr. SAMUEL DONNE carried forward from Ledger F, fo: (242). Additional entries through June 30, 1750 includes cloths, 3 small table mats; 1 lb. of Green Tea; To Old Transfer Notes on MORTONs; (Nov. 27, 1749) To JOHN BATTALEYs Claim as Clerk of the Court Martial; 12 gallons of Wine. The Credit Account shows payments in 1748: By 70 barrels of Corn; By 2009 lbs. of Pork; By JNO. POLLARD for BATTALEY. Account paid in full.

- (p. 24). October 24, 1747. The Debit Account of BENJAMIN DUNCAN shows three entries, two for total of 4 bushels of Salt, and one for Powder & shott. The Credit Account shows one Tobacco payment to pay account in full.

- (p. 25). July 31, 1747. The Debit Account of WILLIAM DODGIN carried forward from Ledger F, fo: (236); with additional entries through 1752 which include a gallon Madeira Wine pr. Note; paid JOSIAH FARGUSON; bushell Salt by yr: Negro; 50 3d. nails; 25 8d. Nails by Capt. SKINKER; 31 panes of Glass; (1752) To your Bond payable to B; MARSHALL. The Credit Account shows 3 pr. Hinges returned; By Gibsons Transfer Note; By yr. Acct. of Taylors work agt. JNO. MORRISON; By Colo. CHAMPE; By WM. BRUCE for Acct. of yr. Execution agt. Capt. ROBINSON; By Ball: of Taylors accot., By an error in 176 lbs. tobo: By cash reced of CATESBY COCKE. Account paid in full.

- (p. 25). July 31, 1747. The Debit Account of Mrs. SARAH DICK carried forward from Ledger F., fo: (14); with additional entries To 1 Oz. Nuns for Capt. DICK by DARCUS TANKERSLEY, To GEO: TANKERSLEYs Obligation; Ballance to T. T. Ledger 34. The Credit Account shows By Cash lodg'd in my hands by Capt. DICK; By GEO: TANKERSLEYs Obligation. Account paid in full.

- (p. 25). July 31, 1747. The Debit Account of LUCY DINGLE carried forward from Ledger F, fo: (12); with additional entries for various kinds of cloth, buttons and a Stear.

The Credit Account shows payments from August 20, 1747 through November 5, 1750 including By Cash by WM. MARSHALL JUNR; By your Parish Claim; By WM. LONGMIRE Cr., By yr. Acct. for bringing 2 wenches to bed; By do for 4 do; By do for 5 do. (A ballance appears due but not noted.)

- (p. 26). July 31, 1747. The Debit Account of FRANCIS DAY carried forward from Ledger F. fo: (257); No additional entries. The Credit Account shows an entry the 2d. of October 1751 By Majr. WAGGENER, (Account paid in full).

- (p. 26). July 31, 1747. The Debit Account of Mrs. ELIZABETH DEGG carried forward from Ledger F, fo: (65); No additional entries. The Credit Account shows an entry dated 1748 By JOHN MARTIN. (Account paid in full.)

- (p. 26). July 31, 1747. The Debit Account of JOHN EMBRY carried forward from Ledger F, fo: (208); No additional entries. No entries in the Credit Account

- (p. 26). July 31, 1747. The Debit Account of ARNOLD EDWARDS carried forward from Ledger F, fo: (4); No additional entries. No entries in the Credit Account

- (p. 27). August 1, 1747. The Debit Account of WILLIAM FURLONG carried forward from Ledger F, fo: (261); A long entry through October 26, 1748 includes a number of entries for cloth, salt, 1 fine felt to SHORTLEY, 1 small felt to do; pr. Womens Shoes to THOS: DEW; pr.mens worsd. hose to do; pd. THOMAS BURNET; pr. Womens shoes 5/6; pr. Womens hose 2/9; 2 thimbles, 1/4 lb. brown thread; 1 tinder box; pr. yarn hose; Cr. OWEN CAMPBELL; Cr. MARTHA HELLIER; 1 clasp knife, powder & shott; 2 barrells Corn at Colo. LOMAX's; pr. wool cards; 2 1/2 yds. Ozna. by yr. Wife; pr. Sissars; pr. womens shoes. The Credit Account shows By THOS: DEW, By tobo: By your Acct. agst. me to this day for Wheat & carting goods; By a Journey to DEEP CREEK; By PATRICK MITCHELL, By 1 pistole, Ballance due & charg'd in fo: (131).

- (p. 27). August 1, 1747. The Debit Account of HENRY FEWELL carried forward from Ledger F, fo: (63); with additional entries for October 5, 1747 including cloth, coat buttons, a pr. mens worsd. hose. The Credit Account shows a payment by ROBT. GREEN, the account paid in full.

- (p. 28). August 1, 1747. The Debit Account of RICHARD FRY carried forward from Ledger F, fo: (254). Entries through April 19, 1750; include 1 pint Japan Mug; 2 bushells Salt by EDWD. BALLANCE; To Cr. HENRY WARE; 1 m. 20d. nails; To cash Mr. RICHD. TUTT; pr. mens gloves; pr. worsd. hose; 1 mans fine hatt; pd. Capt. STROTHER 8 levies; Cr. BRIDGETT KIRTLEY pr. Note; 1 pr. Womens Mittins fine; 1 pr. womens shoes; 8 1/2 yards fine Linnen; 174 yards Red Tammeys; 1 close hair brush; pd. EDWD. JONES; pd. HENRY COPE; The Credit Account shows By Capt. SNEAD; By building me a Boat; by a barrel of Corn;by a FERRY BOAT; By Capt. DIXON. Account paid in full.

- (p. 28). August 1, 1747. The Debit Account of GEORGE FLETCHER carried forward from Ledger F, fo: (90); No additional entries. The Credit Account shows payment on April 20, 1748 by 1 BOYDS HOLE Note; by Cash; (small ballance due.)

- (p. 28). May 1746. The Debit Account of Messrs. SYDENHAM & HODGSON. To Cash pd. you by Mr. FORWARD. Febry: 7, 1747/8. To Sales of 7 hhds. p PERREY; To do 4 hhds. p

WILCOX; To Abatement on Insurance p *HAPPY JENNET* as she sail'd with convoy; (1749) To RICHD. BARNES Excha: Sent you; To do Capt. DONALDSONs; To Cash paid you by LYONEL LYDE. The Credit Account shows By Good p the *GRYMES*; By goods p the Restoration; By do p the *PHILLIS*, By do p the *HAPPY JENNET*, By charges on 7 hhds. cost.

- (p. 29). August 1, 1747. The Debit Account of Mr. RALPH FALKNER carried forward from Ledger F, fo: (151). One additional entry: To Interest on 11:15:9 from March 1747 to 18th Novr: 1748, 8 mos. The Credit Account shows ballance carried forward to folo: /63/

- (p. 29). August 1, 1747. The Debit Account of JOHN FARROL carried forward from Ledger F, fo: (114); with additional entries through May 1750; including purchases of cloth; pr. mens shoes. Cr. RICHD. ROBINSON, 1 felt; 1 pr. yarn hose; 1 felt hat; pd. WM. PARKER. The Credit Account shows one cash payment and By d8 1/2 barrels of Corn; account paid in full

- (p. 29). August 1. 1747. The Debit Account of JOHN FRANKLING carried forward from Ledger F, fo: (200); includes a number of additional entries through April 17, 1749; including cloth, nails, pr. shoe buckles, pr. sleeve buttons; salt; To Cr. ELIAS GRAVIT; To sundrys for ELIAS GRAVIT; To Cr. ELIZA: RIGGINS; The Credit Accounts shows payments by two hogsheads of tobacco and cask; a Crop Note on Gibsons; By Capt. DIXON, by Cash; account paid in full.

- (p. 30). August 1, 1747. The Debit Account of JOSIAH FARGUSON carried forward from Ledger F, fo: (190); with additional entries including 1 blew cloth howsen; 9 barrels of Corn; a bridle bitt omitted in Ledger F; powder & shott; To SARAH SETTLEs Debt; To WM. HUDSONs Debt & costs; To 2 stock locks. The Credit Account carries forward ballance from Ledger F, fo: (190); By sundry claims of tobo: By my Quit rents for Anno 1746; By ye 9 barrels of Corn credit given by his Tobacco accot. By an old Cash ballance

- (p. 30). August 1, 1747. The Debit Account of GEORGE FOX carried forward from Ledger F, fo: (164); with additional entries including; To Sundrys at RANKINS's Outcry; To Cash 1 pistole; To Cr. DANIEL McDONALD 1 bushell salt; cloth, salt, nails, 2 dozen bottles of Wine; 26 1/4 gallons Rum pr. Capt. BENJA: STROTHER; To 1 hhd. Rum qt. 118 Galls. @ 4/6 for wch: Capt. BENJA: STROTHER is security. "All paid in full" The Credit Account shows payments from July 16, 1748 through July 4, 1751; including: By Tobo. in RANKINS's Hogd., cash; hhd. tobacco; cash of WM. HARRISON;

- (p. 30). May 12, 1748. The Debit Account of Mr. JOHN BOUTWELL. To 12 fathom of Rope 8s. The Credit Account shows full payment by ( ) BOWIE.

- (p. 30). 1747. The Debit Account of WILLIAM FULLER carried forward from Ledger F, fo: (112; No additional entries. The Credit Account shows By Capt. GREENs Assumpsett (account paid in full)

- (p. 31).August 1, 1747. The Debit Account of JAMES FREEMAN carried forward from Ledger F, fo: (65). Additional entries include purchase of thread, laces, salt; To Cr. CATHARINE CALVIN; To your Wifes Debt from fo. (64); To pd. 6 levies @ 73 in Parish Book. The Credit Account shows payments through May 22, 1750 of 2 hogds. tobo: 2 casks, 2 1/2 pistoles in cash; by WM. FURLONG; By a crop note. (account paid in full)

- (p. 31). August 1, 1747. The Debit Account of DANIEL FARGUSON, Doctor, carried forward from Ledger F, fo: (56); with additional entries for cloth, 1 pr. best pumps, ribbon, thread, 1 castor hat, 1 bottle wine, 1 qt. Madeira Wine. The Credit Account shows payment October 21, 1748 by cash. Account paid in full.

- (p. 31).December 9, 1747. The Debit Account of JOHN GILLISON. To 1 lb. Salt Petre. The Credit account shows payment in full September 12, 1748.

- (p. 32). August 1, 1747. The Debit Account of Mrs. CATHARINE FRENCH carried forward from Ledger F. fo: (165). No additional entries. The Credit Account shows two payments on April 26, 1751 by Capt. RICHD. HOOE.

- (p. 32). April 23, 1748. The Debit Account of Mr. WILLIAM GERRARD. To 1 pr. mens shoes; to 1 felt. The Credit Account shows no entries

- (p. 32). August 1, 1747. The Debit Account of Mr. WILLIAM FITZHUGH carried forward from Ledger F, fo: (62); with additional entries: To 1 lb. green Tea; pd. an Oyster Man; To 2 lbs. Salt Petre; To 2 whip saw files; The Credit Account shows (1749) By pd. JNO. SHORT 1 Crop Note nett; March 23, 1749/50: By cash. (Account paid)

- (p. 32) (no date). The Debit Account of (blank) FLOOD, Doctor. To Loaf Sugar The Credit Account dated April 8, 1748 By Cash you paid to Mr. SIMPSON. (Account paid)

- (p. 33). August 1, 1747. The Debit Account of RICHARD GREEN carried forward from Ledger F, fo: (255); with additional entries through December 25, 1755 including a number of entries for cloth, powder & shott; 1 felt, 2 pr knee buckles; 1 pr. shoe & knee buckles; 5 yds. tartan; 1 1/2 bushells Salt; 1/4 lb. pepper; pr. yarn hose; Rent for year 1747; To yr. Bond of this date; paid Mrs. JONES her Judgmt. agst. you; To your Rent for 1748; To your Rent for 1749; (also 1750 through 1755). (in 1750) To HENRY FEWELL accot; To Interest; The Credit Account shows a number of payments by Crop notes

- (p. 33). August 1, 1747. The Debit Account of ISAAC GREEN carried forward from Ledger F. fo: (174); with additional entries through November 16, 1748 including cloth, thread, salt, To yr. Brothers Debt in fo: (34); pd. 2 levys; pd. Majr. MONROE; 1 bushel of salt pr. your Son; The Credit Account shows payment July 7, 1748 by 1 hogd. tobo; by the Cask; By Ballance carried to fo: (136).

- (p. 33). March 14, 1747/8. The Debit Account of Mr. JOHN FITZHUGH. To 4 gallons of Madeira Wine; to part of your Wifes Levys & some thread in the Parish Book. The Credit Account shows a cash payment by Capt. FRANS: THORNTON to settle account.

- (p. 34). August 1, 1747. The Debit Account of DANIEL GREEN carried forward from Ledger F. fo. (128); with additional entries through December 10, 1750 including a bushell of Salt, thread, a pen knife, cloth and a bushell of beans. The Credit account shows payments in 1750: By Charg'd to yr. Brothers Account; By a Gibsons Note.

- (p. 34). August 1, 1747; The Debit Account of WILLIAM GREENLEASE carried forward from Ledger F., fo: (81); No additional entries. The Credit Account shows two cash payments in 1748 and on July 12, 1750 By Mr. WM. ROWLES.

- (p. 34). August 1, 1747. The Debit Account of NATHANIEL GRAY carried forward from Ledger F. fo. (118); with additional entries for salt, a kirb bridle, 3 1/2 yds. Drogheda for a bag; June 4, 1750 To 4 1/2 gall. Wine ret'd. in cash. The Credit Account shows payments by DANIEL WHITE SENR; by Colo: CHAMPE and the cash credit, account paid in full.

- p. 34). August 1, 1747. The Debit Account of THOMAS GRIFFIN carried forward from Ledger F, fo: (70); with additional entries of 1 best ivory comb and 2 Linnen Handkerchiefs. The Credit Account shows By Tobacco left with Inspectors; By Widow JONES cash; account paid in full.

- (p. 35). August 1, 1747. The Debit Account of ROBERT GREEN carried forward from Ledger F., fo: (32), with a number of additional entries through November 22, 1749, mostly cloth but including To your Assumpsit for WM. FULLER; 2 worsd. caps; thread, breast buttons, Carolina hatt; The Credit Account shows a credit brought forward from Ledger F., fo: (32); payment by a Note and by cash; payment in full.

- (p. 35). August 1, 1747. The Debit Account of WILLIAM HARRISON carried forward from Ledger F, fo: (256); with a number of additional entries through August 3, 1751; mostly cloth but including To your Promissory Note for SAML: WHEELER; 2 yds. Ozna: yr. Daughter, SARAH; salt, thread, 1 felt, 1 single Girth; pair womens shoes; 1 quart mugg; 1/2 pound powder; 4 lbs. shott; 500 8d. nails; 500 4d. nails; Sundrys bought at RANKINS's Outcry; 9 bushels of beans, a barrel of sugar. The Credit Account shows payments by tobacco and cash; by a pair of Childrens Stockons retd., By FRANCIS STROTHER; By Capt. DIXON for the old Ballance; By part of my Inspection Acct., By PATK: COUTTS.

- (p. 36). August 1, 1747. The Debit Account of HUGH HORTON carried forward from Ledger F., fo: (81), no additional entries. The Credit Account shows payment November 25, 1749 by JOSEPH FRANKLING of part of the Debit.

- (p. 36). August 1, 1747. The Debit Account of ALLFORD HEAD carried forward from Ledger F, fo: (21); no additional entires. No entries in Credit Account.

- (p. 36). August 1, 1747; The Debit Account of MARTHA HELLIER carried forward from Ledger F., fo: (178); with additional entries through April 18, 1749, including cloth, salt, 1 pr. Spectacles; a linnen handkerchief; pr. womens shoes; powder & shot, Cr. Majr. CHAMPE for Doctor ALLISON; paid ISAAC ARNOLD SENR., a felt hatt; The Credit Account shows By your Acct. to this day; By WM. FURLONGs Cr., By LUCEY DINGLE; By cash; By overpaid you for Corn; By your account for bringing five wenches to bed; By GEO: WRINGLESBY; By your Account for bringing Cate to bed; April 18, 1749, By cash.

- (p. 36). August 1, 1747. The Debit Account of ROBERT HALFPENNY carried forward from Ledger F, fo: (113); no additional entires. The Credit Account shows payment made for Debit by 4 barrels of Corn.

- (p. 37). August 3, 1747. The Debit Account of CHARLES HOLDSWORTH carried forward from Ledger F, fo: (155); with additional entries through April 27, 1750, including powder & shot; paper Ink powder; quire paper; Cr. ROBT. STROTHER pr. yr. Note; To 3 cyder casks at RANKINS's Outcry; To your signed Promise for BLACKLEY; 1 fine hatt;

pr. mens shoes, 1/2 doz. knives & forks; 7 yds. Irish Linnen; a looking glass; To JAMES KAYs Acct., To Cash to JAMES KAY. The Credit Account shows payments by cash; by a crop note and by GEORGE WRINGLESBY

- (p. 37). August 3, 1747; The Debit Account of Mr. HOWSON HOOE carried forward from Ledger F., fo: (227); with additional entries including 1 tin funnel, a quire of paper; a grindstone; 2 shoe knives; 1 plain Howsen; 2 bushell of Salt; To one fringed Howsen; The Credit Account shows payments by tobacco; by JOHN STROTHER; By DANIEL WHITEs Note of Credit, by cash; payment in full.

- (p. 38). August 3, 1747. The Debit Account of HENRY HAMBLETON carried forward from Ledger F., fo: (7); with no additional entries. No entries in Credit Account

- (p. 38). August 3, 1747. The Debit Account of WILLIAM HILL, Caroline, carried forward from Ledger F, fo: (206), no additional entries. The Credit Account shows payment in 1748 by cash.

- (p. 38). August 3, 1747. The Debit Account of EDWARD HOYLE carried forward from Ledger F, fo: (158), with no additional entries. No entries in the Credit Account

- (p. 38). August 3, 1747. The Debit Account of WILLIAM HAMBLETON carried forward from Ledger F, fo: (16); not additional entries. The Credit Account shows a partial payment by cash October 6, 1749.

- (p. 39). August 3, 1747. The Debit Account of JOHN HUMPHRYS carried forward from Ledger F, fo: (56); no additional entries. The Credit Account shows amount paid

- (p. 39). May 23, 1748. The Debit Account of WILLIAM HAMPTON for 3 yds. Irish; 2 yds. Brown Holland, 1 Oz. Nuns; 1 best Linen Handkerchief. The Credit Account shows debit paid July 18, 1749 by Colo. SPOTSWOOD.

- (p. 39). August 3, 1747. The Debit Account of WILLIAM HUGHS carried forward from Ledger F, fo: (217); with two additional entries for cash; The Credit Account shows By my Acct. this day; by cash; by Capt. RICHD. TALIAFERROs Note, By T. TURNER JUNR. Account paid in full.

- (p. 39). September 3, 1750. The Debit Account of HESTER JONES. To Balla: from page /40/; To a pipe of Wine; To 4 doz. bottles of Beer; salt, salt petre; 96 gallons of Rum; 102 pds. of Beef; 2 dozen Ale; part of last years levies; 6 bushels of Rye; The Credit Account shows several cash payments, By your Public Claim in the County at 15 p cent for 1750; By Gibsons Inspection; By your County Claim for 1751 deducting your levies & for JOS: JONES; By Transfer Tobo: reced Mr. BRUCE; For your County Claim 1752 pd. by JOS: STROTHER; Balance due 12th February 1754.

- (p. 39). August 3, 1747. The Debit Account of LOVELL HARRISON carried forward from Ledger F., fo: (65); with additional entries of To over paid you in LONGMIREs Cr., To sundrys pr. Day Book. The Credit Account shows By WILLIAM LONGMIRE; By WM. LONGMIRE for Rent; account paid

- (p. 40). August 3, 1747. The Debit Account of Mrs. HESTER JONES carried forward from Ledger F, fo: (253); with additional entries for cloth, sundrys from the Day Book and interest on amount carried forward; To JOSHUA LAMPTONs Acct., To 1 Tierce Rum pr. JNO: FARREL of 74 1/2 gallons; To 3 gallons of Wine, To 1 pipe of Wine (Account through 19 December 1748. The Credit Account shows several cash payments; payments by WM. FURLONG; RICHARD GREEN, ADAM LINDSEY, SUSANNA LONGMIRE, ISAAC ARNOLD JUNR., cash in English Shillings; ballance carried to fol: 39.

- (p. 40). August 3, 1747. The Debit Account of DAVID JONES carried forward from Ledger F, fo: (26); with additional entries To yr: Wifes Debt; 3 1/2 yds. Irish, ballance from Day Book; 1 bushel of Wheat to OWEN CAMPBELL; cash 15d., bushel of Salt. The Credit Account shows By Capt. DIXON for EDWD. JONES; By ROBT. WALKER; By getting 1900 Clapboards; By 2 empty hhds., By work done to this day; By one years Wages as Miller

- (p. 40). August 3, 1747. The Debit Account of WILLIAM BLACKLEY. To fell short in your levy; To 1 bushell of Salt; To yr. Rent for 1747; To your Rent for the year 1748. The Credit Account shows two tobacco payments and by tobacco payments October 16, 1749 by JAMES STIGLER, CHAS. HOLDSWORTH; JAS: JOHNSON, ROBT. STROTHER; ISAAC CALL; JNO: ANDERSON, TIM: LYON By Charged ALEXR: SNELLING JUNR.

- (p. 41). August 3, 1747. The Debit Account of ROBERT JOHNSON carried forward from Ledger F, fo: (264); with additional entries for cloth; pins, thread for yr: Wife; 100 6d. nails by MARTIN; quire of paper, bushel of salt; paid RICHD. ROBINSON; To sundrys bought at RANKINS's Outcry; To 3 1/2 yds. Drogheda for NORMAN; an Ivory comb; a linen Handkerchief for CHURCHILL; 1 clasp knife. The Credit Account shows payments by hogsheads of tobacco; by cash; by transfer note, by 1 bag stem'd tobo; (carried to page (118).

- (p. 41). August 3, 1747. The Debit Account of EDWARD JONES, King George, carried forward from Ledger F, fo: (47); no additional entries; The Credit Account shows a payment by RICHD. FRY (ballance still due)

- (p. 41). November 26, 1747. The Debit Account of THOMAS JORDAN for cloth, buttons, thread (account through May 20, 1749). The Credit Account shows a payment by JOSEPH TUTT and by Capt. DIXON (ballance still due)

- (p. 42). August 3, 1747. The Debit Account of ROBERT INGLES carried forward from Ledger F., fo: (119); with two additional entries; 100 8d. nails and to sundrys. The Credit Account shows a partial payment by Transfer Note April 17, 1747. (Apparently at some time later the following was added): July 4th 1744; To your Bond for yr. balla. due in Book F, fol /119/ payable 1st March following; To 2 months Interest; May 1st 1746; 50 6d. nails; 1/2 bushels of Salt; To your 10 1/2 months Interest of 1204 pds. of tobacco; To 100 8d. nails; June 1757: To Interest & cost of suit & Attorneys fees. The Credit account shows payments by tobacco, transfer Notes. (ballance due)

- (p. 42). August 3, 1747. The Debit Account of CHARLES JONES carried forward from Ledger F, fo: (159), no additional entries; no entries in Credit Account

- (p. 42). August 3, 1747. The Debit Account of JOHN JOHNSON, Prince William, carried forward from Ledger F, fo: (161), with additional entries for 6 3/4 yds. Bubdois, check, thrad, 2 prs. plaid hose; pr. womens shoes; pr. yarn hose, 1 horn comb; 8 3/4 yds. fine Linnen. The Credit Account shows Debit paid by cask, by Laying 2 Negro women, by Building a Quarter.

- (p. 42). August 3, 1747. The Debit Account of BAILEY JOHNSON carried forward from Ledger F, fo: (161), no additional entries. The Credit Account shows payment of Debit by Cash pd FRA: WATTS.

- (p. 43). August 3, 1747; The Debit Account of WILLIAM JAMESON carried foreard from Ledger F, fo: (265), with additional entries including a number of cloth items; 12 yds. flower'd Callimanco; 1 brass pepper box; 1 bushel of salt; thread, coat buttons, Cr. EDWD. ELMES pr. your Note; To your Rent for 1747; 3 felt hats; pr. womens shoes; 200 8d. nails, 1 m. pins & 1 hair sive; (the account goes through November 14, 1748). The Credit Account shows several payments by tobacco; by cash; By 12 bushels of Barley; by 30 gallons of Cyder; by one tobacco transfer note; by 6 gallons of Vinegar. (ballance due).

- (p. 43). August 3, 1747. The Debit Account of LEWIS JONES carried forward from Ledger F, fo: (267); with additional entries for Salt, cloth, After Settlement & Bond given; To 12 1/2 yds. Gray Cloth; 3 hhds. shells; (May 7, 1750) 2 years interest on Bond; 6 levies. The Credit Account shows payment in full by tobaccopayments, Inspectors Note; by Bond given May 7, 1748; by cash for 3 hdds. Shells; by Mauling 2000 rails; by cash.

- (p. 44). August 3, 1747. The Debit Account of Mr. ROBERT JACKSON carried forward from Ledger F, fo: (212); with two additional entries; To 35 gallons Ale; To 32 gallons Ale. The Credit Account shows Credit brought forward from Ledger F, fo: (212), but no amount or other credits shown.

- (p. 44). August 3, 1747. The Debit Account of EDWARD JONES, Plaisterer, carried forward from Ledger F, fo: (140); no additional entries; no entries in Credit Account

- (p. 44). January 15, 1747/8. The Debit Account of WILLIAM HEMMINGS, Hobs's Hole, To 62 galls. Ale; To 59 Galls. do. The Credit Account shows payment by Cash.

- (p. 45). August 3, 1747. The Debit Accounty of JUDY JOHNSON carried forward from Ledger F, fo: (89); with additional entries for Cloth; salt. 1 levy; 3 yds. Broad Cloth for WM. JOHNSON; Rent for the year 1746 omitted; nails, rent for 1748, 1749, 1750 & 1751; Cash paid ISAAC ARNOLD; To pd. Capt. DIXON. The Credit Account which shows payments through May 7, 1752 by crop notes; hdds. of tobacco; (ballance due).

- (p. 45). August 3, 1747; The Debit Account of JOHN JOHNSON, Leeds Town, carried forward from Ledger F, fo: (194); with purchas January 15, 1747/8 of 81 galls. of Ale; The Credit Accounts shows a number of payments by Cash; By Mr. ROBERT VAULX, By part of JOHN MORISONs Board

- (p. 45). August 3, 1747. The Debit Account of Capt. THOMAS JOHNSON carried forward from Ledger F, fo: (190); with additional entries; a pipe Wine; 2 pr. Childrens Hose; 2 rugs, thread, 2 best snaffel bridles; 1 pr. blankets, pr. womens shoes; an Iron pott; a bed Cord. The Credit Account shows By Cash at Caroline Court 12 1/2 pistoles; By cash of EDMD. PENDLETON 3 pistoles & 1 dollar; By cash; By Colo. GRYMES Order to Caroline Sheriff; carried to fo: /130/

- (p. 46). August 3, 1747. The Debit Account of ANTHONY KITCHEN carried forward from Ledger F., fo: (146); and To Cash August 4th 1749; The Credit Account shows two cash payments to settle account

- (p. 46). August 3, 1747. The Debit Account of SAMUEL KENDALL carried forward from Ledger F., fo: (238); with additional entries: To your Assumpsit for JOHN CONNERY; for cloth, breast buttons, 1 1/2 bushell Salt; 100 20d. nails; To Cr. Capt. SKINKER; To Cr. ISAAC SETTLE; To your Bond given this day; 1 fur'd hat & band; 1 Carolina hat; The Credit Account shows payment in full by payments in Cash, 1 crop hogd. tobo; By yr. Accot. agst. RANKINS Estate; by a Constables Fee; by Cash.

- (p. 46). August 3, 1747. The Debit Account of SAMUEL KELLY carried forward from Ledger F, fo: (193), no additional entries. No entries in Credit Account

- (p. 47). August 4, 1747. The Debit Account of JOHN KENDALL carried forward from Ledger F, fo: (210); with two additional entries: To 100 3d. nails; To 1/2 bushell Salt. The Credit Account shows payment in full By Tobo: By EDMOND DONAHOE; By cash.

- (p. 47). August 4, 1747. The Debit Account of MICHAEL KELLY carried forward from Ledger F, fo: (97); no additional entries; no entries in Credit Account

- (p. 47). August 4, 1747. The Debit Account of JAMES KAY JUNR. carried forward from Ledger F, fo: (80); with additional entry August 14, 1749 for 1/2 bushell Salt. The Credit Account shows payment in full By CHAS: HOLDSWORTHs Account

- (p. 47). August 4, 1747. The Debit Account of STEPHEN LATHAM SENR. carried forward from Ledger F, fo: (58); with additional entries for nails, cloth, a linen handkerchief, 1/4 lb. Brown thread. The Credit Account shows payment in full: By cash by FRANKLIN LATHAM; By charg'd FRANKLING LATHAM in his Acct.

- (p. 47). January 16, 1747/8. The Debit Account of WILLIAM ARROWSMITH. To 7 yds. Irish @ 3/2; To 8 yds. Drogheda @ 1/6; 1/8 Whit'd thread; 1/4 lb. Brown thread; To yr. Promissory Note for SAML. WHEELER; To 1 felt, 1 bushell of Sale 3/6; To the above tobacco for SAML. WHEELER. The Credit Account shows full payment By 1 Mattox Transfer Note reced of GEO: HARRISON; By Boggs Hole Transfer Note

- (p. 48). August 4, 1747. The Debit Account of ADAM LINDSEY carried forward from Ledger F, fo: (120); with a number of additional entries: To 1 felt for SAML. WHARTON; 9 3/4 yds. Irish @ 3/4; 1 small felt; 2 bushells of Salt pr. Note; To paid Mr. JOSEPH MORTON; To pd. HARRY TURNER; To 100 20d. nails; 100 8d. nails, 100 3d. nails; To 35 squares of Glass 10 by 9; paid Mrs. JONES yr. Order; pd. GEORGE TODD 253 lbs. tobo: @ 13/ To 1 broad Ax; To 2 whip saw files; To 4 hand saw files; To 1 weeding hoe; pd. Colo. CHAMPE; To 1 small Rasp; The Credit Account shows payment in full by cash (1 Dble. loon); By your acct. to this day; by Cash; By your account to this day for work done at the Mill; By Colo. CHAMPE Cr. not allowed.

- (p. 48). August 4, 1747. The Debit Account of Colo. LUNSFORD LOMAX carried forward from Ledger F., fo: (135); with additional entries: To paid your Note to JAMES WRIGHT; To 1 sayne Rope & cask, To cash; To 1 Grindstone by ABRAHAM WILSON, To 7 1/4 lbs. Hops; To 1 yrs. Interest on your Bond; (July 24th 1750): To Jack's work from this morning to Augt. 12th, 17 days. The Credit Account shows payment in full: By your Credit brought forward from Ledger F, fo: (135); By Capt. WARD; By THOS: BARTLET for 6 barrels of Corn; By ROBT. MONDAY for 2 barrels of Corn; By ISAAC ARNOLD for 2 barrels of Corn; By WM. FURLONG for 2 barrels of Corn; By Mr. JOS: SIMPSON; By cash.

- (p. 49). August 4, 1747. The Debit Account of JAMES LEE carried forward from Ledger F, fo: (158); no additional entries; no entries in Credit Account

- (p. 49). August 4, 1747. The Debit Account of FRANKLING LATHAM carried forward from Ledger F, fo: (215); with additional entries through October 3, 1748 which include salt; 1 felt, cloth; To Cr. yr. Fathers Account by yr, own Order; To 2 felts No. 3. To 1 fine hat. The Credit Account shows payment in full; By 2 Caves Crop Notes; By 4 Cash payments

- (p. 49). August a4, 1747. The Debit Account of RICHARD LEE, in STAFFORD, carried forward from Ledger F, fo: (89); no additional entires; no entries in Credit Account.

- (p. 50). August 4, 1747. The Debit Account of WILLIAM LONGMIRE, carried forward from Ledger F., fo: (249); additional entries mostly for cloth; also 2 butcher knives 1 pr knee buckles, 1 qt. Oyl; 3 boys small felts; thread, salt; quire of paper; Cr. JAMES STIGLER; 2 1/2 yds. Ozna: to ROBT. BENSON; To Cr. LUCEY DINGLE; To Cr. ELIZA: GREENWOOD; To Cr. Majr. CHAMPE; 1 felt hat boys; 1 pr womens gloves; The Credit Account shows payment in full: By tobo; By yr. Credt. Ledger F fol. /249/; By your wages for 1747; By an allowance on Sundrys. By Wages for 10 months.

- (p. 50). October 1748. The Debit Account of Colo. JOHN LEWIS. To cash pd. at WILLIAMSBURG. The Credit Account shows payment in full: By Cash reced of RICHD. ROY for his Mothers Bond at Interest for 21:10:0

- (p. 51). August 4, 1747. The Debit Account of JOSHUA LAMPTON carried forward from Ledger F, fo: (159); with additional entries for 1/2 yd. Scarlett Tammys; 1 pr. Knee buckles, 4 laces. The Credit Account shows payment is full: By Cash; By Mrs. JONES.

- (p. 51). August 3, 1747. The Debit Account of JOHN LEWIS, Boatwright, carried forward from Ledger F. fo: (203); no additional entries; no entries in Credit Account.

- (p. 51). August 3, 1747. The Debit Account of MURDY McCOY carried forward from Ledger F, fo: (77); no additional entries; The Credit Account shows payment in full By Cash pd. FRAS: HOOE.

- (p. 52). August 4, 1747. The Debit Account of BENJAMIN MARSHALL carried forward from Ledger F, fo: (111); with a number of additional entries including cloth, salt, a mans fine hat; To Cr: NATHANIEL WILLIAMS pr. yr. Note; pr. mens yarn hoes @ 2/9; To Cr. JOHN ALLSUP pr. yr. Note; nails, thread, ivory comb; To Cr. your Brother of this date never charged; pd. 3 levys; To GEO: HARRISONs Debt on Bond; To yr. Levy; To yr. Promise for MICHL: SKINNER; To GEO: HARRISONs ballance The Credit Account shows payments by Hogsheads of tobacco; by Cask, by Cash; By ISAAC ARNOLD JUNR; By MOSES RANKINS; By JNO. GRAY

- (p. 52). August 4, 1747. The Debit Account of Mr. JOHN MOORE carried forward from Ledger F, fo: (17) with additional entries including 1 pr Girls small shoes; cloth, nails, salt, gun powder; To 1/2 yd. Shalloon by ANTHO: FICKLING; buttonms; 1085 foot Inch Plank; 1 Knot Drum line; To cash pd. Mr. FINNEY; To Cr. JOHN BROWN, To 25 bushels of Salt; To 6 bottles of Wine; To 40 dollars; To 250 8d. nails; To 1009 feet of Inch Plank; To 50 pds. Sugar; 2 bottles train Oyl; To 2 books; To Cap. JOS: STROTHERs Order; To 12 squares of Glass; The Credit Account shows payment in full: By 1 quarter Beef; By cash; By 1018 feet 1 1/4 inch Plank @ 50/; By 2015 feet Inch do @ 45/; By 1 hogshd. tobacco; By the Cask; By 2 barrels of Tarr; By 5 Pistoles; By 60 barrels of Corn; By cash; By 75 barrels of Corn @ 9/6; By 117 balla: JNO: BROWNs Debt.

- (p. 53). August 4, 1747. The Debit Account of WILLIAM MARSHALL SENR. carried forward from Ledger F, fo: (259); with additional entries including: To your assumpsit for RICHD. ROBINSONs Levy; To 1 curb bridle; paid JAMES SCURLOCK; cloth, nails, salt; buttons; thread, 1 Tin funnel; 1 boys felt; quire of paper; To Cr. ISAAC SETTLE; powder & shot; To 2 lbs. Hops; To your Rent for the year 1747; To pr. yarn hose, To pr. mens shoes; Topr Womens worsd. hose; To pd. Capt. WM. TALIAFERRO; To your Rent for the year 1748; To pd. 6 levys. The Credit Account shows: By THOMAS BARTLETT for yr. Judgmt. agst. him; By do in tobo: By 1 transfer Note; By 1 hogshd. tobo: By the cask; By a Crop note; By Cr. ROBT. JOHNSON; By SCURLOCK's Acct. not allowed; By 2 pistoles; By 1 hhd. of tobacco.

- (p. 53). August 4, 1747. The Debit Account of ROBERT MILLER carried forward from Ledger F, fo: (20); with one additional entry; To Cash pd. H. TURNER; The Credit Account shows debit paid in full May 20th 1748: By OLIVER TOWLES

- (p. 54). August 4, 1747. The Debit Account of JOHN McCORMICK carried forward from Ledger F, fo: (92) with a number of additional entries including: buttons, a pocket knife & fork a thimble; cloth, salt, To Cr. DAVID ROBINSON; shot & powder; To Cr. Capt. WATTS; 1 mans Hat; 1 pr. mens worsd. hose; 1/2 m. pins; 1 bridle, nails; To pd. yr. Rent to Capt. JOHN WATTS; To pd. your levy for 1748; To pd. JNO: RODGERS; To pd. JNO: STEVENS; To pd. JOSEPH TUTT; To yr. Rent for 1749; To DAVID ROBINSONs Order; (Debit account through June 9th 1750); The Credit Account shows payments in tobacco, transfer notes; By 1 pr. Stockons ret'd;

-. (p. 54). August 4, 1747. The Debit Account of WILLIAM MARSHALL, Son of EDWARD; carried forward from Ledger F, fo: (106); with additional entries including 1/2 bushel of Salt; To your Rent for the year 1747; To pd. 1 levy; To your Rent for 1748; To your Levy; The Credit Account shows payments in cask and tobacco.

- (p. 54); November 9,. 1747. The Debit Account of EDWARD MARSHALL SENR. includes To 3/4 yds. Broad Cloth @ 11/ yr. Son, BEN: To 1 Stk. Hair by yr. Son, EDWARD; To one hk. Silk by BEN: (Jany: 1752): To Cash yr. Son, BEN. The Credit Account shows payment by Tobo: overpaid in your Levys; By 1/2 of Building a Corn House; By 6 hhds. setting up

- (p. 55). August 4, 1747. The Debit Account of DENNIS MAHORNER carried forward from Ledger F, fo: (104); no additional entries, no entries in Credit Account.

- (p. 55); August 4, 1747. The Debit Account of ELIZABETH MIFLIN, Now JAMES COPE; carried forward from Ledger F, fo: (107); with three additional entries; for salt, for 3 1/2 yds. of Check; for 50 10d. nails. The Credit account shows payment by tobacco.

- (p. 55). August 4, 1747. The Debit Account of Capt. JOHN MICOU carried forward from Ledger F, fo: (124); with additional entries including Interest on ballance carried over; To a pr. of London best shoes LEO: HILL; To Cash pd. JOS: STROTHER; To 8 1/2 lbs. Hops pr. yr. Son; To 5 3/4 lbs. Hops pr. THOS: EVANS; The Credit Account shows payment: By Majr. MURDOCK for Chocolate; By Capt. WARD; By Capt. ROBINSON; By REYNOLDS for Corn; By WM. JOHNSON; By cash

- (p. 55). August 4, 1747. The Debit Account of BENJAMIN MASSEY carried forward from Ledger F. fo: (58); with 3 additional entries: Bond Given this day; To Interest; To cost of suit. The Credit Account shows payments: By a Whortons Note; By WITHERS CONWAY; By do to ballance account

- (p. 55). May 7, 1748. The Debit Account of Major GEORGE LEE for 2 yds. of Blew broad cloth @ 14/6. The Credit Account shows full payment: By HARRY TURNER

- (p. 56). August 4, 1747. The Debit Account of JOHN MARSHALL carried forward from Ledger F, fo: (178), no additional entries; no entries in Credit Account

- (p. 56). August 4, 1747. The Debit Account of ROBERT MONDAY carried forward from Ledger F, fo: (263); with additional entries including salt, sundrys bought at RANKINS's Outcry; To 2 barrels of Corn at Colo. LOMAX's; coat buttons; To pd. 3 levys for 1748; To sundrys pr. ballance your account; The Credit Account shows full payment by cash and tobacco payments; By Cash by WM. LONGMIRE; By ROBERT CALLs Credit; By RANKINS Acct. proved; By Capt. EDWARD DIXON November 14, 1749.

- (p. 56). August 4, 1747. The Debit Account of WILLIAM MUMFORD carried forward from Ledger F, fo: (196); no additional entries. The Credit Account shows the debit of one pound: By Cash of Majr. SKINKER

- (p. 56). (In the Debit account only the name Mr. GEORGE ROCK appears). The Credit Account shows December 28, 1748: By 64 lbs. Chocalate; By 29 lbs. do. rat eaten

- (p. 57). August 4, 1747. The Debit Account of Majr. JEREMIAH MURDOCK carried forward from Ledger F, fo: (247); with additional entries including: : To 4 yds. Worsd. ferrett @ 3d; To 3 lbs. Salt Petre by GUY; To 4 lbs. Chocolate of Capt. MICOU; 4 galls. Wine; 3 1/4 of Ale; 2 pds. Chocolate; (other entries of wine and chocolate through February 12, 1752.) The Credit Accounts shows payments by cash; By Capt. EDWARD DIXON; By cash of WM. HUNTER; By an order of Capt. DIXON; By Mr. SIMPSON for prizing a tranfer hhd.

- (p. 57). August 4, 1747. The Debit Account of JAMES MAXWELL carried forward from Ledger F., fo: (103). with a number of additional entries including: cloth; pr. of worsd. hose; To paid JAMES SCURLOCK yr. Bill to him; 1 mans fine hat; 1 pen knife; cash for 2 steers; paid WM. MARDERS pr. Note; To ballance in a Japand. pint Mug; Cr. WM. MARDERS by your own order; Cr. Mr. CHARLES ASHTON pr. yr. own order; an ivory comb; a womans fur'd hat; 1 band for do; 2 lbs. powder. The Credit Account shows Credit brought forward from Ledger F, fo: (103); By 2 steers; By CHARLES ASHTONs order disallowed; (Jany. 7th 1750); By CUTHBERT SANDYS.

- (p. 58). August 4, 1747. The Debit Account of HENRY MACHEN carried forward from Ledger F, fo. (38), with additional entries for 2 doz. corks, 1 Dble. hand bridle; powder and shott; another 2 doz. corks; 4 lbs. single refined Sugar; a quire of paper; 1/2 lb. Powder by yr. Sister in Law; cloth, nails; The Credit Account shows: By your Wifes Parish Claim; By 40 lbs. Butter; by Colo. CHAS. CARTER paid in full August 4, 1749.

- (p. 58). August 4, 1747. The Debit Account of Capt. ANDREW MONROE carried forward from Ledger F, fo. (76); with additional entries for 1 1/2 gallons of Madeira Wine @ 6/; To balla: remaining on 18 hdds. of tobo: of 900 wt. after a bail of goods reced; To your assumpsit for THOS: ROBINS; pd. S. SKINKER Sheriffs fees; To Cash pr. JAMES NAUGHTY; To Cash pr. Colo. CHAS. CARTER; To Cash to JAMS: PASLEY; To pd. Capt. DIXON for 7151 pds. tobo @ 2d., To pd ROBT. CALL for his attendance v. BROWN; To pd. JOSHUA FERGUSON; pd. POLLARD; To a pipe of Wine; To pd. FURLONG for carting; The Credit Account: By paid THOMAS VIVION in Bills of Exchange; By 35 pr. cent on do; By pd. JNO: SHORT 3 hhds. tobo:, By ISAAC GREEN; By cash; By Cash to K. G. Court; By your Excha: on LYDE;

- (p. 58). August 4, 1747. The Debit Account of EDWARD MASSEY carried forward from Ledger F, with no additional entries. The Credit Account shows payment in full: By THOS: ROBINSON

- (p. 59). August 4, 1747. The Debit Account of EDWARD MARSHALL, Son of EDWARD, To yr. signed Settlement as pr. Ledger F, fo. (123), To 1 clasp knife; To 1 pr. yarn hose; To 1/8 Colld. thread; To 1 band buckle, 2 oz. whitd. thread; To pr. gloves rat eaten; The Credit Account shows By 1 months work; By 1/2 build a corn house; By Cash; By GEO: TANKERSLEY; Debit paid in full

- (p. 59). August 4, 1747. The Debit Account of WILLIAM MARDERS carried forward from Ledger F, with additional entries for: To 1 horn comb; To 2 shoe knives; cloth, buttons, thread, salt, To 1 Still at RANKINS Sale; To pd. Capt. WATTS; To 1 fine hat; To sundrys pr. Day Book; The Credit Account shows: By JAMES MAXWELL; By Cash; By HESTER STONE Credit for you; By 2 Gibsons Notes; By 2 Mattox Notes.

- (p. 59). August 4, 1747; The Debit Account of Mrs. ELIZABETH McCARTIE carried forward from Ledger F, fo. (68); with additional entries for a pr. of Gloves, a pr. of Mittens; a pack of cards. The Credit Account shows payment in full By paid in Cattle; By cash.

- (p. 60). 1747. The Debit Account of JOHN MORISON carried forward from Ledger F., fo: (262); with additional entries beginning July 27, 1747: To pd. WM. FURLONG for going to Town for a Dedimus; To 1 pr. London Pumps best; To 1 pr. Scissors; a number of kinds of cloth; buttons. "To paid SAML. DINGLE his Taylors Acct., to this day September 4, 1747. The Above Acct. allowed in Court Sept. 4, 1747." To Expences in going to HOBS HOLE to Examine Capt. FARGUSON; To 1 Oz. Nuns by Mrs. SARAH; pr. shoes; pd. FARGUSON a Secretarys Fee; To 1 fine hat; To 1 1/2 yds. Dowlass for lineing Breeches @ 2/4; To Mrs. FISHPOOL for yr. Board; To pd. Mr. SIMPSON for yr. Schooling; To 1 four bladed knife; To Expences going to WILLIAMSBURGH and returning; To 2 pair of thread hose you had of Mr. Bowie @ 4/6; To paid Doctor FARGUSON his Account; "The above Account allowed in Court August the 5th 1748." To pd. Mr. JAMES POWERS; pd. Mr. Attorney; pd. Mr. MERCER; To cash to the Overseer; (carried to fo; /129/); no entries in a Credit Account.

- (p. 61). August 4, 1747. The Debit Account of Mr. GEORGE MORTON carried forward from Ledger F, fo: (54); with an additional entry: To your Debt from do. Sterling 1:16:0. The Credit Account shows: By Cash; By JOSIAS FARGUSON, By Cash made Sterling to pay debit in full.

- (p. 61). August 4, 1747. The Debit Account of DAVID MITCHELL carried forward from Ledger F, fo: (159); no additional entries and no entries in Credit Account.

- (p. 61). August 4, 1747. The Debit Account of Mr. PATRICK MITCHELL carried forward from Ledger F, fo: (34); with additional entries for Cash; To the balla: as pr. Mr. WALKER's Settlemt. of an old Acct., To 145 pds. of tobo: To 1/3 of 105 galls. Rum; To 30 gallons Ale; To 220 feet 6 inches Inch Plank; To paid DANIEL WHITE yr. Note; To 205 foot Inch Plank; To pd. WM. FURLONG; To pd. Capt. KELSICK; April 27, 1749: To one loaf Sugar. The Credit Account shows: By your Credit from Ledger F, fo: (34); By REVD. MR. ROSE; By an adz, a hammer, By 1/3 of 105 Galls. rum; 3 cash payments; By 425 foot Plank, By 500 bushells Salt @ 20d. Debit paid.

- (p. 62). August 4, 1747. The Debit Account of THOMAS MONDAY brought forward from Ledger F, fo: (150); with additional entries for cloth, cash, 1 fine hat, a pr. Mens hose; The Credit Account shows By months Work @ 25/. Debit paid.

- (p. 62). August 4, 1747. The Debit Account of CORNELIUS McCARTIE brought forward from Ledger F, fo: (217), with two additional entries: To paid your Bill to JAMES SCURLOCK; To pd. your Bill to JOHN ROACH. The Credit Account shows: By your Credit brot. forward from Ledger F, fo: (217); By Cash By the above 1000 tobo: Small balance

- (p. 62). August 4, 1747. The Debit Account of PETER NEWGENT brought forward from Ledger F, fo: (105), no additional entries; The Credit Account shows: By Cash for Ballance

- (p. 63). September 2, 1747. The Debit Account of WILLIAM NORMAN brought forward from Ledger F, fo: (176); with additional entries for Cloth, 1/2 lb. single refind. Sugar; To cost of suit and Attorneys fee. The Credit Account shows two cash payments; By yr. Accot. for 6 days Work making a pr. of Leather Breeches.

- (p. 63). August 4, 1747. The Debit Account of MESSRS. NEAL & FALKNER brot. forward from Ledger F, fo: (151); with additional entries To Ballance from fol: /29/; To interest on 11:15:9; for total Debit of 242: 0: 1:. The Credit account shows payment of 243:0: 0: by Cash November 18th 1748.

- (p. 63). August 4, 1747. The Debit Account of WILLIAM OWENS JUNR. brot: forward from Ledger F., fo: (66); no additional entries; no entries in Credit Account

- (p. 63). August 4, 1747. The Debit Account of WILLIAM OWENS SENR. brot. froward from Ledger F., fo: (160); no additional entries; no entries in Credit Account

- p. 63). 1748. The Debit Account of the WASHINGTON PARISH COLLECTORS. To Majr. WILLIAM WALKERs Order; To Tobo: pd. JNO: MARTIN by Mrs. DEGGS; to JNO: MARTINs Acct. with me; "This account is ballanced." The Credit Account shows: By 1 Crop Note of JNO: MARTIN; (other payments of JNO: MARTIN); "This Account is ballanced."

- (p. 64). August 4, 1747. The Debit Account of ROBERT PECK brot. forward from Ledger F. fo: (139); with additional entries for powder and shott; salt; To your Promissory Note for SAML. WHEELER; To Sundrys bought at RANKINS's Outcry; To 1 best Linen Handkerchief by yr Son, JOHN; pins, cloth, buckles, 1 felt hatt; To sundry pr. Day Book by yr. Wife; To Colo. FAIRFAX's Order; 3 barrels of Corn at the Mill; To my Promissory Note wch: I lent you & pd. to PHILIP ALEXANDER; To your Sterling Debt; The Credit Account shows several tobacco payments; By GEORGE WRINGLESBY;

- (p. 64). August 4, 1747. The Debit Account of ISAAC PITMAN (Widdows since his Decease); brot. forward from Ledger F., fo: (239); with two additional entries: To 1 Dble. Reind. Bridle; To 3 1/2 yds. Drogheda; The Credit Account shows payment in full: By Charg'd JAMES FREEMAN in his Account. (ISAAC PITMANs Ballance at his death 12: 6: 7 1/2. Credit Account: By Mr. RIDING since his decease hogd. tobo: & cask.

- (p. 64). August 4, 1747. The Debit Account of WILLIAM PAYNE SENR., brot. from Ledger F, fo: (71); no additional entries; no entries in Credit Account.

- (p. 65). August 5, 1747. The Debit Account of JOHN PERRYMAN brot. from Ledger F., fo: (98), no additional entries; no entries in Credit Account

- (p. 65). August 5, 1747. The Debit Account of FRANCIS PAYNE brot. from Ledger F., fo: (101), no additional entries; no entries in Credit Account

- (p. 65), August 5, 1747. The Debit Account of WILLIAM PAYNE JUNR. brot. from Ledger F., fo: (107); no additional entries, no entries in Credit Account

- (p. 66). August 5, 1747. The Debit Account of JOHN PRICE brot. from Ledger F., fo: (112); with an additional entry December 2, 1749: To 2 yrs. 3 months Interest; To your bond this day taken with interest; The Credit Account shows By your Bond this day taken (December 2, 1749); April 5th 1751; By Mr. WM. ROWLEY in full.

- (p. 66). August 5, 1747. The Debit Account of RICHARD PRICE brot. from Ledger F., fo: (122); with additional entries: To 6 pr. cent of 782 to make it Crop; To costs of Suit; To 2 yrs. 3 months Interest; December 2, 1749: To your bond taken this day with Interest. The Credit Account shows December 2, 1749 By your Bond taken this day; April 5th 1751; By Mr. WM. ROWLEY in full.

- (p. 66). August 5, 1747. The Debit Account of JOHN PAVIOR ballance from Ledger F., fo: (114), no additional entries, no entries in Credit Account.

- (p. 67). August 5, 1747. The Debit Account of JAMES PURCELL: To your Debt from Ledger F, fo: (141); The Credit Account shows payment in full: By Mr. TRIPLETT August 6, 1748.

- (p. 67). 1748. The Debit Account of JAMES BERRY of Stafford. To your Mother, GRACE BERRYs, Debit. No entry in Credit Account

- (p. 67). August 5, 1747. The Debit Account of THOMAS PRICE ballance brot. from Ledger F., fo: (165); no additional entries; no entry in Credit Account

- (p. 67). August 5, 1747. The Debit Account of CHARLES PAYNE brot. from Ledger F, fo: (166); with an additional entry: To fees on Admr. yr. Estate. The Credit Account shows payment in full: By a Crop Note on Boyds Hole; By a Transfer do; By a present made to balla:

- (p. 67). January 1, 1747/8. The Debit Account of GEORGE TODD. To 60 gallons of Beer; To 1 bushell of Salt; To Coll. BENJA: ROBINSONs Order. The Credit Account shows July 28, 1748: By ADAM LINDSEY; By JAMES BOWIE; October 17, 1748: By Cash

- (p. 68). August 5, 1747. The Debit Account of EVAN PRICE ballance brot. forward from Ledger F, fo: 207: with additional entries: To 75 pr. cent on 2: 6: 2:; To Sundrys bought at RANKINS's Outcry; June 2d. 1751: To Cash pd. LOVELL WHITE pr. yr. Note. The Credit Account shows: August 19th 1748; "By your Trouble in Demanded Sundry old Debts," By Crying RANKINS goods; By do WHEELERs; by Cash; By 20 head of Sheep

-. (68). August 5, 1747; The Debit Account of WILLIAM PARKER brot. from Ledger F, fo: (116); with additional entries: To Cr. ANDREW THOMPSON pr. yr. Note; To 250 foot Inch Plank; salt, beef, tallow; To pd. yr. Ordr. to JOHN MILLER; The Credit Account shows February 16, 1747/8: By Cash; By Mr. CAMMACK; By WM. LONGMIREs Account; By JOS; BERRY JUNR., By yr. Accot. for Taylors Work to this day; By JOHN FARROL; then three entries through May 7, 1755 for his account

- (p. 68). August 5, 1747. The Debit Account of Mr. JOHN PARISH Debt brot. from Ledger F, fo: (177); no additional entries; no entries in Credit Account

- (p. 69). August 5, 1747. The Debit Account of BIRKITT PRATT brot. from Ledger F, fo: (27); with two additional entries: To 2 1/2 bushells Sale pr. Note by JNO: BRYAN; 1750: To yr. Promisory Note to MOSES RANKINS. The Credit Account shows cash payment July 21,1750 for Debit in full.

- (p. 69). August 5, 1747. The Debit Account of WILLIAM QUISENBURY Debt. from Ledger F, fo: (108); with one additional entry: To your Rent for the year 1747; No entries in the Credit Account

- (p. 69). August 5, 1747. The Debit Account of ANN QUISENBURY Acct. brot. from Ledger F, fo: (3); with an additional entry for 6 1/4 yds. of Callico @ 5/6. The Credit Account shows payment in full: By Mr. JORDAN.

- (p. 70). August 5, 1747. The Debit Account of JOHN RANKINS ballance brot. from Ledger F. fo: (24); with additional entries for a felt hat; several kinds and quantities of cloth; 1 pr. steel buckles, 1 two foot rule; 1/2 pd. powder, 1 fine hatt, To your Debt to your Fathers Estate; The Credit Account shows October 2, 1748: By ISAAC ARNOLD JUNR., By Work done at the Rich Bottoms; Sept. 26, 1750: By cash of Mrs. JONES; By charged in the Day Book

- (p. 70). August 5, 1747. The Debit Account of Colo. WILLIAM RANDOLPH Esqr., Debt brot. from Ledger F, fo: (30); with additional entries : To pd. BENJ: SETTLE; To pd. JOSIAH FARGUSON; To 300 6d. 300 10d. 300 8d nails; To pd. Majr. HARRY TURNER; To Cash pd. H: WARE; (three payments made in 1750); The Credit Account shows Credit brot. from Ledger F, fo: (30); By 1203 pds. of Pork @ 12/6; By 276 pds. do; By 8 hoggs; By 160 bushells of Corn; By 4 barrels of Corn; By Parish Book; By a Roys Note; By Gibsons Note

- (p. 70). September 25, 1747. The Debit Account of CATHARINE CALVIN. (seven entries for purchase of cloth); 1 pr. mens worsd. Hose; 1 pr. Womens worsd. hose; The Credit Account shows payments: By JAMES FREEMANs Credit; By WM. COATEN; By 4 months 2/3d. Work @ 6/9 pr. month; By Quilting a Coat for MRS. SARAH.

- (p. 71). August 5, 1747; The Debit Account of JOHN RODGERS ballance brot. from Ledger F, fo: (143), with additional entries for cloth; buttons, powder and shot and To Cost of Suit; The Credit Account shows payment September 7, 1747 by Cash and By Capt. DIXON for Ballance

- (71). August 5, 1747. The Debit Account of WILLIAM RANKINS ballance brot. from Ledger F, fo: (77); with additional entries for payment of 4 levies and Cr. your Bond to ballance: The Credit Account shows: By HARRY TURNER; By yr. Mothers ballance; account paid

- (p. 71). April 27, 1748. The Debit Account of NIGHTINGALE MEEDS. To 7 yds. Drogheda @ 1/6; ; To 3 1/2 yds. Irish @ 3/2; The Credit Account shows payment in full: By WILLIAM FURLONG July 14, 1749.

(p. 72). August 5, 1747. The Debit Account of THOMAS ROY ballance brot. from Ledger F, fo: (78); with additional entries for 25 gallons of Ale; a bushel of salt; 5 gallons of Ale put in your Cask; To 2 lbs. Hops for yr. Brewing; To 4 1/2 gallons of Wine; To 1 pr. boys Shooes for BOOKERY; To 4 lbs. Spanish Brown Mixt. in Oyl at 4/; To 50 3d. nails; To 2 bottles of Clarrett; To 21 gallons of Molasses; To 15 red paint mixt; more hops in 1749; more salt in 1751. The Credit Account shows: By 1 pr. Boys Shoes return'd, By JAMES WHITE; By Cash, By Mr. CAMMACK

- (p. 72). August 5, 1747. The Debit Account of CHRISTOPHER RODGERS SENR. ballance from Ledger F, fo: (83); with additional entries: To yr. costs of suit; August 31, 1751 To pd XT. RODGERS JUNR. To the balla. of tobo: accot. The Credit Account shows payments by a hogd. of tobo and cask; By Cash recd. of Colo. GAWIN CORBIN.

- (p. 72). August 5, 1747. The Debit Account of JOHN ROACH ballance brot. from Ledger F, fo: (84); with additional entries for salt, 1 lb. Dble. refined Sugar; 1 fine hatt; 1 linen handkerchief; thread; 500 10d. nials, 500 6d. nails; 1/2 bushel of salt; To pd. Majr. CHAMPE; To 1 bushel of salt pr. your Son; To 1 boys felt hat. The Credit Account shows payments By 1 Gibsons Transfer; By JOHN STROTHER; By 1 hogd. tobo and cask; March 30, 1747/8 By JAMES ARNOLDs Cr.. Carried to page (139).

- (p. 73). August 13, 1747. The Debit Account of CHARLES RIGGINS. Your ballance brot. from Day Book to this date; To Sundrys for yr:self & SAML. EVANS from Day Book; 1748: To 1 quire of paper pr. JOS: EMBREY; To 12 bushels of Salt. The Credit Account shows payments: By Cask July 9, 1748; By Cash pd. FRANS: HOOE 1749.

- (p. 73). August 5, 1747. The Debit Account of ROBERT RANKINS ballance brot. from Ledger F, fo: (232) with a number of additional entries including powder and shott; cloth, salt, silk, To 2 yds. Red Half Thicks by NICHO: GREEN @ 3/5; thread; 2 pr. mens Yarn hose @ 5/6; pr. womens do 2/9; linen handkerchief @ 2/; 1 do at 1/6; To pd. DANIEL WHITE SENR. his Exo., To pd. WILLIAM WHARTON his Exo., To pd. ROBT. MONDAY pr. Acct. proved; To pd. Capt. SMITHER 2 levies; To paid FRA: STROTHER his Judgmt., To pd.

WM. EDWARDS his Judgmt., cost of do; To pd. MARY McKENNIE her Judgmt., cost of do; To pd. Majr. MURDOCK his Judgmt., cost of do: To pd. HARRY TURNER his fee for Admr.; To paid EVAN PRICE for Crying at the Sale; To pd. SAML. KENDALL pr. account prov'd, To pd. EDW: TEMPLEMAN proved accot., To pr. administration fee; To MARY McKENNY's costs; To Widdo: RANKINS accot; To do. 2 levies; To RICHD. GREEN; To pd. WM. RANKINS to balla: this account. The Credit Account shows a payment by a hogd. tobo and cask; By yr. part of a light Hogd. wth: Fox Note; by Cask; Credit your Administration Account when reced: By WM. MARDERS; by Mr. ASHTON, By CHARLES HOLDSWORTH; By Mr. WREN; By GABRIEL JOHNSON; By WM. HARRISON; By GEORGE HARRISON; By WM. WHITE; by ISAAC ARNOLD SENR; By ROBERT MONDAY; By WILLIAM PECK SENR., By RICHD. GREEN; By GEORGE FOX; By JOHN PIPER, By ISAAC ARNOLD JUNR; By ROBT. JOHNSON SENR., By ROBT. PECK; By EVAN PRICE; By T. T., By Dr. BANKHEAD for Vinegar; By WM. RANKINS, WM. STROTHER & BENJA: STROTHER; By MARY McKENNYs cost twice charg'd; By Cash reced JAMES RANKINS; Memo: this ballances this Accot.

- (p. 74). August 5, 1747. The Debit Account of CHRISTOPHER RODGERS JUNR., Debt brot. from Ledger F., fo: (144); with additional entries: To paid ANTHO: KITCHEN his Attenda: agt. PRICE. cloth, buttons; 1 shoe knife; thread, silk, salt. To 1 weeks absence. The Credit Account shows Credit from Ledger F, fo. (144); in 1749: By 2 months 1/4 wages; by 2 days wages this day; 1751: By yr. Mother

- (p. 74). August 5, 1747. The Debit Account of JAMES RANKINS ballance brot. from Ledger F, fo: (156); with additional entries for cloth; a hatt; pr. yarn hose; 3 yds. brown Linen @ 1/3; thread, buttons, To 1 1/2 yds. bro: linen @ 15d. by JNO: RANKINS; To 3 prs. yarn hose; To yr. Debt to your Fathers Estate 1: 10: 0:. The Credit Account shows payment of Debit: By 2 Potomack Notes; By ISAAC ARNOLD JUNR., By Work done at the Rich Bottoms; By Tobo: pt. of a Note.

- (p. 74). August 5, 1747; The Debit Account of RICHARD RAWLINGS Debt brot. from Ledger F, fo: (108), no additional entries; The Credit Account show payment of Debit by a Note.

- (p. 75). August 5, 1747. The Debit Account of DAVID ROBINSON ballance brot. from Ledger F, fo: (169); with additional entries for 1 1/8 yds. Check @ 2/2; To yr. Levy for Anno 1749; To part of JNO: BROWNs Cr. disallowed; 1752: The Credit Account shows payment of the Debit before 1752 By JOHN McCORMICKs Cr., By THOMAS BARTLETTs Cr., By Cash; By Capt. BENJA: STROTHER; By JNO: McCORMICK in pt. of yr. Levy; 1752 entry: By ROBT. JOHNSON for ballance

- (p. 75); August 5, 1747. The Debit Account of Mr. GEORGE RIDING ballance brot. from Ledger F, fo: (253); with additional entries for cloth; nails, buttons, pr. small scissors; salt, narrow axe, Wine for your Sick Child; 100 8d. nails; pd. 11 levys @ 73; To 2 qts. Madeira Wine by yr. Son; To a Transfer Note had of Inspectors; To 1 fine hat by yr. Son; To 12 levies @ 67; The Credit Account shows payment of Debit: By 1 Crop Note, By the Cask; By 1 hogd. tobo: By the Cask; By a Crop note. By cash

- (p. 76). August 5, 1747. The Debit Account of THOMAS ROBBINS Debt brot. from Ledger F., fo: (80); with additional entries for a Sifter; 14 mettle buttons; a skillet, 2 pds. Powder; silk, 1/4 gallons Molasses @ 3/6; 1 ivory comb; pr. mens worsd. stocks:, 1 bushel of Salt for ANN RUSSELL; To pd. WM. WREN; 1 knife; cloth; pr. thread hose. The Credit

Account shows payment of Debit: By Capt. MONROE; By Cash; in 1753 by cash, a Pistole; in 1754, by Cash at Capt. DIXONs; By Capt. DIXON.

- (p. 77). August 5, 1747. The Debit Account of Colo. BENJAMIN ROBINSON ballance brot. from Ledger F, fo: (207); with additional entries for 1 pr. best London Pumps yr. Son, JOS.: 4 bushells of Salt pr. Note; 1 lb. Bohea Tea; 200 8d. nails for inspecting yr. tobo: The Credit Account shows a payment June 10, 1748 By yr. Order on GEO: TODD.

- (p. 77). August 5, 1747. The Debit Account of WILLIAM ROBINS ballance brot. from Ledger F, fo: (55), no additional entries; no entries in Credit Account

- (p. 78). August 5, 1747. The Debit Account of JAMES SCURLOCK ballance brot. from Ledger F, fo: (264); with additional entries: To 1 yr. Plaid by SARAH TURNER to yr Wife; To WM. MARSHALLs Accot. to you not allow'd by him. The Credit Account shows payments: By JAMES MAXWELL if allow'd by him; By CORNELIUS McCARKE is allow'd by him; By WM. MARSHALL SENR. if allow'd by him; By yr. Judgmt. agst. RANKINS Estate

- (p. 78). August 5, 1747. The Debit Account of STROTHER SETTLE SENR. ballance brought from Ledger F, fo: (18); not additional entries; The Credit Account shows payment by Cash of Debit.

- (p. 78). August 5, 1747. The Debit Account of STROTHER SETTLE SENR. ballance brought from Ledger F, fo: (35); with four additional entries for cloth, thread and a pr. of worsd. hose; The Credit Account shows payment of Debit March 26, 1748: By Capt. FRANCIS THORNTON

- (p. 79). August 5, 1747. The Debit Account of HESTER STONE ballance from Ledger F, fo: (59), no additional entries; The Credit Account shows payment of Debit: By paid in a Mattox Transferr Note

- (p. 79). August 5, 1747. The Debit of JOHN SMITH, Prince William, ballance brot. from Ledger F, fo: (94); with two additional entries for June 13, 1748 of 3 7/8 yards of Check @ 2/2; and 1 1/2 yards of Check @ 2/. The Credit Account shows payment of Debit: By 1 Quantyco Crop Note; By the cask; By pd. Majr. WAGENER

- (p. 79). August 5, 1747. The Debit Account of MARGARET SETTLE ballance brot. from Ledger F, fo: (72), no additional entries; no entries in Credit Account

- (p. 79). August 5, 1747. The Debit Account of JOHN LOWELL ballance brot. from Ledger F, fo: (110), no additional entries; no entries in Credit Account

- (p. 80). August 5, 1747. The Debit Account of JOSEPH SETTLE ballance brot. from Ledger F, fo: (100); with a number of additional entries including: 1/2 doz. Pewter Plates; cloth, paper, salt, buttons, To 1/2 bushell Salt Delivd' by JNO: MORRISON at Christmas; To 1/2 yrd. Irish yr. Daughter @ 2/8; 1 knife & fork; 1 clasp knife; To 3 yds. Check by yr Wife @ 2/2; May 19, 1748: To 2 yds. Check yr. Daughter, ELIZA: @ 2/. The Credit Account shows payment of Debit: By Tobo; By 3 Chickens; By Cash; By H. WARE.

- (p. 80). August 5, 1747. The Debit Account of JOHN SINCLAIR Debt brot. from Ledger F., fo: (122); no additional entries; no entries in Credit Account

- (p. 80). August 5, 1747. The Debit Account of JOHN SOUTHARD ballance brot. from Ledger F, fo: (125); with additional entries for 1 1/2 bushells of Salt @ 3/6; To your Promissory Note for SAM. WHEELER, cloth and thread. The Credit Account shows a payment May 19, 1949 By Cash; but not in full.

- (p. 81). August 6, 1747. The Debit Account of ROBERT SMITH, Stafford, ballance brot. from Ledger F, fo: (128), with no additional entries, no entries in Credit Account

- (p. 81). August 6, 1747. The Debit Account of JOHN STROTHER, Debt brot. from Ledger F. fo: (160); with several additional entries including buttoms, knee buckles, cloth; To pd. WM. WHEELER by yr. order; yarn hose; To Cr. FRA: BALTROP by yr. Note; To Cr. JOHN ROACH; To pd. Mrs. JONES by yr. Note; To pd. FRA: BALTROP by yr. 2 Notes 30/ each; To pd. HOWSON HOOE by yr Note; To Quitrents for one year; To paid Major CHAMPE; The Credit Account shows payment of Debit November 25, 1747: By WM. WHEELER; By 121 acres of Land

- (p. 81). August 6, 1747. The Debit Account of JOSEPH SPICER Ballance brot. from Ledger F, fo: (132); no additional entries; no entries in Credit Account

- (p. 81). November 21, 1747. The Debit Account of JAMES CASH. To 1 1/2 bushell Salt; To 1 bushell Salt yr. Negro man; (2 more entries for Salt); The Credit Account shows payment of Debit by Cash.

- (p. 82). August 6, 1747. The Debit Account of WILLIAM SETTLE SENR. ballance brot. from Ledger F, fo: (147); no additional entries; The Credit Account shows partial payment of the Debit April 8, 1751 By a Horse

- (p. 82). August 6, 1747. The Debit Account of ISAAC SETTLE ballance brot. from Ledger F., fo: (175); with additional entries for nails; cloth, To 6 yds. Drogheda by yr. Daughter; To 3 falls by yr Son; powder and shott by ANTHO: FICKLING; 1 boys felt, one weeding hoe; (1751): To my order on Capt. DIXON. The Credit Account shows payment of the Debit: By 2 Empty Hogds; By CHARLES WHARTON; By WM. MARSHALL SENR., By Cash; By 9 head of Cattle.

- (p. 82). August 6, 1747. The Debit Account of Capt. SAMUEL SKINKER ballance brot. from Ledger F, fo: (251); with additional entries including: To 2 bushells Salt lent as from do: (paid); To JOHN WITHERS Debt in part; To the Vestrys order on you; To 30 lbs. Oatmeal; To 1 pack Cards by Guy; To JOHN STROTHERs Land; To 1/2 lb. Powder by Johnny; To 1 pr. Kid Gloves by Mrs. MOLLY; To 3 bushells Lime; To 1 pr. small girls shoes by Mrs. MOLLY; The Credit Account shows payment of Debit: By Colo. WM. BEVERLEY; By 2 lbs. Salt Petre returned in kind; By paid Majr. CHAMPE for WITHERS; By THOMAS BARTLETT; By Cash; By JOSEPH TUTT for Court Martial Fine; By Major JOHN CHAMPE; By 1 Quarter Beef; (carried to page (125).

- (p. 83). August 6, 1747. The Debit Account of WILLIAM SETTLE, Son of FRANCIS, ballance brot. from Ledger F, fo: (145), no additional entries; The Credit Account shows payment of Debit by Cash March 10th 1755.

- (p. 83). August 6, 1747. The Debit Account of THOMAS ZACHARY ballance brot. from Ledger F., fo: (241); with additional entries including: cloth, salt, nails, thread, and 3 levies; March 2d 1749: Then settled Accots. with THOS: TURNER & the ballance due to him is 7:4:10 1/2; wch: I promise to pay on demand witness my hand THOMAS his mark T ZACHARY. Witness JNO: BATTALEY. Account continues: To cost of suit; To pd BENJA. MARSHALL, Exr. GEO: HARRISON; May 4th 1750: To pd. 15 s. & 7d. tobo. The Credit Account shows payments by Crop notes; By JNO: WREN SENR; By 1 Crop note on Accot. of GEO: HARRISON; cost of do suit computed at 85 lbs. tobacco; By WM. JAMESON; by Capt. DIXON

(p. 83). November 9, 1747. The Debit Account of THOMAS DEW. To fell short in paymt. of yr. Levy; To Cr. MEREDITH HELM by WM. FURLONG; To 1 felt hat, To Cr. WM. FURLONG for sundrys he took up for you on November 9; The Credit Account shows one payment 1748; By: JOHN TRIPLETT (account paid in full.)

(p. 84.).August 6, 1747. The Debit Account of JOSEPH STROTHER SENR. ballance from Ledger F, fo: (220); To fell short in your Levy as pr do.; To Cr. WM. SMITH by yr. Order; July 15th 1749: To Cr. JAMS: ARNOLD; 27th: To paid OWEN CAMPBELL pr. your Order The Credit Account shows payment by 3 transfer Notes; by Cash, By overpd. in Levys; by Capt. DIXON. (account paid in full).

(p. 84). August 6, 1747. The Debit Account of SARAH SETTLE Debt from Ledger F, fo. (2); no additional entires: the Credit Account shows an undated payment by JOSIAH FERGUSON of the Debit Account.

(p. 84). August 6, 1747. The Debit Account of JOHN SHOTWELL ballance from Ledger F., fo: (206); no additional entries; the Credit Account shows payment of the Ballance October 4, 1749 By Mr. WILLIAM HUNTER.

(p. 85), August 19, 1747. The Debit Account of Mr. JOHN TRIPLETT ballance from Ledger F, fo. (165); with additional Debits for 1 pr. womens shoes; pins, thread, 2 pr. womens coarse gloves; silk, fine Irish, 5 1/4 yds. best blew Shalloon @ 2/6; 2 bushells Salt @ 3/6; 1 pr. womens worsd. hose; pr. mens yarn hose; To Cr. THOS: NIXON pr. yr. Note; To Cash paid you by Majr: Champe; To Credit JNO: FORGUS pr. Note; To Cr. JAMES PURCELL; To THOS: DEWs Account; The Credit Account shows a ballance of Tobacco from Ledger F, fo. (165); By Colo: CHAMPE (Sterling payment of 112:10:0; By your Bond payable 10th June; By Interest on your Debt; March 19, 1750: To 5 quarts of Wine

(p. 85). August 21, 1747. The Debit Account of BENJAMIN SETTLE your Acct. from Ledger F, fo: (138); with additional debits for 1 pr. Dble. Channeld. Pumps; Linen, Garlix, Shalloon, 2 doz. coat buttons, 1 oz. blue thread; 1/4 lb. white thread; The Credit Account shows for payment By Cash; (Carrd: to page 141.)

(p. 85), December 19, 1747. The Debit Account of JOHN ROSE, MARTHA HELLIERs Son in Law; To 10 1/2 yds. Drogheda @ 1/6; 0:15:9; The Credit account shows no entries

(p. 86). August 21, 1747. The Debit Account of JOHN SHORT; To 93 lbs. Rice as pr. Ledger F, page 9153 @ 1 1/2d; December 7: To one pipe of Wine; To 1 bed cord; The Credit Account shows two cash payments to pay debit in full.

(p. 86). August 21, 1747. The Debit Account of AQUILLA SNELLING. ballance from Ledger F, fo: (152); with additionals debts for cloth, To 7 yds. Check @ 2/2 by yr. Brother;

thread, pr. mens shoes, pr. words. hose; a mans Hat. The Credit Account shows payment in full July 14, 1749: By Colo. BENJAMIN ROBINSON

(p. 86). August 21, 1747. The Debit Account of JOSEPH STROTHER JUNR. ballance from Ledger F, fo: (59); with additional debits for 1 1/2 bushells Salt pr. Note; To Cr. MARGT. DONAHOE by yr. Order; March 2d. 1748: To cash; The Credit Account shows payment in full April 20th 1748 By Capt. JNO: MICOU.

(p. 87). August 21, 1747. The Debit Account of JOHN STRANGE, Overseer ELK RUN; yr. Acct. brot. from Ledger F, fo. (183); with 3 additionals debits for fine Check, for 2 yds. Irish, To 1 oz. Nuns; The Credit Account shows payment by yr. Share of 6013 tobo: being 10 1/2 shares; By Cash for ballance

(p. 87). August 21, 1747. The Debit Account of WILLIAM SMITH your ballance brot. from Ledger F, fo: (3); no additional entries. The Credit Accoount shows payment April 31 1748 by Capt. JOSEPH STROTHERS Cr.

(p. 87). August 21, 1747. The Debit Account of REVD. JOSEPH SIMPSON your Acct. from page (266), in Ledger F; with additional debits for 5 gallons Wine; pd. ROBT. WALKER, Cash recd. of DOCTOR FLOOD; To 4 3 1/2 galls of Madeira Wine @ 5/6; To 22 gallons of Wine & Cask; To pd. yr. Ordr: to Colo: LOMAX; To one bell mettle Skillet; To 147 squares of Glass; To 40 dollars in Cash; To cash for THOMPSON to pay GOODMAN; To 1 1/2 yds. Irish Linen pr. ELIZA: BENSON; To pd. JOHN BATTALEY for Drawing a Sett of Deeds; To cash pd. Majr: SKINKER; The Credit Account shows Credit brot. from Ledger F, fo: 266; pr. OLIVER TOWLES; By JNO: MORISONs Schooling; By Capt. FRAS. THORNTON; By yr. Excha. on JOS: TAYLOR; By JOHN MORISONs Schooling; By part of JOHN MORISONs Board; By JNO. MORISONs Acct. for books, paper & shoes; (Account paid).

(On the Credit side of p. 87, the following appears: Febry. ye 23d. 1747. One years School; 3 quires of paper; 2 pair of Double channeld. pumps; Virgil net Delph; Justin, Ceesars Comt; History of Scotland; To one years School (5: 0: 0); To one quire of paper; To 9 months & 2 weeks Board (6: 0: 0); To 5 months School; To one Horace at 10/, one Greek Testys: Cashs reced of Mr. TOLES for Pictures bought of SINGLETON; Handlys Physick; Cash reced of Mr. THORNTON; for Tobacco. The Entry appears to pertain to the REVD. JOSEPH SIMPSON.)

(p. 88). August 22, 1747. The Debit Account of Mrs. SARAH SMITH; To 41 bushells of Slime as pr. Ledgr: F, fo. 23. No additional entries. The Credit Account shows payment in full: March 23, 1747/8 By Cash.

(p. 88). August 22, 1747. The Debit Account of BENJAMIN STROTHER JUNR. To your Acct. brot. from Ledger F, fo. (83). No additional entries. The Credit Account shows payment in full June 8, 1747 By Cash

(p. 88). December 7, 1747. The Debit Account of JAMES STIGLER. To 1 bushell Salt; To 1 boys felt. The Credit Account shows payment in full April 27, 1748 By WILLIAM LONGMIRE; By Cash.

(p. 88). August 22, 1747. The Debit Account of Mrs. SLAUGHTER; To 50 1/2 lbs. Wool as pr Ledger F, fo. (14), @ 8d; no additional entries. The Debit account shows payment in full in 1748: By ROBT. JACKSON

(p. 89). August 22, 1747. The Debit Account of WILLIAM TAYLOR. To your ballance brot. from Ledger F, fo: (20), no additional entries; The Credit Account shows no entries.

(p. 89). August 22, 1747. The Debit Account of GEORGE TANKERSLEY. To your ballance brot. from Ledger F, fo. (129); To 1 yd. Irish by DORCAS; To 1 yd. Shaloon by REUBEN; salt, hops, thread, coat buttons, bottle of wine; check, To 1 Cow; To 3 bushells of Barley; To 4 bottles of Wine, To 105 pds. of Beef; The Credit Account shows payments by 1 1/2 bushells of Pease; cash, 5 bushells of Pease; By my Inspection Account; the Beef and Wine paid by Cash.

(p. 89). January 12, 1747/8. The Debit Account of Mr. JOHN SINGLETON. To 48 gallons Ale; To 62 gallons of Ale. The Credit Account shows payment: By Cash for ballance, 5: 10: 0.

(p. 90). August 22, 1747. The Debit Account of JOHN THORNLEY. To your Acct. brot. from Ledger F, fo: (112); with additional entries for Salt, silk, coat buttons, 5 yds. of Shaloon @ 2/4; To 7 yds. Irish @ 2/8; To your Rent for the year 1746 omitted; To your Rent for the year 1747; additional purchases of Salt in 1749 and 100 8d. nails. The Credit Account shows: By your Credit brot. from Ledger F, fo: (112); By 1 Gibsons Transfer Note; By Capt. EDWARD DIXON. (Payment in full of debit.)

(p. 90). August 22, 1747. The Debit Account of Capt. WILLIAM TALIAFERRO. To your ballance brot. from Ledger F, fo: (130); with additional entries for 2 hhds. tobacco, To RICHD. ROBINSONs Accot. with me; To an Error in Colo. ARMISTEADs Cr. in Book F, fol: /130/; salt & 6 doz. Corks. In 1748: 1 lb. Bohea Tea; 11 lbs. Large white Rope; 1 Gross Corks lent; 5 yds. of Red binding @ 2d; To pd. Mr. HARRY TURNER for Molassus; 3 lbs. Turkey Coffee; 2 lbs. Chocolate; 5 1/2 lbs. hops, 30 gallons Beer. The Credit Account shows payment in full: By Colo. ARMSTEAD for 3 quarters Beef; 3000 feet of Scantling; By JOHN WREN JUNR; By Cash; By WM. MARSHALL SENR; By Colo. WOODFORD; By Ballance charged in fo: /146/.

(p. 91). August 1747. The Debit Account of Capt. FRANCIS THORNTON. To your Acct.brought from Ledger F, fo: (257); with additional entries including 7 hhds. tobo: Lent; 1 pr. Stays pr. Note; silk, shalloon, men worsd. hose; breast mettle buttons; loaf dble. refd. Sugar; 1 lb. Green Tea; 2 bushells Salt; pr. womens hose; 1/2 lb. Pepper; 1 peice Diaper Tape; powder & shott by JNO: McCORMICK; 1 sockett Chissell, 500 10d. Nails The Credit Account shows: To Interest on your Bond one year this day; To Mr. SIMPSONs Order; (other Interest payments); To cash for return'd shoes; (Carried to Page 119).

(p. 91). August 22, 1747. The Debit Account of DANIEL TAYLOR. To your ballance brot. from Ledger F, fo: (111); with additional entries for Salt, cloth, thread through November 25, 1748. The Credit Account shows three payments in Cash; By overpaid in your levy

(p. 91), November 25, 1747. The Debit Account of Mr. FRANCIS TALIAFERRO. To 2 dozen Coat Buttons (only entry). The Credit Account shows payment in full by Cash

(p. 92). 1747. The Debit Account of Capt. OLIVER TOWLES. To your Debt brot. from Ledger F, fo. (269); followed by numerous entries including 1 pipe of Wine; 2 dozen

Bottles lent; 1 Quarter of Lamb; 28 foot 1/4 inch Plank, 16 bottles of English Beer; 1 Tea Pott; 1500 3d. nails; 1 m. 6d. nails; Silk Handkercheif by JNO: SMART; 1 Linnen Handkercheif by do; 1 pr. best worsd. hose to do; To paid Colo. WOODFORD; To 1 cask of Cyder 104 gallons @ 6; To 2 doz. wine glasses @ 8/; coat buttons, silk, various kinds of cloth; To sundrys for BENJA: KNIGHT from my Book; To sundrys for WM. GORDON; To do for JNO: McHENRY; To 30 galls of Cyder @ 6d; To Cr. HENRY JOHNSON pr. your Order; To 31 1/2 gallons Ale & 6 bottles; To 1 mans fine hatt by JNO: SMART; To 30 gallons of Ale; To Cr. JOHN McHENRY pr. yr. Note; To Cr. JOHN SMART pr. yr. Note; To Cr. BENJA: KNIGHT pr. yr. Note; To 20 gallons of Ale; To 30 gallons of Beer; 2 prs. boys shoes; (several other entries for Beer, Ale and Wine), 61 gallons French Brandy @ 4/6; 1 pr. of Shoes to Negro Jammey; (The Debit of this account 437: 5: 1 1/2. The Credit Account shows payments of 462: 11: 8 1/2 by Credit brot. from Ledger F, fo: (269); By JOHN MILLERs Bond; By a barrel of Flower wt. 181 Nett; By 48 hhds. of Shells; By 14 yds. of Crape; By 70 hhds. of Shells; By Taylors Work formerly omitted; By 5 gallons of Linseed Oyl; By Freight for 10 Tun of Stone 15/; By Joiners Work for Sash frames; By freight for 7 tuns of Stone; By Mr. JOHN MARTIN for 13 yds. Crape by WEEDON ARNOLD; By coopers work for 6 cask; By THOS: TURNER JUNR., By Cash of PATK. MITCHELL; By Cash 1 dbleloon; By 2 crop Notes; (Carried to page (122).

(p. 93). August 22, 1747. The Debit Account of THOMAS THATCHER. To your ballance brot. from Ledger F, fo: (265); with numerous additional entries including salt, cloth, nails, 1 Copy book; 1 clasp knife; pr. scissors; thread; powder & shott; paper. The Credit Account shows payments: By Cash of Mr. BENJA: GRYMES; By a hhd. of tobo: Augt. 8th 1749: By JNO: WREN.

(p. 93). August 22, 1747. The Debit Account of Capt. ANTHONY THORNTON. To your ballance brot. from Ledger F, fo: (127), no additional entries. The Credit Account shows full payment by Cash Augt. 20th 1748.

(p. 93). September 21, 1747. The Debit Account of REVD. MR. ROBT. ROSE. To paid Mr. PATRICK MITCHELL; Int. 8 months. The Credit Account shows full payment in 1748 By Capt. WARD.

(p. 94). August 22, 1747. The Debit Account of WILLIAM TURLAND. To your ballance brot. from Ledger F, fo: (49); with two additional entries for Salt. The Credit account shows payment in full by Cash February 4, 1748/9.

(p. 94). August 22, 1747. The Debit Account of DARBY TOOL. To your ballance brought from Ledger F, fo: (242); with two additional entries for Tartan and Irish. The Credit account shows payment in full By HARRY TURNER

(p. 94). March 22, 1747/8. The Debit Account of Mr. ROBERT VAULX. To cash paid JAMES WALKER; To 4 1/2 gallons of Wine @ 6/; To cash paid HARRY TURNER; (other Wine purchases). The Credit Account shows payment in full: By 5584 foot of Inch Plank @ 5/; By 1098 feet of 1 1/2 Plank @ 5/; By 2628 Inch do @ 5/; Deduct freight.

(p. 94). May 4, 1746. The Debit Account of Colo. WM. FAIRFAX; To 160 1/2 lbs. hops; To cash pr. yr. Order to JNO: SUTTON; To cash pd. Majr. CHAMPE; May 1949, two purchases of Tea. The Credit Account shows payment for items (except Tea) May 1748: By Cash reced of the Caroline Sheriff on Accot. of JNO: MILLER

(p. 95). August 26, 1747. The Debit Account of ROBERT TALIAFERRO (Mattapony); To yr. Accompt. brot. from Ledger F, fo: (34); no additional entries; The Credit Account shows payment in full January 3, 1747/8: By WM. BOWLER.

(p. 95). August 26, 1747. The Debit Account of ELLINOR TAYLOR. To your ballance brought from Ledger F, fo: (56), no additional entries. The Credit Account has no entries.

(p. 95). August 26, 1747. The Debit Account of CHARLES WHARTON. To yr. ballance brot. from Ledger F, fo: (81); with additional entries including sugar, cloth, thread, powder, pins, salt, a meal sifter; a clasp knife; To Cr. ISAAC SETTLE; To 6 1/2 yds. Holland Check @ 3/6 by JNO: WHARTON; Ballance due now in Cash; due for Rent. The Credit Account includes payments By making 28 pair shoes; By mending yr. Chair Harness; By mending 2 pr pumps; By tobo: By 12 pr. shoes making; By WM. FURLONG; By a Crop Note; By Ballance Sterling acct. as above pd. By DAVID WILSON; By yr. Wives Knitting; By making 12 pr. Shoes; By JAS. JONES; which pays for a barrell of Corn, 275 ft. plank.

(p. 96). August 1747. The Debit Account of DANIEL WHITE SENR. To your ballance brot. from Ledger F, fo: (262); with additional entries including: To paid RICHARD BERNARD as from Do; To paid FOXHALL STURMAN as from Do; cloth, a razor, To your Promissory Note for SAML. WHEELER; cloth, silk, thread; To Cr. LAWRENCE DOWNTON pr. Note; 1 felt; quire of paper, 250 6d nails; To paid NATHANIEL GRAY; May 19, 1750; To 2 bottles of Wine. The Credit Account shows payment in full By Cash; By 1 hogd. tobo: by the Cask; By yr. Exo. agt. RANKINs Estate; By 3 Mattox Notes; By Gibsons Inspection; By do 24 lbs. tobo:

(p. 96). September 16, 1747. The Debit Account of MAJR. BAILER; To 1 Pipe of Wine, 25 pistoles Error; To 7 1/2 yds. garlix; May 1751: To 1 pd. fine Hyson Tea; July 10: To 1 pd. do Lent. The Credit Account shows payment in full by two cash payments and by 1 pd. Tea return'd.

(p. 97). August 26, 1747. The Debit Account of MAJR. WILLIAM WALKER. To your ballance brot. from Ledger F, fo: (252), with numerous additional entries including 2 horse collars; To yr. Order to pay HARRY TURNER; To yr. Order to pay JAMES BOWIE; To 1 doz. Wine glasses; To 8 bushells Corn at the Mill @ 7/6; To a pr. of Mill Stones; To OLIVER TOWLES Order for Capping; nails, pr. shoes to yr. man; Cash received of JOHN SHORT; To paid WM. PINN; To 3 Bricklayers Trowells; a felt hatt; 1 m. 6d. nails pr. JAS. HARPER; To paid WILLIAM PINN; To 1 carpenters Chissell pr. JAS: WREN; nails pr. HARPER; nails prL JNO: CATLETT; To 6 m. Shingles; To Cash pd. for 5000 feet of Plank; To 2500 shingles pd. CARSON for the Prison; To 8 1/2 barrels of Corn from the Mill; To 17700 shingles for the Church; To your Bond to LEEDS TOWN JUSTICES; To 4 yrs. 8 months Interest; To 45 feet of Flagstone; To 40 feet of 2 Inch Oak plank; Total Debit 338: 2: 6. The Credit Account shows payments to total 338: 1: 0: By Smiths Accot. to this Day; By yr. Order on WASHINGTON PARISH Collectors for 22000 @ 9/6; By Colo. WOODFORD; By an allowance in the 8d. nails; By Painters work; By yr. Order on the Sheriff of WESTMORELAND COUNTY for 11348 @ 12/6; By do HANOVER PARISH Collectors for 19000; By 1000 feet 1 1/4 Plank; By 1800 do Inch

(p. 97). April 20, 1748. The Debit Account of Mr. RICHARD TUTT. To a ballance on a former Acct. from Ledger D, fo. (208); with three additionals entries: To Cash of Mr. BENJA: GRYMES; To Cash by JNO: BATTALEY; To Ballance all Accots. to this Day. The Credit Account shows payments which include: By ton of Stone as pr. yr. Acct., By RICHD. FRY; By 20 ton of Stone by GASKINS; By 18 ton of do by PETER LEE; By 20 ton of do "balanced." 1751. By 12 tun Stone; By 12 tun do; By 24 do p INGRAM & NICOLS.

(p. 98). August 26, 1747. The Debit Account of GEORGE WILLIAMS, To your ballance brot. from Ledger F, fo. (97); the above tobo: The Credit Account shows payment in full 7br. 10, 1751 By ROBT. RAE.

(p. 98). January 30, 1748/9. The Debit Account of MOSES PITMAN. To 1 bushell Salt by JAS: JONES. The Credit Account shows partial payment same date by Cash.

(p. 98). August 26, 1747. The Debit Account of JOSEPH WHARTON. To your ballance brot. from Ledger F, fo: (101); with a number of additional items including mostly various kinds of cloth; To 10 lbs. Wool by WM. FURLONG; powder & shott; April 3d. 1750; To Cash at Spotsylvania Court; To cash pd. RICHD. BARNES; The Credit Account shows payment in full May 5, 1750; By 50 acres of Land 38: 0: 0.

(p. 99). August 26, 1747. The Debit Account of COLO. WILLIAM WOODFORD. To your ballance brot. from Ledger F, fo: (31); with a number of additiona entries including Too 1 lb. Bohea Tea 14/; To 1 lb. Green do: 18/; To pd. Mr. GILCHRIST; To ROBT. WALKERs Cr. allowed before; 5 m. 10d. nails; To paid Majr. WALKER; salt, 2 packs cards, 25 gallons Wine; a grindstone; 1 lb. Bohea Tea; To pd. H. TURNER. To 30 gallons of Wine & cask; To pd. Gibsons Inspection; To a Barrell of Sugar, To 1 keg Vinegar; The Credit Account shows a num-ber of entries including: By OLIVER TOWLES; By ROBT. WALKER Cash; By 60 barrels of Corn @ 27/6; By an allowance on Mill Stones; By yr. Excha; on SYDENHAM & HODGSON; By 2 hhds. of tobo: sold at ROYS WAREHOUSE Public Sale; April 10th 1751: By HENRY DRAKEs Note; By JNO: WREN.

(p. 99). August 26, 1747. The Debit Account of Mr. ROBERT WALKER. To your ballance brot. from Ledger F, fo. (250) with additional entries including To 1 felt No. 3, 1 do No. 4; 1 m. 6d nails; To 1 pr. Shoes to JAS: COSWELL 6/6 pr. yr. Note; To 1 pr. Buckles to Do 1/3; To Cr. LEWIS JONES's Negro pr. yr. Note; To pr. Mens Shoes JAMES LINDSEY; To pr. Mens Gloves; 1 best Curb Bridle; 30 gallons Beer; cloth, thread, To 1 Silk Handkerchief by JAS: LINDSEY; To 30 gallons Beer; To 30 gallons Beer; To 1 frying pan; salt, cloth, broad axes; To Cr. JAMES COSWELL pr. Note; To Cr. BEN: REEVES pr. yr. Note; To 1 pr. Shoes pr. Note to JAMES LINDSEY; To your Rent for the year 1747; To 4 gallons of Wine; To Cr. DANIEL WHITE by yr. Note; To Cr. STEPHEN CASH by yr. Note; To 4 gallons Madeira Wine; The Credit Account shows payment: By your Account agst. me to this Day; By HARRY TURNER Cr. to THOS. ROY in Error; By the Revd. Mr. SIMPSON; By Capt. SNEAD; By a pair of Chair wheels &c., By a small Quarter Beef; By yr. Accot. agst.me to this day; By Ballance due T. T. & Carried to page (126).

(p. 100). August 26, 1747. The Debit Account of WILLIAM WHITE. To your ballance brot. from ledger F., fo. (270); with additional entries including cloth; pr. worsd. hose; pr. mens gloves, a silver laced hat; To Cr. JOHN KENDALL pr. yr. Note; To yr. Debt to HARRY TURNER; To goods bought at RANKINs Sale; To my Judgmt. agst. WHARTON & you; To cost of WHARTONs Suit; June 9, 1748: To 1 mans hatt; The Credit Account shows payment which include: By a Negro girl bought at Out Cry; By THOMAS BUTLER; By CHAS. ASHTON; By 1 hhd. tobacco; May 3d. 1750: By BIRKET PRATT.

(p. 100). August 26, 1747. The Debit Account of WILLIAM WHEELER. To your ballance brot. from Ledger F, fo: (66); with additional entries which include: To your Promissory Note for yr. Son, SAMUEL; cloth, salt, nails, shot, To Cr. JNO. STROTHER; The Credit Account shows payment in full: By JNO: STROTHER; By tobacco; By 1 hhd. tobacco; By the cask; By an allowance on Nails p Day Book

(p. 101). August 26, 1747. The Debit Account of DANIEL WHITE, King George. To yr. ballance brot. from Ledger F, fo. (53), with additiona entries for 4 bushells of Salt; To JOS: DODDs Order; To Transfer notes; To yr. Debit in Parish Book; To JAS: ALLENs Levy; To paid JOEL ANCORAM; To paid WM. DODGINS; To pd. WM. BRUCE for Clks. Note. The Credit Account shows payment: By ROBERT WALKERs Note; By PATK. WHITEHALL; By cash; By yr. Cr. in Parish Book; By the Cask & prizing.

(p. 101). August 26, 1747. The Debit Account of JAMES WHITE. To your ballance from Ledger F, fo: (56); with two additional entries: To pd. THOMAS ROY; To cash pd. JAS. LEWIS The Credit Account shows full payment: By a Roys Crop Note; By the Cask

(p. 101). April 14, 1748. The Debit Account of SAMUEL WHARTON. A number of entries are for cloth; thread, 1 quarter Beef; a bushell Salt; 1250 10d. 100 20d. nails; a felt hat, a broad ax; To pd. yr. levy 69 Tobo: To my Note to PAT: COUTTS. The Credit Account shows full payment: By yr. Account for Mill Work to this Day; By 64 acres of Land, 48: 0: 0: By 17 1/2 days work to this time. (Debit & Credit: 50: 3: 4:)

(p. 102). August 26, 1747. The Debit Account of HENRY WARE. To your ballance brot. from Ledger F, fo: (67); with additional entries including nails, 3 yds. Cotton @ 3/; To paid JOSIAH FARGUSON; 1 hank silk; thread; To 1 bushell Salt pr. JOHN SETTLE; To pd. Majr. SKINKER; To 6 ells Wrapper; To 1 side Leather; To 1 bottle Wine; To yr. Obligation to LUKE BURFORD; To 2 pds. Chocolate; To 3 pds. do; To pd. JOS: SUTTLE; The Credit Account shows payment in full: By a Wrong charge of 758 tobo: wch: should be charged the Estate; By RICHARD FRY; By 63 1/2 barrels Corn; By 4 barrels of Corn to DAVIDSON; By 20 pds. Bacon, 1/2 bushel pease.

(p. 102). August 26, 1747. The Debit Account of JOHN WILLIS. To yr. ballance from Ledger F, fo: (79); with two entries for 1 Stock lock, To 1 ditto. The Credit Account shows full payment: By 97 lbs. tobacco; By cash; By F. JETT

(p. 102). August 26, 1747. The Debit Account of RICHARD WALKER. To yr. ballance brot. from Ledger F, fo. (86); no additional entries. No entries in the Credit Account.

(p. 103). August 26, 1747. The Debit Account of SAMUEL WHEELER. To yr. ballance brot. from Ledger F. fo. (120); with an additional entry: To pd. WM. HARRISON for his case of yr. Stock. The Credit Account shows payments: By JOHN WEBB; by JNO: ARROWSMITH; By WM. HARRISON; By DANIEL WHITE; By WILLIAM WHEELER.

(p. 103). August 26, 1747. The Debit Account of JOSEPH WHEELER. To yr. ballance brot. from Ledger F, fo: (98); no additiona entries; no entries in Credit Account

(p. 103). August 26, 1747. The Debit Account of DANIEL WHITE JUNR. To yr. ballance brot. from Ledger F, fo: (135); with additional entries including salt, cloth, shoe buckles, hilling hoes; small buttons; powder & shot; The Credit Account shows full payment by tobacco; By Empty hhds; Then a further Debit May 24, 1750 for cloth and salt.

(p. 103). August 26, 1747. The Debit Account of SARAH WISDALL. To your Debt brot. from Ledgr. F, fo: (149); with additional entries including: To Cr. you as pr Contra: To your Rent for the year 1747; To 1/2 bushell Salt, To 2 1/2 yards Ozn. @ 15d; December 25th 1749: To yr. Rent for 1749, (500 lbs. tobacco). The Debit Account shows payment in full: By your Credit brought from Ledger F, fo: (149); By your ballance due to you in tobo: By CHRISTOPHER LAST; By 1 pr. Gloves & 1 pr. Stockings; By yr. Parish Claim for the year 1747; By Cutting Negroes Cloth; December 25th 1749: By yr. Parish Claim (500 lbs. of tobacco.)

(p. 104). August 26, 1747. The Debit Account of FRANCIS WOFENDALL. To your ballance brot. from Ledger F, fo: (237). with additional entries including: To 4 levies for yr. self & FRA: STROTHER @ 42; 1small felt, cloth, salt; To 7 yds. Check by JNO: DONOHOE @ 2/2; thread; To 1 1/2 bushell Salt by JNO: DONOHOE @ 3/6; To 1 pr. womans wash gloves; To 100 8d. nails; To yr. Promissory Note of this date; To a Carolina Hatt after the above Note; To 3 broadhoes; The Credit Account shows payments By tobacco & Cash; By 32 1/2 lbs. Feathers omitted in Ledger F, fo. (237); By a Crop note;

(p. 104). May 17, 1748. The Debit Account of Capt. WARD. To 4 Quarters of Beef. wt. 373. The Credit Account shows: "ballance in Cash."

(p. 104). August 26, 1747. The Debit Account of JOHN WELSH, of COBLERS MOUNTAIN. To your ballance brot. from Ledger F, fo: (154), no additional entries and no entries in the Credit Account

(p. 105). August 26, 1747. The Debit Account of JOHN WREN SENR. To your ballance brot. from Ledger F, fo: (202); with additional entries including nails, sugar, salt, To 1/2 m. Pins to JERE: BROWN; To one Kettle at RANKINs. Out Cry; To 1 yrs. Rent; To an Old Note; To 1 Steer; To 7 hhds. Shells; To balla: tobo: accot. The Credit Account shows full payment By yr. Account from Inspectors Book; By 2 qts. of Brandy not Accounted for, By your Inspectors Account to this Day; By Majr. JNO: TALIAFERRO; By a Balla: in Excha: in cash;

(p. 105). August 26, 1747. The Debit Account of WILLIAM WHARTON. To your ballance brot. from Ledger F, fo: (33); with additional entry: To the Tobo: Article; the Credit Account shows partial payment of Debit By Tobo: By yr Exo. agst. RANKINs Estate

(p. 106). August 26, 1747. The Debit Account of BENJAMIN WEEDON. To your ballance brot. from Ledger F, fo: (74); no additional entries. The Credit Account shows payment in full September 25th 1749: By Cash of WEEDON ARNOLD; By do.

(p. 106). August 26, 1747. The Debit Account of CHARLES WRIGHT. To your Accompt brot. from ledger F, fo: (80), with additional entries including To 2 pr. yarn hose pr. F. ROBBINS; To 1 yard Shallon @ 2/6; To 1 1/2 dozen mettle Coat buttons @ 15d; To 2 doz. Vest ditto @ 8d., To green thread, 1 pr. buckles @ 1/3. The Credit Account shows full payment May 17, 1748 by a hogd. tobo. and Cash; October 26, 1749, By cash.

(p. 106). August 26, 1747. The Debit Account of BENJA: WOODWARD. To yr. ballance brot. from Ledger F, fo: (218), with one additional entry January 14, 1747/8: To 111 gallons of Ale. The Credit Account shows payment in full by four cash payments, the last October 2, 1751.

(p. 107). August 26, 1747. The Debit Account of WILLIAM WREN. To your Debt brot. from Ledger F, fo: (54); with additional entries including: To 3 dozen Coat Buttons; To pd. ROBT. MONDAY pr. yr. Order; October 14, 1747: To a Marriage Lycense, Governors Dues; several debits for Cash; July 27, 1749: To overpd. you for 46 lbs. Beef. The Credit Account shows payment in full: By Credt brot. from Ledger F, fo: (54); By your Beef Acct., By 35 lbs. of Tallow; By THOMAS ROBBINS; By Acct. for Beef; By 46 lbs. Beef; By ISAAC ARNOLD JUNR., By 787 lbs. of Beef; By 12 Heads

(p. 107); August 26, 1747. The Debit Account of GEORGE WRINGLESBY. To your ballance brot. from Ledger F, fo: (82); with numerous additional entries including cloth, salt, pins, laces, 1 1/2 yds. Check by Negro Joe; To 100 10d. nails; brown thread; powder & shott; pr. womens worsted stockings; To 1/2 yd. Cotton by SARAH GRAVES; To 1 hilling hoe pr. SARAH GRAVES; quire paper; To paid ROBERT PECK; To paid Mr. JAS. BOWIE; August 29, 1749: To Cr. JOSH. DODD pr. yr. Note; The Credit Account shows payment in full of 24: 10: 1 1/4: By yr. Womens Stockings returned; By your last years ballance; By your share & 1/2 of tobo: this year; By H. REYNOLDS order for his Parish Claim; By your Parish Claim; By Ballanced charged fo. (151).

(p. 108). August 26, 1747. The Debit Account of JOHN WREN JUNR. To your Ballance brot. from Ledger F, fo: (266); with a number of additional entries including To 5 yds. Shalloon @ 2/6 yr. Wife; To Cr. LEWIS JONES 2 1/2 yds. Drogheda @ 1/6; To 1 Linnen Handkerchief; To 1 pr. Shoes to ANDREW; 1/2 lb. Powder; pr. mens shoes; a felt hat; 1 mans fine hatt; 1 1/2 bushell Salt; To 12 1/2 yds. Dowlass by yr. Wife; To paid Capt. WM. TALIAFERRO; To pr. worsd. hose; To 1/4 lb. Powder, 1 lb. Shott yr. Wife; To 2 yds. Callico yr. Wife @ 5/6; To pr. womens shoes pr. yr. Wife; November 3, 1749: To 1 Cow 1: 12: 3; The Credit Account shows partial payment by a cash payment and By yr. Accot. of Work to this Day being 3 months

(p. 108). August 26, 1747. The Debit Account of FRANCIS WATTS, Prince William; To your Debt brought from Ledger F, fo: (18); with three additional entries : To 1 Tobo: Box; To Cash; To pd. Colo. CHAMPE; The Credit Account shows a Credit from Ledger F, fo: (18); By yr. 2 shares for Anno 1746; By part of a Horse unpaid

(p. 108). January 8, 1747/8. The Debit Account of PETER LEE. A number of entries including: salt, sheeting, cloth, pr. mens pumps; pr. womens shoes; 1 clasp knife; 1 hank twine; After settlement a fine hat; 2 silk handkerchiefs; additional cloth. The Credit Account shows a total payment of 16: 6: 0 (the settlement amount); balance due of 3: 5: 0; with eight payments of 154 tons of Stone; 38 hhds. of Shells @ 2/6.

(p. 109). July 27, 1747. The Debit and Credit Accounts of ALEXANDER SNELLING SENR. has been crossed out.

(p. 109). July 27, 1747. The Debit Account of ALEXANDER SNELLING JUNR. A number of entries including a quire of paper; cloth, shott, pr.mens shoes; pr. garters, 1 padd lock; furrd. hatt; powder. mans hatt, womans shoes; a weeding hoe; To yr. Wife's Acct.

The Credit Account has one entry Janury 9, 1747/8; By 1 womans furr'd hatt & band return'd. A second entry of July 14, 1748 has been marked out.

(p. 110). August 1, 1747. The Debit Account of HANOVER PARISH. A number of entries including: To 5 bottles red Wine brot. from Ledger F, fo: (130); To 12 1/2 yds. Holland for a Surplace @ 7/10; To 1 Ounce Nuns; To paid Mrs. MACHEN for making the Surplace allowed by the Vestry Septr. 30: 1747; To paid WM. PARKS for Advertizing the letting of the Church; To 3 delinquents; To Curing THOS: JORDANs Legs; To 1 Bottle of Claret; To 10 yds. Drogheda for STEPHEN MANSFIELD @ 1/6; To 5 yards Manx frieze for STEPHEN MANSFIELD @ 2/6; other entries for cloth and thread; To goods Capt. B. STROTHER had last year; June 6, 1749: To 1 bottle Wine; The Credit Account shows partial payment: By Capt. SKINKER by the Vestrys Order; By the Vestrys Order; By 1100 pds. tobo.

(p. 110). August 5, 1747. The Debit Account of JOSEPH TUTT. A number of entries including: To 200 3d. Nails; To Cr. DORCUS CAMPBELL by yr. Wifes order; thread, pins, powder, sugar; pr. scissors; 1 firmer Chissell; 1 felt, 2 grindstone; plaid hose, childs hose, yarn hose, pr. mens hose; July 11, 1749; To THOMAS JORDANs Order accepted; The Credit Account shows payments by a hogd. of tobo: By overpd. in your Levys; By a Crop note; By a Transfer Note; By Cash;

(p. 111). August 6, 1747. The Debit Account of ELIZABETH DUFF. Part of the Debit Account has been crossed out; the remaining entries include: To paid MOSES RANKINS Levy; To Cr. THOMAS ROBINSON pr. yr. Note; (BENJAMIN RUSH and OWEN CAMPBELL mentioned in crossed out portion). The Credit Account has been marked out.

(p. 111). August 6, 1747. The Debit Account of MOSES RANKINS. A number of entries including: cloth, a pen knife, a linnen handkerchief; 3 dozen coat buttons, thread, vest buttons; The Credit Account shows payment: By ELIZABETH DUFF; By 4 Potomack Transfer Notes; By Ballance carr'd to folo: (137).

(p. 111).September 21, 1747. The Debit Account of Mr. JOHN MERCER. 5 bushells Barley; 5 Bushells Barley; 4 lbs. Turkey Coffee; To pd. THOS: BUTLER by yr. Note; To 1 Watch Key; To Cash pd. you by HARRY TURNER at WMS:BURGH. The Credit Account shows payments: By Cash 3 Pistoles; By a fee of JNO: MORISON; By yr Accot. agt. Old Morison.

(A scrap of paper apparently unrelated to the Debit or Credit entries on page 111, partially torn: "The Bearer pray send 1/4 or 1/2 lb. Green (torn) CHAMPE who is at prst. very sick. Your humble Servt. CHARLES YATES. Lambs Creek, 11th June 1749." Another scrap of paper with many numbers but only the words: "At a Court held for WMS:BURG the 3d June 1749."

(p. 112). August 10, 1747. The Debit Account of THOMAS HARPER. Several entries including: To Cash; To paid JOHN FOX for his Attendance; To Cr: yr. Brother, SAMUEL, by yr. Note for sundrys; To 1 pr. Womens shoes by JO: DEANE yr Note; The Credit Account shows payments: By your Credit brot. from Ledger F, fo: (228); By 2 hogds. tobacco; By cash. Account appears to be paid.

(p. 112). January 27, 1747/8. The Debit Account of Mr. RICHARD TALIAFERRO at Mill:. Two entries: To 2 1/2 bushells Salt pr. Note; To Cash pd. CHAS. TAYLOR. The Credit Account shows payment August 18th 1748; By CHARLES TAYLOR

(p. 113). (no date). The Debit Account of JOHN WITHERS. To your Debt brot. from Ledger F, fo: (244); no additional entries. The Credit Account shows payment in full: By Capt. SKINKER, By Cash reced of WM. ROWLEY.

(p. 113). September 12, 1747. The Debit Account of MASSEY THOMAS. A number of items including: To 1 bushell Salt by yr. Son; ivory comb; horn comb, thread; clasp knife; cloth, yarn and plaid hose; Carolina hat; Carry'd forward p. 134; The Credit Account shows a payment August 2, 1748: By 1 Mattox Note.

(p. 113). September 21, 1747. The Debit Account of MAXIMILIAN ROBINSON. Several items include: To 7 yds. Irish @ 2/8 by WM. DODGINS; 1 lb. green Tea; a dble. rein'd bridle; pound of hyson Tea; To JOHN MICOUs Judgment; To yr. Bond; To 6 months Interest; To 9 1/4 gallons Wine @ 5/6; To Cask for Corn on Capt. PERRINs Accot; To Cash pr. Negro Ben; April 13, 1750; To Cash; The Credit Account shows payments for Debit of 3: 14: 6 By yr. Order on the Collectors of Hanover Parish; By Cash; July 26, 1749: By Cash of H. TURNER. The Debit of 102: 17: 6; April 1750 By 1646 bushels of Corn @ 1/3.

(p. 114). September 28, 1747. The Debit Account of Mr. CATESBY COCK. Several entries including: To a pr. Hair Cloths; To pd. Ferryman; To Cash pd. H. TURNER; To cash pd. FRANS: BALTROP; To a pr. furr'd gloves; To pd. T. ROY for Ferriages; To a pair of Sleeve buttons; The Credit Account shows full payment: By Cash of Mr. HARRY TURNER from Ledger F, fo: (35); June 1750, By cash; October 15, 1751: By a case of Pickles.

(p. 114). September 28, 1747. The Debit Account of Mr. CHARLES DICK. Several entries include: To Tobacco put in your hogd: To reprizing do; To 65 gallons Ale; To 2 dozen & 1 linnen handkerchiefs; To 3 dozen & 3 do; cloth, To 63 gallons Ale; January 30th 1753: To 67 gallons of Ale. The Credit Account shows a payment March 25, 1748 By JOS: STROTHERS JUNR., July 1750; By a Mortons Transfer Note; December 1752 By (blank) pds. of Butter.

(p. 114). January 14, 1747/8. The Debit Account of Mr. CUTHBERT SANDYS shows entry for 62 1/2 gallons of Ale @ 3: 2: 6; and February 18, 1748/9 To 64 gallons of Ale @ 3: 4: 0; The Credit Account shows payment of first debit by Cash April 5, 1748.

(p. 115). October 12, 1747. The Debit Account of JOSEPH FRANKLING. Several entries, nearly all for cloth; also To HUGH HORTONs Order; To 2 Butcher Knives; To 1 broad Hoe 4/6 by yr. Brother, JOHN. The Credit Account shows payments by tobo; by Cash; May 28th 1750 by a Note.

(p. 115). November 13, 1747. The Debit Account of JOHN ROSE, King George. Two entries: To 1 bushell Salt; To 1 hk. Silk. The Credit Account (undated) shows two payments in cash for debit.

(p. 115). November 23, 1749. The Debit Account of Mr. EDMUND TAYLER, Caroline Four entries: To 111 gallons Run @ 3/6; To 1 barrel Sugar Nt. 253 @ 37/6; To 1 cask of Rum; To 1 barrel of Sugar Nt. 268. The Credit Account shows payment of the Debit of 48: 17: 8: in 1749 and 1750: By Cash of JNO: PENDLETON; By Cash of yr. Brother; By Cash.

(p. 116). December 7, 1747. The Debit Account of CHRISTOPHER LAST. A number of entries including cloth; thread, a grindstone, a Linen Handkerchief; 1/4 lb. Pepper;

To 2 1/2 yds. Check to HANNAH; 1 meal sifter; 30 gallons Beer; To pd. Negro Joe; To Cr. PENELOPE JONES pr. yr. Note; To Cr. SARAH WISDALL by yr. Note; To yr. Rent for 1748; To pd. HARRY TURNER for Clerks Fees @ 14/. The Credit Account shows payment in full: By 4 days work; July 30, 1748: By Capt. SKINKER; By HENRY JOHNSON; August 3, By Cash; By ROBT. WALKER.

(p. 116). January 8, 1747/8. The Debit Account of Capt. BENJAMIN STROTHER. Several entries include cloth, pr.mens shoes; thread, yarn hose; salt; June 28th 1750: To DAVID ROBINSONs Order; To yr. Promise for WM. RANKINS; January 16, 1751: To yr. Promise for GEO: FOX. The Credit Account shows an undated entry: By Hanover Parish; 1750 By Cash.

(p. 117). February 2,1747/8. The Debit Account of Mr. JOHN MARTION, Maddox; One entry: To 13 yds. Crape had at Towles @ 2/. The Credit Account shows one entry: By Charg'd in Fo. (77) the amount of the debit.

(p. 117). February 16, 1747/8. The Debit Account of WILLIAM COATON. A lengthy account including: cloth; buttons, handkerchiefs, To Cr. CATHARINE CALVIN; Cash; pd. Negro joe; 1 fine hatt; To pd. WM. PIN for 1 bushell Oysters; To pd. ELIZA: BARTLETT; To Cr. WM. MARSHALL JUNR., To Cr. ELIZA: BARTLETT; To Cr. WM. FURLONGs Harry; a razor; pr. buckles, 1/2 m. pins; 1 stock lock; garters, paper, The Credit Account shows payment in full: March 30, 1748 By work done from this day to April 9th; Began to work again this day to May 26; By ROBERT WALKER; July 2d: By 25 1/2 days work to this day; To 14 days work; By 29 1/2 days work from Augt. 20th 1748; April 20, 1748, This day began work; By 6 1/2 days work first week; By ballance charged fo: (146).

(p. 118). April 4, 1748. The Debit Account of HENRY JOHNSON. A number of entries including: cloth, cash; thread, ticken, thread hose; worsd. hose; Cr. KITT LAST; handsaw file; To paid Mr. BOWIE; linnen handkerchief; brass ink pot; pd yr. levy for the year 1748; To paid LUKE BURFORD yr. Acct., 1 pr. mens pumps; To pd. Mr. GILCHRIST; To pd. your Levy for the year 1749; The Credit Account shows payments: By yr. Wages from this day; May 27th 1749 By yr. Wages from 30th Jany. to this day except 7 1/2 days (total payments for Wages: 25: 3: 5.)

(p. 118). May 20, 1748. The Debit Account of ROBERT JOHNS. To your ballance brought from page (41), with a number of additional entries including: salt, cloth; To Cr. CHRISTOPHER LAST pr. yr. Note; sheeting, thread, buttons, felt hat; 1 snaffell bridle; To paid WM. LONGMIRE; To Cr. OWEN CAMPBELL; To sundrys bought at RANKINS Outcry; To pd. WILLIAM FURLONG; April 7th 1750: To pd. H. WARE; To pd. Majr.MURDOCK. The Credit Account shows payments: By WM. MARSHALL SENR @ 14/; tobacco & cask, crop note; for payment of 25: 0: 10 debit.

(p. 119). March 17, 1747/8. The Debit Account of Capt. FRANCIS THORNTON. To 7 hogds. tobo: lent as pr: Page (91) with a number of additional entries including: cloths, brass mettle buttons, To pd. STROTHER SETTLE JUNR; a linen handkerchief; powder & shtt; 1 lb. fine green Tea; 2 lbs. Chocolate; sugar; bottle of Wine for yr. Mother; To EDMUND DUNAHOEs balla:, To prizing 5 hhds. of tobo: To 250 10d. nails for do: To 5 hhds. of Shells for *The Globe*. The Credit Account shows payment in full: By 2 hogds. tobo as pr. page (91); By Credit in the Parish Book; By part of Mr. SIMPSONs Order for 4: 15: 6 disallowed; By Cash you pd. Colo. PRESLY THORNTON; By a Saddle & Bridle for MORRISON; July 20th 1756: By FRAS: JAMES.

(p. 119). March 24, 1747/8. The Debit Account of ZACCHEUS WHARTON. A number of entries including: To 9 1/2 yds. Drogheda by yr. Mother @ 1/6; thread, To 1 pr. worsd. Hose by yr. Mother; powder and shott; handkerchief; coat buttons, brest buttons, various kinds and amounts of cloth; March 21, 1750/51: To cash 33: 1: 3 1/2; The Credit Account shows payment March 25, 1749 By Cash, 0: 17: 9; May 5,1750; By 50 acres of Land 38: 0: 0.

(p. 120). July 28, 1742. The Debit Account of Majr. ROBT. TUCKER. To cash you recd. of JOSIAH SMITH for Stone Steps; To 3 lbs. Candlewick you sold; To 1 hhd. cut & dried tobo: wt. Nt. 800*; August 5th 1744. To cash paid ANDW: ANDERSON by yr. Order; January 18th 1746/7 To Cash paid you by MARK TALBOTT; March 25th 1747; To 514 lbs. Cut tobo sold to sundrys; To cash sent you by HARRY TURNER. The Credit Account shows April 1744: By 5 barrels Pork sold for you; By cash reced of JAMES CROSBIE; By Clap Boards; Janry. 25, 1744/5: By 12 empty barrels; Febry. 21, 1745/6: By allowance to SWEENY for 800 boards for deficiency in lying; By freight of Boards &c. (Account paid) (Only account on this page)

(p. 121). January 29, 1747/8. The Debit Account of JOHN CARMACK. A number of entries including sugar, green tea; pickles, green taffety, ribbon,cloth, thread, paper, 1 gallon madeira wine; 2 gallons wine, 2 quarts Rum; 1 gallon Rum; To Dr. FERGUSONs Order; To pd. Mr. JAMES BOWIE; To pd. THOS: ROY; To pd. Mr. PATRICK MITCHELL; To pd. Mr. GRAY; To pd. CHARLES TAYLOR, 1 felt for PEGGY; To a pr. mens shoes to PEGGY; The Credit Account shows partial payment of Debit: By cash; By Cash from WM. DAWES; By WM. FURLONG; By Capt. SNEAD; By a loaf of Sugar twice charged.

(p. 122). 1748. The Debit Account of Mr. OLIVER TOWLES. To yr. Debt brought from fo: (92); April 27: To 28 gallons Brandy @ 4/; and a number of additional entries including: To pd. ROBT. MILLER; 2 gallons 5 pints Wine, paper, 30 gallons Brandy; cloth, thread, 2 1/2 gallons Madeira Wine; To 1 fine Ht by Mr. CARMACK; To pd. GEORGE HOOMES for Corn; To pd. EDWD. JONES 17 days wages; To 1 felt for Negro Jeremy by Mr. CARMACK To Cash pd. Mr. JENNINGS; To cash pd. WM. GERRARD; To Mr. JENNINGs further claim; To your Debt to the TRUSTEES of PORT ROYAL 253: 16: 4:, Interest on do. from June 24, 1745; 76: 2: 6:, March 2d. 1750: To paid JAMES BOWIE, To paid ROBT. GILCHRIST; June 16, 1751; To pd. yr. Ordr. to H. TURNER; To Secretarys Fees on HEARDs Bill in Chancery; To pd. Colo. B: ROBINSONs fees; To pd. Colo. BEVERLEY for E. JENNINGS; October 18, 1752; To balla: due O. TOWLES as this day settled 82: 17: 1/2; Test: T. TURNER; OLIVER TOWLES, Balla: carried to folo: /158/; The Credit Account shows payments: April 29th 1748 By your Credit brought from fo: 92; By Cash; By Majr. WM. WALKER; By Gibsons Note; By Mr. PATK. MITCHELL; By. WM. GERRARD; By Mr. JNO: WASHINGTON; By 1 doz: plates China; By 1 crop note Wt. 1155 @ 14d; By Capt. LIKELY; By GEO: HOOMES cash twice charg'd; July 1750: By Mr. CARMACK; By 6 chains bought; March 3d. 1750/1: By WM. ALLISONs & JNO: BOWIEs Bond; By JOHN MICOU; By Colo. JNO: BAYLOR; By Colo. WOODFORD; By JNO: MICOUs Bond; By Colo. LOMAX on Mr. B. GRYMES; By Mr. WM. GRAY for P. MITCHELL; By 2 pistoles you paid BOULWARE; By 1 do he recd. of JNO: ARMESTEAD; By WM. GRAY for P. MITCHELL; By 2 years Rent reced of WM. JOHNSON; October 18th 1752: By an error in THO: LOTTs acct. Debit and Credit in this Account: 752: 16: 2 1/2.

(p. 123). April 29, 1748. The Debit Account of THOMAS BARTLETT. To your ballance brought from page (5); with additional entries including cloth, ribbon, salt, corn, To pd. JOSIAH FARGUSON for Clerks Fees; To pd. Capt. STROTHER for 5 levies; To pd.

WILLIAM GORING pr. yr. Note; pr. womens gloves, nails, oyl, salt, To Cr. JAMES HALL; July 11, 1750: Then settled all accots & due to me. The Credit Account shows an entry June 3d. 1751; By Capt. DIXON ballanced this day.

- (p. 123). May 4, 1748. The Debit Account of Mr. ROBERT HARRISON. To one gallon Madeira Wine by yr. Brother, GEORGE. The Credit Account shows payment by cash May 25th 1749.

(p. 124). February 29, 1747/8. The Debit Account of WILLIAM PINN. To yr. Acct. from both of the day book; with additional entries for cloth, breast buttons, 2 hks. Silk, a brass pepper box; a fine hat; To overpaid you in 14 hhds. of Shells; The Credit Account shows payment in full: By your Credit from back of the Day Book; By bushell Oysters; By 2 bushells do; By 1 Do for COATON; By 2 Turkeys; By 3 Turkeys; By Majr. WILLIAM WALKER, By 20 hogsheads Shells; By, Majr. WILL: WALKER.

(p. 124). June 20, 1748; The Debit Account of Capt. JOHN WATTS, Maddox. The several entries include 1 gallon of Madeira Wine; 6 gallons Madeira Wine by Letter; 1 lb. Green Tea best; 2 Transfer Notes on Maddox; cloth, paper, gross of corks; 3 gallons Wine The Credit Account shows payments in 1748 and 1749: By JOHN McCORMICK; By 1 Brays Transferr; By JNO. McCORMACK for Rent; June 1750; By do for do.

(p. 125). 1748. The Debit Account of Mr. GEORGE HARRISON. To your Obligation for RANKINS; October 11, 1748; To cloth; 1750; To interest on his Bond: The Credit Account shows payments by Tobacco; By THOS. SACRY.

(p. 125). August 12, 1748. The Debit Account of Capt. SAMUEL SKINKER. To 2 1/2 lbs. Dble. Refd. Sugar as pr. page (82); with additional entries for cash, powder & shot, pair girls shoes; thread; nails, a Heifer; salt, a pack of Cards; pr. of Gloves to SAMUEL; 3/4 lbs. Candlewick; 1 dozen bottles Wine; pr. scissors to MISS MOLLY @ 1/4; pr. of wash Gloves to SAMUEL; pd. Capt. FRAS: THORNTON; 2 prs. womens shoes; To part of the duty on a pipe of Wine; To 2 pr. Hinges returned; To 1/2 lb. Chocolate @ 1/3; The Credit Account shows payments from September 9, 1748 through August 20, 1751; By Cash recd. of Colo. BEVERLEY; By 256 lbs. Beef; By the Heifer returned; By HENRY WARE; By 1 Brays Transfer Note; By Parish Book balla:, By Sheriffs fees to this day; By cash in part of MICOUs Bond

(p. 126), July 27, 1748. The Debit Account of Mr. ROBERT WALKER. To your ballance due this day settled page (99); with numerous additional entries from August 3, 1748 to April 26, 1753 including To Cr. KITT LAST pr yr. note; shott, salt, nails, your Rent for year 1748; pr shoes to JNO: ROBINSON; 4 Chizells, 3 plain irons and hank of Silk for SPENCE MONROE; 1 hatt pr. Note to JAS. ARNOLD; various kinds and amounts of cloth; your Rent for the year 1749; your rent for the year 1750; 10 pds. hopps; To iron lent 123 pds; To 64 feet Plank; To your rent for 1751; 5 sides of leather; 17 1/2 pds. hopps; your rent for 1752; 1 m. brass nails; The Credit Account shows payment in full by entries from August 3, 1748 to September 3, 1753; By part of DANL. WHITEs Credit disallowed; By Cash reced of Colo. GAWIN CORBIN; April 6th 1751: By yr. accot. settled to this day; By Mr. ROBT. ROSE; By SAML. SKINKER; By work done to this day; By 70 lbs. Beef;

(p. 127). September 13, 1748. The Debit Account of Mr. WILLIAM JORDAN. To 23 hogds. tobo: deliv'd Capt. DIXONs then at Gibsons Warehouse; (the 23 hogsheads are listed with the amounts in each cask and the initials stamped on the casks); January 23, 1748/9; To 1 cask Ale quantity 65 gallons. The Credit Account shows payment December 1748; By HARRY TURNER for ballance.

(p. 128). September 27, 1748. The Debit Account of Collo. NATH; HARRISON. The account has a number of entries including: 3 bushells of Barley; 42 gallons of Ale, a curry comb & brush; 4 bushells of Corn; 20 bushells of Salt, 3 bushells of Pease; cloth, To a Sow; To the balla: of MAJR. WALKERs Bond; To 12 m. 4d. nails; To a Lock for the Church; The Credit Account shows payments: By 13 bushels of Barley; By Cash; By 31 bushels of Barley; By cash of Mr. WM. DAVIS for 10 bushels Wheat; By a quarter Beef; By 10 bushels Rye; 15 May 1752; By cash.

(p. 128). September 29, 1748. The Debit Account of JEREMY BROWN. To 72 bushels of Salt; To 1 rugg; To 1 1/2 yards Check; To 3 yards Drogheda; To 1/2 bushel of Salt charged on back of the Day Book; to Cash; The Credit Account shows payment in full from April 12, 1749 to May 3, 1750: By 54 lbs. tobacco; By 4 bushells of Beans; By tobo:

(p. 129). 1748. The Debit Account of JOHN MORRISON. To your Debt brot. from fo: (60: with numerous additional entries beginning November 4, 1748, including 2 hammers, 2 saws, 7 narrow hoes; 4 broad do; 1 broad Ax., 10 pr. plaid hose; 1 pr. dble. channell Pumps @ 10/; 11 sutes making for Negroes @ 18d., To making 10 do. boys & girls @ 15d., To 21 shirts & shifts making @ 4d; To 472 yds. broad cloth @ 13d;; 6 yds. Shalloon @ 2/3; 1 1/2 doz. coat, 1 doz. Vest buttons; 3 hks. hair; 2 hks. silk, thread; To pd. Mr. DINGLE yr. Tayles Accot., To pd. Mr. MERCER; quire of paper; pr. worsd. stockings; mens wash gloves; To a Scarlet Broadcloth great Coat; To Expences in going over to PRINCE GEORGE & WMS:BURG 20 days; (a number of additional entries for cloth, thread &c.,) Allowed by the Court Octr. 6, 1749. To pd. B. WALLER for compounding the appeal (Debit: 181: 4: 11). By yr. Account settled in Court; making 4 shirts; To cash to the Overseer; making 5 Negro mens sutes; making 5 womens Jackets & Pettycoats; Cash paid Capt. PEACHEY's Messenger for his Expences &c., pd. yr. Overseer & Boys Ferriages at ROYs, To 5 months Schooling & Board; To pd. Mr. SIMPSON for books, paper & shoes; To pd. Mr. DINGLE his Taylers Account, To pd. Mr. DODGINS his do; To his Coffin Sheet &c., died the 15th about 10 a clock at night (January 15, 1749/50); To 6 months Board; To paid Mr. JAMES BOWIE his accot., Cloth pr. MILES THWEAT; Allowed by the Court Octr. 7, 1750 49: 8: 6 1/2:, To paid PARSON WILEY; To paid WM. DODGINS his Taylors Accot., To paid Doctr. ALLISON; (carried to page 157); The Credit Account shows payments from April 1749 to February 6, 1750/51: By 3 Crop notes; By Cash reced of Mr. DEWEY; By yr. Brother, ALEXR. part of the Law Suit & charges &c.; By yr. Sister JANEs do;, By cash found after yr. death; By cash reced of MILES THWEAT;

(p. 130). November 9, 1748. The Debit Account of Capt. THOS: JOHNSON. To your balla: due brot. from fo: /45/, with additional entries for scarlet silk, nails, 58 gallons Rum; barrel of Sugar Wt. 213 lbs; 25 yds. fine Irish, 1 lb. Green Tea; 1 lb. Bohea Tea; 58 gallons Rum; 1 pipe of Madeira Wine; 79 gallons Rum; 64 gallons Cyder; 67 gallons Ale; 31 gallons Molasses @ 3/; 6 lbs. Chocolate; 6 dozen & 4 bottles of Ale; 50 gallons Cyder; 4 gallons Ale; 1 Quarter Beef; 112 gallons Rum; cash reced of Capt. JOHN MICOU; 12 1/2 dozen Liverpool Ale; pr. mens pumps; 110 gallons Rum; 316 pds. Sugar; 1 saddle; 1 steer; 116 gallons Rum; a pipe Wine; 30 gallons Ale; 97 gallons Cyder; 1 years Rent of ye Ordinary; The Credit Account shows payments from December 19, 1748 to December 21, 1749; By Cash for your Ordinary; (numerous cash payments), By Capt. THOMAS JOHNSON;

paid HARRY TURNER; carried to /fol/ (152).

(p. 131). November 10, 1748. The Debit Account of WM. FURLONG; To your Balla: due in fo: (27); with a number of additional entries through January 1755 including a pair of ribb'd yarn hose, 1 worsd. cap; 1 pr. worsd. Stockings No. 1; 1 pr. wash'd gloves; a set of shoe & knee buckles; pr. of garters; salt, thread, cloth, a knife; a hatt; To pd. CHARLES WHARTON; To pd. Capt. THORNTON on Accot. of DUNAHOE; To pd. SAML. FREEMAN; To pd. NIGHTINGALE MEEDS; To 3 barrells of Corn @ 8d, To 1/2 bushel beans; To 9 1/2 pds. dried beef; To 211 lbs. pork; To pd. ANN MARSHALL; To 3 1/2 bushels of corn more than your share; (the last entry is dated December 20, 1764; To ballance to your Credit in EDWD. DIXONs Ledger A 15: 15: 6. The Credit Account shows payments from March 14, 1748/9 to 1756 including payments: By crop notes; By Cash; By ISAAC ARNOLD SENR., BY ROBERT JOHNSTON; By Carting Mr. DAVIS's Wheat &c., By Carting Line to the Glebe &c., By Carting 4 pipe of Wine for Colo. MONROE; By making 2000 nails; By carting goods from Maddox; By sheering Sheep 2 yrs., By Colo. WOODFORD; By making 6 m. nails; By making 3 m. do; By 6 1/2 months wages; By boarding 4 months; 3/4 boarding LINDSEYs men; By your Parish Claim; By a County Claim; By ballance charged pr. Contract; 1756: By your 1 1/2 share of 1195 tobo: By sundrys pr. your Accot. sworn to Vizt. 3800 Rails mauling, curing a Horse of a Fistula

(p. 132). 1748. The Debit Account of JAMES PEAD. To a womans furr'd hat & band; To 2 pair womans washt. gloves; December 17, 1748: To 2 pair Womans ditto; To 1 felt @ 1/4, 1 ditto @ 2/8; 1751: To oyl & paint. The Credit Account shows payment in full by three cash payments

(p. 132), October 22, 1748. The Debit Account of JOHN DONOHOE. To 1 1/2 yds. Drogheda @ 18d., To 1 1/4 yds. Shaloon @ 2/4; vest buttons, knee buckles, brass buttons, felt hatt; thread; 1/2 yd. white Linnen @ 2/7; pr. plaid gloves; 2 1/2 yds. Oznabrigs @ 1/3; pr. mens wash gloves; The Credit Account shows payment in full April 22, 1749: By FRAS: WOFFENDALE

(p. 132). November 14, 1748. The Debit Account of BENJA: THOMAS. To 7 yds. bro. Irish Lin: @ 1/7; To sundrys. The Credit Account shows payment in full of the 12/7 1/2 debit March 4, 1748/9: By MOSES RANKINS.

(p. 133). November 17, 1748. The Debit Account of Capt. PERRIN. The account has several entries through March 16, 1748/9 including a 72 gallon Cask @ 5/; To coopering of 7 casks; To pd. HENRY JOHNSON for distilling; To Cash paid you by HARRY TURNER; To 9 yds. Oznabrigs; To 50 feet of Plank & fixing the bulk heads; To 200 20d. nails; To 323 barrels of Corn @ 8d. (Stated in fol: /145); The Credit Account shows a number of payments from November 1748 till March 1749 of the debit including: By ballance of Accot. sent you; By HENRY DRAKE for 132 gallons Rum; By HENRY DRAKE for 4 pipes Wine; By Capt. THOS: JOHNSON for 1 ditto; By Capt. DICKINSON for 60 gallons Rum; By Capt. EDWD. DIXON for 64 gallons do; By LUKE BURFORD for 64 do; By Capt. NICHOLSON for 56 do; By GEO: FOX for 26 do; By Jno: Short for 1 pipe Wine; By JOS: WHARTON for do; By FRAS: BALTROP for 60 galls wine; To Capt. THOS: JOHNSON for 58 gallons do: To 5 pipes of Wine sent last March; By MRS. COLEMAN 1 pipe of Wine; By 6 hhds. Rum & 4 barrels of Sugar; By MRS. JONES one pipe of Wine (Vide fol: 145);

(p. 133). November 12, 1748. the Debit Account of CAPT. DIXON; To 64 gallons of Rum @ 4/; To paid H: BERRY his Accot; cloth, salt, buttons, tobo: boxes; dozen red painted snuff boxes; a cask of Rum; a Cask of Sugar; To 2 bushells Sale to WM. BERRYMAN; To 4 yds. brown Holland for G. TANKERSLEY @ 10d; dozen mens worsted hose; powder & shot; 1749: Debt for Transfer tobo: To WM. MARSHALLs Order; To tobo: prized in the hhd; The Credit Account shows several payments by Cash; By WM. WREN JUNR; By Colo. MONROE; (This accot. crr'd fo. 147).

(p. 134). December 22, 1748. The Debit Account of CAPT. DIXON. This account shows a number of hogsheads of tobacco with the cask marks and the places stores such as at Roys, at Gibsons, at Brays, at Caves, at Maddox &c. The Credit Account shows a number of payments by Crop Notes. with names; ROBT. JOHNSON, J: BOON's, JAMESONs, T. SACRYs, R: GREENs; ROBT. PECK; FRA: WOFFENDALEs.

(p. 134) November 28, 1748. The Debit Account of MASSEY THOMAS. Several entries in this account including a pen knife, pr. garters, 1/2 bushel Salt; To Ballance from folo (113); To 1 pr smallest yarn hose pr. Son; To 100 10d. nails; January 12, 1750: To Cash. The Credit Account shows payment in full June 12, 1750 By a Crop Note and three shillings cash.

(p. 135). May 1746. The Debit Account of SYDENHAM & HODGSON. Several entries in this account including To Cash you recd. of Mr. FORWARD; To sales of 7 hhds. by PERREY; To do of 4 by WILCOX; To Abatement on Insurance by WILCOX as he sail'd wth: convoy; To RICHD: BARNEs Excha: on yr. selves; To Capt. DONALDSONs do sent you; July 1750: To my order on LYONEL LYDE. The Credit Account shows the Debit of 212: 14: 6: paid in full between 1746 and January 1749/50 by goods pr. Restoration; By do pr. the *GRYMES*; ; By do pr. the *PHILLIS*, ; By do pr. the *HAPPY JENNET*; By Charges on 7 hhds. casks; By a draw; By goods by the *HAPPY RETURN*

(p. 135). December 1748. The Debit Account of ISAAC ARNOLD SENR. To your ballance brot. from page (1); with a number of additional entries for buckles, a rugg, cash, linnen, cloth. To your rent for the year 1748; 2 narrow hoes; ivory comb; To goods bought at RANKINS Estate; To paid your Levy for 1748; To paid WM. FURLONG; To 16 yds. white sheeting not charg'd in fol: /1/; To sundrys as per the Day Book; To 1 womans saddle & furniture laced; To Oyster Shells; 2 pad locks; mettle buttons; nails, your Rent for the year 1749; 1 hhd. oyster shells; 1/2 barrel Corn; 4 earthen ware dishes & 2 plates; To 2 saucers, 3 salts, 1 Tin funnell; your rent for 1750; 2 bushels of Beans; yr. Levy; quit rents for 1751. The Credit Account shows a number of payments from January 3, 1748/9 to July 1751 including By MARTHA HELLIER; By 2 hhds. tobp: Crop notes; empty hogsheads;

(p. 136). December 17, 1748. The Debit Account of ISAAC GREEN. To yr. ballance brot. from page (33). with a number of additional entries including a pr. mens shoes; a mans fine hatt; various kinds and amounts of cloth; thread, ivory comb, horn comb; razor, 3 handkerchiefs; pound of powder; 3 lbs. shott; pair womans pumps; pair womans wash gloves; boys felt, a rug, 2 gallons molasses; bushel Salt pr. Son; pr. Womans wash mittens pr. MARY SETTLE; pd. two levies; To 1 do for DANIEL; To pd. ELIZA: BROWN; To pd. ELIZA: BARTLETT; The Credit Account shows 18 yards Check returned December 28, 1748; a pair of womans wash gloves returned; By 1 hogshead of tobacco; By 1 crop note; By a Transfer note; By ELIZA: BARTLETT; August 13, 1753: By Capt. DIXON.

(p. 136). December 19, 1748. The Debit Account of JOEL ANCHORAM. Several entries including salt, white sheeting, yr. rent for 1749; 4 chisells; 1/4 yd. plaid; yr. Rent for Anno. 1750; yr. Rent for 1751; yr. Rent for 1752. The Credit Account shows: May 7th 1750: By yr. Accot. of Work to this day; By Cash; May 19, 1753; By yr. Accot. for Work done to this day; By balla: of a former Accot;, July 16, 1753: By cash pd. Capt. DIXON in ballance to May 19th 1753.

(p. 137). December 22, 1748. The Debit Account of MOSES RANKINS. To yr. Ballance brot. from fol: (111) settled; with a number of additional entries including cloth, mens shoes; a saddle, a knife, stockings knee buckles; buttons, To pd. BENJA: THOMAS; To paid ELIZABETH DUFF; To pd. BENJA: MARSHALL; To yr. levy 50 lbs. tobo: To cost of suit. The Credit Account shows four payments in 1749 & 1750; By 1 hhd. tobacco, By cash; By BIRKET PRATT; By 8 months service.

(p. 137). January 15, 1748/9. The Debit Account of ELIZA: RANKINS. There are several entries including a Sifter pr. Note; salt, cloth, thread, To 2 young cattle; The Credit account show one undated entry: By settled in the Administration Account

(p. 138). January 2, 1748/9. The Debit Account of MRS. BETTY COLEMAN. One entry: To 1 pipe of Wine 26; 0: 0. The Credit Account shows one entry March 20, 1748/9: By Cash pr. Capt. WM. JOHNSON 26: 0: 0.

(p. 138). March 20, 1748/9. The Debit Account of Capt. WILLIAM JOHNSON. One entry: To 1 hhd. Rum quantity 109 gallons @ 4/6, 24: 10: 6; The Credit Account shows one entry: May 12, 1749: By Cash 24: 10: 6.

(p. 138). January 6, 1748/9. The Debit Account of WILLIAM LONGMIRE deced Estate. shows several entries including: To paid WM. PARKER for Taylors Account; various kinds and amounts of cloth; thread, pr. buckles; To paid your Rent; To paid two levys; To JAMES JOHNSONs Promise for WIDOW BLACKLEY; To paid MRS. JONES. The Credit Account shows payment of debit of 8: 18: 2 1/2 on January 21 & 23, 1748/9; By tobacco; By your Credit brought from fol: (50); By tobacco; By paid in your Husbands Claim

(p. 138). June 6, 1749. The Debit Account of EDWARD PARROT. There are several entries in this account including: To my Note for 3 barrells Corn paid; for thread, cloth, pins, a mans felt, 2 boys felts, pr. garters, To yr. Levy; To sundrys from Day Book. The Credit Account shows the Debit of 5: 8: 0: paid in October 1749: By your Parish Claim

(p. 139). January 9, 1748/9. The Debit Account of JOHN ROACH. To 250 10d. nails; to 100 4d. nails; to your ballance brot. from page 72; To 1/2 bushell Salt; To a bushell of Salt by yr. Son; The Credit Account shows partial payment of 2: 5: 6: of a total 2: 10: 3 1/2 By a Gibsons Transfer Note on June 6, 1749; By Cash on March 2, 1750/51.

(p. 139). March 14, 1748/9. The Debit Account of Mr. THOS: TURNER JUNR. Entries through June 3, 1755 include To a case knives & forks; 1750: To my order on JAMES HUNTER; 1753: To Cash deliver'd you for DR. LYNN; To pd. ROBT. JACKSON 23: 10: 0: Sterling; To pd. Mr. CHAS. DICK; To pd. PETER COPELAND; 1755: To pd. Mr. B. GRYMES; To pd. Capt. THOS. ROGERS; To pd. Mr. ROBT. JACKSON. The Credit Account shows payments through 1755: By 35 barrels of Corn @ 6/3; By cash pd. Mr. GRYMES Overseer; By Colo. FRAS: TALIAFERRO for 4 Bonds amounting in the whole to Serling 1150: 0: 0; By 30 pr. cent on do., By Colo. FRAS. THORNTON.

(p. 139). January 11, 1748/9. The Debit Account of MICHAEL SKINNER. Several entries in the account including cloth, plaid hose, thread, a rugg, paid yr. last years levy; To your Brother, JOHNs, Debt. The Credit Account shows the payment of the debit of 8: 9: 8: September 2, 1749 By 1 hhd. of Tobo. on Gibsons and cask; January 16, 1750/1: By cash; July 1754 by BENJA: MARSHALL.

The above account of THOMAS TURNER JUNR. is continued beginning on June 3, 1755: To pd. Mr. ROBT. JACKSON; To 30 pr. cent Int. on do; To pd. ALEXR. CAMPBELL for WM. WALKER; To pd. CUTHBERT SANDYS; To pd. MAJR. TUTT for H. TURNER; To pd. COLO: CHAMPE; To pd. Mr. CHAS. DICK; To pd. MARK TALBOTT; To pd. DR. HEATH; To pd. ANTHO: STROTHER; To pd. Mr. FEILDING LEWIS; To pd. Colo. JNO: THORNTON; To pd. JOHN MITCHELL for H: LENOX; To pd. Capt. THOS: ROGERS; To paid Mr. JAMES HUNTER; 1758: To EDWD. DIXON; May 1759: To Collo: JOHN CHAMPE as pr. his Accot; To Interest on do. 1760: The E. D. Store Account; To Mrs. TURNERs Acct. wth. EDWD. DIXON; To do for good bot: at the Sale of Estate; To Capt. WILLIAM DICKS accot., To Balla: of Colo. TALIAFERROs Bond of 1757 due when deld. Capt. A. THORNTON; To balla: of Majr. H. TURNERs Accot; To Rent of land bought of Capt. ANTHO: STROTHER;

This entry carries the following notation: "This Account is settled in Colo. TURNERs Estate Ledger 1767; and all proper Credits given for Interest of TALIAFERRO Bonds &c."

(p. 140). January 14, 1748/9. The Debit Account of JOHN BATTALEY. This account shows a number of entries including a pr. of worsd. hose; a pr. of shoes; a pr. buckles; 2 pr. gloves; cloth, 2 small knives; pr. pumps; To paid ELIZA: BENSON; To pd. HARRY TURNER; To paid CAPT. DIXON. The Credit Account shows payment of the Debit of 21: 11: 6 1/2 By the REVD. Mr. SIMPSON; By yr. Parish Claim; By yr. Do as Clerk of the Court Martial; By one years wages; By Cash for balla:

(p. 140). April 25, 1749. The Debit Account of OWEN CAMPBELL. To your ballance brot. from fo: (18); with additional entries through December 5, 1750; including 1 whip saw file; 1 cross cut saw; 1 hand saw; 1 Carolina hatt; 3 dozen buttons; thread, cloth, salt, boys felt, The Credit Account shows payment of the debit of 6: 19: 0 1/2 by payments in 1749: By ELIZA: DUFF; By Capt. JOSEPH STROTHER; By yr. Acct. for Smiths work to this day; in 1750: By overpd. in yr. levies; By yr. Accot. of work to this day.

(p. 141). January 25, 1748/9. The Debit Account of Mr. ROBERT GILCHRIST, shows several entries through January 15, 1752 including salt, beef, a dozen vest buttons by THOS: EVANS; (and total 571 beef); The Credit Account shows payment May 30, 1749: By HENRY JOHNSON

(p. 141). January 27, 1748/9. The Debit Account of LUKE BURFORD includes 1 barrell Ale qt. 29 galls, To your Ballce: brot. from fol. 18, To 1 hhd. rum qt. 113 gallons @ 4/6; To 5 gallons & 3/4 of Molasses @ 3/. The Credit Account shows payment of the Debit of 41: 13: 9 1/2 by five cash payments; By HENRY WARDs. Obligation for 9: 0: 0: April 5, 1750: By Capt. THOS: ROY.

(p. 141). April 17, 1749. The Debit Account of BENJA: SETTLE. To your Ballance from page (85); cloth, buttons, a broad hoe; thread; The Credit Account shows payment of the Debit of 2: 11: 6; December 8, 1749: By Capt. EDWARD DIXON.

(p. 142). July 7, 1748. The Debit Account of Mr. HARRY TURNER. This account shows several entries thrugh August 5, 1749 including 1 bundle Mohair of TOWLEs, 6 baggs Buttons No. 1; 6 do No. 2; 8 do No. 3; 2 do No. 4; 2 casks dble. refined Sugar wt. 291 lbs; pr of Shoes for PETER; pr. yarn stockings; 2 lbs. Bohea Tea, cloth; To Capt. THOMAS VIVIONs Bond; Interest on ditto; To DARBY TOOLs promisary Note 0: 19: 5: The Credit Account shows payments in 1749: By WILLIAM WHEELER, By FRAS: STROTHER; By goods @ 6/; July 6, 1750: By Colo. RANDOLPHs Exrs., By 310 barrels Corn @ 6/8.

(p. 142). February 3, 1748/9. The Debit Account of JOHN MILLER contains several entries through July 26, 1752, mostly wine, some ale, 1/2 dozen pewter plates, 1/2 dozen knives & forks; The Credit Account shows payment of the Debit of 10: 4: 6 by seven cash payments thrugh July 26, 1751.

(p. 142). June 9, 1749. The Debit Account of BURDITT CLIFTON. Two entries: To 1 gross corks; To Salt. The Credit Account shows payment of the Debit of 0: 5: 8: on June 9, 1749 by Cash.

(p. 142). April 29, 1749. The Debit Account of JAMES WRIGHT. One entry for a mans fine hatt for 14/. The Credit Account shows no entries.

(p. 143). February 13, 1748/9. The Debit Account of Mr. ALEXR. McPHEARSON. One entry: To 6 lbs. Chocolate @ 2/6. The Credit Account shows payment of the 15/ Debit May 12, 1749: By cash.dd

(p. 143). February 18, 1748/9. The Debit Account of JOHN SKINNER. Two entries: To 1 pr. blanketts, 17/6; To 1 Rugg 10/. The Credit Account shows payment of the Debit of 1: 7: 6 September 2, 1749: By MICHL. SKINNER.

(p. 143). September 21, 1749. The Debit Account of Colo. PRESLEY THORNTON. Two entries: To cash pd. you at the LEEDS TOWN RACES, 100: 2: 6: ; To cash pd. your by Capt. FRAS: THORNTON. The Credit Account shows payament of the first debit of 100: 2: 6: By yr. Wifes part of the General Courts decree agt. the PORT ROYAL Land.

(p. 144). March 4, 1748/9. The Debit Account of ISAAC ARNOLD JUNR. To 3 fathom Rope; To ballance from fol: /3/; with additional entries including 3 felt hatts; thread, cloth, powder & shot, ivory comb, mens worsd. hose; pr. mens gloves; nails, To pd. WM. WREN; mettle coat buttons; salt; March 10, 1749/50: To ballance of all Accots. this day settled in cash pr. Contra: 3: 14: 7 1/2; To pd. BENJA. MARSHALL; to pd. ESTER JONES; To Corn, To JAMES ARNOLDs Acct., The Credit Account shows payment of the additional debits, 8: 9: 8 1/2 after settlement on April 2, 1751: By Capt. DIXON.

(p. 145). November 17, 1748. The Debit Account of Capt. JNO: PERRIN & SON. A lengthy account including: To 72 gallon cask; To coopering 7 rum Casks; To pd. for distilling 3 casks rum; To cash pd. you by HARRY TURNER; To 9 yds. Ozna:, To Twine; To 50 foot Plank & 200 20d. nails; To 323 barrels of Corn @ 8d., To commission of 660: 0: 0: at 28 pr. Cent; To do on 323 barrels of corn @ 2 1//2; To cash at yr. own house; To cash paid you by HARRY TURNER; To a pair of Shoes to ABRAHAM TIPPET; To cash to yr. Boy; To a hank of twine & meal; To 2080 bushels Corn by James Sloop; To 1552 bushels Corn by *Cupid;* To 1955 do by *Brocklebank;* To 1500 bushels freight sent; To 1620 bushels of Corn by *James,* To 20 pds. of bacon & 1/2 bushel pease; To pd. JOS: BERRY 30 bushels; To do.

MARTHA HAMPTON 70 1/2 bushels; To RICHD. BUCKNER 30 bushels, To JOHN CORBIN 148:4 bushels; To MAX: ROBINSON 329:1 bushes; To Colo. RANDOLPH 93 bushels; To HENRY WARE 300 freight; To pd. JNO. CORBIN 31 bushels. October 12, 1750. The above acct. given in To my Commissions on 380: 0. 0 @ 28 pr. cent; Vide page /152/. The Credit Account shows payments from 1748 to October 1750. By ballance of Accots. sent you; By 5 pipes of Wine By 520 gallons of Rum; By 2 barrels of Sugar; By cash recd. of ROBT. GILCHRIST; By 1 hhd. Rum sold to EDMUND TAYLOR for 111 galls. Rum @ 3/6; By WM. JOHNSON for 1 pipe Wine; By EDMUND TAYLOR 112 1/2 galls. Rum; By do 1 barrel of Sugar Nt. 268; By WEEDON & HILTON for 106 galls. Rum @ 3/6; By JOS: BERRY for 42 galls. do; By JAMES MARTIN 108 galls. Rum; By JNO: MOORE 50 lbs. Sugar; By 1 pipe to WM. JOHNSON; By 30 galls. Wine to JAMES BOWIE; By 30 do to RICHD. BUCKNER; By 30 do to Capt. DIXON; By 30 do to JAMES WHARTON; By 30 do to ROBT. GILCHRIST; By Mr. GEORGE BLACK cash; By 33 galls. ARCHL. McPHERSON; By 22 galls. Capt. DICKINSON; By Majr. SKINKER; By do for freight from Madeira; By Colo. PRESLEY THORNTON; By 30 galls. Wine MUNGO ROY; By 30 galls. Wine HENRY DRAKE; By Mr. WM. DAVIS 30 galls. Wine; By GEO: BLACK do; By MRS. JONES, 1 pipe of Wine; By 2 pipes do;. Memo: The above small quantitys were drawn from 4 pipes & ran 325 galls.

(p. 146). May 5, 1749. The Debit Account of WILLIAM COATON. To your ballance brot. from fo: 117; with additional entries including cloth, a mans hatt; pr. womans lamb gloves; powder & shott; a handkerchief; thread; a case of knives & forks; To Cash paid ISAAC ARNOLD SENR. for Pork; To Credit in page /117/ 6 1/2 work; The Credit Account shows payments through 1750: By work on the Palisade; By do at the Brick Kiln; By do burning Bricks; By work from this day done in 22 weeks as pr Accot. kept by Mr. BATTALEY; being four months 1 week; By Capt. JNO: MICOU.

(p. 146). June 9, 1749. The Debit Account of Capt. WILLM. TALIAFERRO. To ballce. of yr. Acct. from fo (90); with additional entries including: To Cash; To do reced. of WILL: ROWE; To Cash pd. H. TURNER on Acct. MAJR. BAYLOR; To 3 prs. Childres hose damgd., To 6 3/4 lbs. hopps; The Credit Account shows payment of the Debit of 0: 5: 7 1/2; June 14, 1749 By work done in PORT ROYALL; January 1, 1747/50; By Cash in Error.

(p. 147). July 17, 1749. The Debit Account of Capt. DIXON. To your Accot. brot. from page (100), with numerous additional entries including cloth; To MAJR. MURDOCKs Debt; To 1 lantern, To Cr. ROBERT MUNDAY; To Interest on ROBERT MUNDAYs Bond; To Cr. JOHN BROWN; To Cr. JOHN THORNLEY; To Cr. JOHN FRANKLING; To Cr. BENJA. SETTLE; To 5 shammy skins; To DANIEL WHITEs order; To EDWD. JONES order; To THOS: PEATROSS Order; To 30 galls. Wine; To THOS: JORDANs order; To 10 galls. Jamaica Rum; To 83 galls. Rum @ 4/; To WIDDOW THATCHERs Order; To JOHN ROGERS do; To JOHN HOLLOWAY for Shells; To JOHN FRANKLINGs order; To ANN MARSHALLs order omitted; To THOS. SACRYs do; To Colo. LOMAXes do; To ISAAC ARNOLD JUNR. do; To Cr. ELIZA: BROWN; To Cr. FRANS: WOFFENDALE; To Cr. ELIZA: BARTLETT; To MAJOR MURDOCKs order; To Cash reced of Messrs. MILLS & BOWLER on Accot. of T. TOWLES for Strettle; To Cr. CHAS. WHARTON; To Cr. JOS: ROBINSON, To Cash of WM. BOWLER & my self; To 10 bottles Citron Water; (last entry August 29, 1752). The Credit Account shows Cr. from page (133); By yr. Exchange on Mr. YOUNGER payable to Colo. CHAMPE; By 25 pr. cent on do; By WM. WREN agt. ADAM LINSDEY; By JNO: BATTALEY; By cash pd. for Corn; By pd. DICK SIMMONDS; By pd. ROBT. PARKER; (last entry July 28, 1752).

(p. 148). August 4, 1749. The Debit Account of JAMES MURREY. Eleven entries for cloth, ivory comb, snaffle bridle; blankett, womans pumps, small buttons; The Credit Account shows payment of the 2: 0: 6: debit: By your share and half of tobo: the weight of the whole crop being 2838 among 10 sharers & a half is 405 lbs. tobacco.

(p. 148). August 4, 1749. The Debit Account of Mr. PATRICK COUTTS. The several entries include cloth; cash 18 1/2 pistoles; (4 entries for Beef totalling 1064 pounds); To cash Cr. pr. yr. Accot; To do in part of 3 hhds. Tobacco; To 110 galls. Rum. The Credit Account shows payment August 14, 1749 By sundrys reced of him; By Capt. THOS: JOHNSON; By cash; January 4, 1750/1; By ALEXR. MORISONS Passage; By Cash reced.

(p. 149). September 26, 1749. The Debit Account of JOSIAH GASCOINE. Five entries for pr. womans pumps; 3 yards Irish Brown Linen; 1/2 m. 10d. nails, 1 pewter dish & Bason; To Cash; The Credit Account shows payment of the Debit of 3: 5: 0: September 26, 1749: By 26 hhds. Shells @ 2/6.

(p. 149). December 18, 1749. The Debit Account of Mr. JOHN SMITH, Middlesex. One entry: To 1 cask of Ale qt. 74 galls. @ 1/. The Credit Account shows payment of the Debit of 3: 14: 0 by PETER ROBINSON.

(p. 149). November 10, 1749. The Debit Account of CHRIST: ROBINSON, Middlesex. One entry: To 1 barrel Ale, 30 galls. The Credit Account shows payment of the Debit of 1: 10: 0: by PETER ROBINSON.

(p. 149). December 18, 1749. The Debit Account of Mr. JAMES SCORSBIE. Two entries. To 3 casks of Ale qt. 74 galls; To 2 do of Beer qt. 53 galls. The Credt Account shows payment of the Debit of 4: 7: 0: by Cash.

(p. 149). December 19, 1749. The Debit Account of Mr. JAMES MARTIN. One entry. To 110 galls. Rum @ 3/6. The Credit Account shows payment of the Debit of 19: 5: 0 by Cash.

(p. 150) September 19, 1747. The Debit Account of ELIZABETH DUFF. Several entries including: To Cr. THOS: ROBINSON pr. yr. Note; To sundrys pr. Day Book; To 2 bushels of Salt pr. B: RUSH; To 3 boys felts; To pd. OWEN CAMPBELL pr. yr. Note; To 1 pd. Powder & Shott; To Tobacco Order The Friends; June 12, 1750: To Cash pd. BENJA: RUSH; 1747: The Friends on Acct. & Order of ELIZA: DUFF; To pd. yr. Order to WM. HARRISON in Salt; 1753: To pd. a WESTMORELAND Clks. Note; The Credit Account shows payment of one Debit of 12: 12: 3 by Tobacco due to E: DUFF; By an old Gibsons Note sold; By MOSES RANKINS; By overpd. in yr. Levies; The other Debit of 11: 16: 8 paid: By Tobo: left with me by ELIZA: DUFF; October 1749: By do pr. do.

(p. 150). January 16, 1749/50. The Debit Account of the REVD. MR. WM. DAVIS. Several entries through August 11, 1750 include: To a Horse 7: 10: 6; To 698 pds. of Pork nett; To 1/2 lb. Salt. Petre. 1 1/2 bushel Salt; To a keg of Butter nett 73 @ 6d.; To 4 pds. Chocolate; To a copper Chocolate pott; To 75 lbs. Butter; To 30 galls. Wine; To several Books; Debit 24: 14: 7. The Credit Account shows payments on March 7th 1749/50 of 10: 0: 6:, By Mr. JOS: BERRY JUNR; By the horse returned;

(p. 151). 1749. The Debit Account of GEORGE WRINGLESBY. To your ballance brot. from fo: (107); with several additional entries including: To paid ENOCH BERRY; To pr. WM. SHERMAN Cash pr. yr. Note; 7 yards Check @ 1/4; 7 yards Dowlass @ 1/8, thread, To Cash pd. Majr. TALIAFERRO; The Credit Account shows two payments one on December 1, 1749: By Cash recd. of Colo. GAWIN CORBIN for Corn bot. of Majr. TALIAFERRO; the other August 9, 1750: By Capt. JOS: STROTHER for 10/.

(p. 151). November 20, 1749. The Debit Account of WILLIAM JAMESON. To your ballance brot. from fo: (43). with additional entries including 200 10d. nails; yr. rent for anno 1749; 3 pr. plaid hose; To 51 pds. tobo: ballce. in Tobo: To pd. THOS; SACRY; To yr. rent for anno 1750; The Credit Account shows payment of the Debit of 25: 3: 4 1/2: By 6 gallons Vinegar; By ballance from fol (43); By three crop notes; By tobo:

(p. 151). March 1749. The Debit Account of Mr. ROBT. TODD. To 164 1/2 bushels of pease; To pd. Mr. SCOTT for ballance; 1750: RICHD. SIMMONDS; July 7th: To Cash; March 18, 1750/51: To cash for ballance. The Credit Account shows payment of the Debit of 1: 6: 8: July 7th: By 8 days work to this day; by 3 1/2 do.

(p. 151). January 10, 1752. The Debit Account of ANN WREN. To paid Capt. GARNETT an order of ESSEX Court agt. yr. Husband; August 1753: To paid Mr. JAMES POWER a fee; To a Negro Girl (19: 0: 0:), To 30 pr. cent on do: To Duty on do. (Debit of 28: 8: 9). The Credit Account shows payment of 80: 0: 0: January 10th 1752: By Cash reced. of Capt. JAMES GARNETT for yr. Land.

(p. 152). December 8, 1748. The Debit Account of MESSRS. THOS: & WM. JOHNSON. To Ballce. brot. from fo: (130) with additional entries through April 2, 1751 including a pipe of Wine; a qt. of Beef; 13 1/2 goot of 1 1/4 plank, 14 doz. empty bottles; your Rent one year 9 days; The Credit Account shows payment of the Debit of 189: 14: 0 on December 30, 1749 By cash; June 1750 By 3 bottles of Arrack; December 15th: By Bond of this Date;

(p. 152). December 21, 1750/1. The Debit Account of JOHN PERRIN & SON. To 1 bushel 1/2 of pease; To agallon of Rum; To commission of 1572 barrels of Corn; To Ullage allowed on wine; To 212 barrels of Corn by HENRY TODD; To commission for selling, storage & collecting the debts. (Vide page /156/. The Credit Account shows payments from October 27, 1750 including By Cr. from fol: /145/ & given in; By EDWARD KNOWLES Sugar; By JAMES GRAY do. By GEO: BLACK; By JNO: BRYAN 1 hhd. rum 109 galls;, By FRAS. BALTROP 1 hhd. Rum 114 1/2 galls; By PATK. COUTTS 1 do. 112 1/2 galls; By JAMES MARTIN 1 do 113 do; By ROSE TALIAFERRO 1 do 112 do; By WM. BOWLWARE 1 do 110 do; By HOWSON HOOE 1 do 109 1/2 do; By THOS. THORP 1 barrel Sugar 318 lbs. nett; By WM. HARRISON 1 barrel Sugar 269 lbs;

(p. 153). October 1749. The Debit Account of ALEXR. MORRISON. To your part of Expenses in the Law Suit brought agt. MR. DEWEY it being 51: 7: 0; your 1/3; To pd. PATK. COUTTS for yr. Passage; To a Silk Cap; To 4 months board; To Bills of Excha; sent Mr. WM. STRACHAN; To 30 pr. cent on do; The Credit Account shows payments in October 1749: By yr. part of the Personal Estate being 100: 0:0: October 25, 1751: By MILES THWEAT

(p. 153). October 1749. The Debit Account of JANE MORRISON. To yr. part of Expences in the Law Suit brought agst. MR. DEWEY, it being 51: 7: 0:, your 1/3; August 8, 1751: To Bills of Exchange pd. Capt. JOHN THOMSON by virtue of a Power of Attorney to him; To 30 pr. cent on do; Vide page /157); The Credit Account shows October 1949: By yr. part of the Personal Estate being 100: 0: 0:

(p. 153). January 31, 1749/50. The Debit Account of HANOVER PARISH; To 3 pr. Door hinges; To 1 double spring bolt lock; To pd. ZACH: WHARTON for Church Land 500; To pd. for 100 squares of Glass; To a bottle red Wine; To pd. FURLONG for cartin Lime; cloth, thread, stockings; a bottle of Wine; To a Ring to WINNY WMS: for the boy; To (cloth) GEORGE GILES; To paid WINNY WILLIAMS for boarding PARSON HARVEY & for burying him; To nails for his Coffing; To pd. MRS. TUTT for curing G. GILES; To pd. COLO. CHAMPE towards Church plate; To 30 feet Plank; This Account Levied Octr. 1751.

(p. 153). January 20, 1749/50. The Debit Account of JAMES DELPECK. To a gall: 1 pint Madeira Wine; To 1 loaf of Surgar; To cash; The Credit Account shows April 1750: By yr. Physic Account payment in full of 5: 8: 0.

(p. 153). June 25, 1750. The Debit Account of Capt. WM. DICKINSON; To Storage 6 weeks; To flat hire do; To 30 galls. Wine & Cask; To 210 ft. inch Plank; (four entries for Beef totalling 216 pounds); The Credit Account shows: August 1750: By Colo. NATHL. HARRISON; By cash for ballance: (The account is not totalled and Colo. HARRISONs amount of payment not shown.)

(p. 154). February 28, 1750/1; The Debit Account of Capt. McCLEAN To 1 Quarter of Beef; To 2 bushels of Pease; To 400 billets; To 200 billets: The Credit Account shows payment in April 1751: By cash in Account of 2: 12: 4.

(p. 154). March 13, 1750/1. The Debit Account of JOEL BERRY: (one entry); To pd. yr. order to ROGERS 1: 10: 0; The Credit Account shows two cash payments June 7 1751 and 4 November 1751 of the Debit amount.

(p. 154). March 29, 1751. The Debit Account of Mr. JAMES BLAIR of Maddox; To Cash paid you by Capt. DIXON; To paid your Order to FRAS: MILLER; To Interest to 23d June; The Credit Account shows payment of the 89: 4: 8 debit August 17, 1751: By DR. BANKHEAD; 82: 10: 5; By Cash to ballance

(p. 154). March 30, 1751. The Debit Account of Mr. DAVID CRAIG. To cash paid yr. Order to JNO: BLAGGE; To cash delivered you; To cash pd. H. TURNER by yr Order; By cash pd. JOHN BLAGGE; To Cash at Wd. Court; July 3: To cash. Ballanced by H. TURNER. The Credit Account shows: 1751: By yr Excha. for 25 pr. cent on do; August 18: By Cash; By H. TURNER for Ballance.

(p. 154). April 6, 1751: The Debit Account of the Revd. Mr. ROBERT ROSE; (one entry): To Cr. ROBT. WALKER 28: 0: 0. The Credit Account shows full payment June 1751: By Cash reced ANDW. ANDERSON; By do p JNO: MILLER.

(p. 154). January 6, 1752. The Debit Account of DAVID MILLER. To a rug; To cloth; To white thread; To pd. CHARLES WHARTON; To cash pd. JNO: MATHEWS, 1 boys felt; 1 doz.

buttons & some thread; February 7, 1753: To pd. JNO: STEVENS; To pd. CHARLES WHARTON; To 3 qts. Rum; The Credit Account shows payment Janury 6, 1752: By a years wages as Miller; January 6, 1753; By do; Feburary 6, 1753; By 1 months do. By 84 pds. of Tobacco @ 12/6. for full payment of 13: 0: 6.

(p. 155). July 2, 1751. The Debit Account of STAFFORD LIGHTBURNE; To yr. Debt from Book (blank) fol: (blank); 9: 15: 4; The Credit Account shows July 2, 1751: By Cash of WM. MARSHALL; December 15, 1752; By Do of LEWIS JONES

(p. 155). October 1751. The Debit Account of the COLLECTORS of HANOVER PARISH (all amounts in tobacco) To my Claim in the Parish; To paid THOS: STANHOPE his do; To paid MARY GRIFFIN her do; To paid WINNY JONES's do; To KEYS, PEEDs. & STROTHERs Claims; To JNO: STEWARD & B. FEWELLs Claim; To Mrs. JONES's County Claim, (10,640 lbs. of tobacco); The Credit Account June 9th 1752; By DANL. WHITE; By ISAAC ARNOLD JUNR; July 25th: By 30 Leases; By JNO: WARE; By JNO: & JAMS: RANKINS; By SAML. WHARTON Levy; By transfer notes. (Account balanced).

(p. 155). November 6, 1751. The Debit Account of JOHN MILLER; To ballance yr. Bond; To 3 1/2 gall: Wine; To 2 doz: Ale; To 120 pds. of Beef; To 2 doz. of bottled Ale; To 89 galls. of Wine; To 100 Lemons; (This account contains numerous entries for Wine); The Credit Account shows a number of cash payments; payment by ZACHY. TALIAFFEROs Bill for 5: 18: 0; By a Qt. Beef & 1/4 Lamb; By Cash for the Lemons; By cash for the ballance Debit of 18: 19: 6 1/2 paid.

(p. 155). December 18, 1751. The Debit Account of RUSH MARSHALL: To 1/2 a barrel of Corn; To 2 1/2 yds. white Linen; To Cash 15: 7 1/2; July 27th: To cash of Capt. DIXON; The Credit Account shows 1751: By yr. Wages from Decr: 7 months 10: 10: 0 which pays the Debit.

(p. 156). April 9, 1749; The Debit Account of JOHN PERRIN & SON. (The first part of the Debit account is marked out). April 9, 1749: To cash I paid you at yr. House; To cash paid you by HARRY TURNER; To cash paid your Son at WMSBURG; To a pair of shoes to ABRAHAM TYPPET; To cash to yr. boy; To a hank of twine & some meal; To pd. H. WARE for 20 lbs. bacon & 1/2 bushel pease; To 1572 barrels 2 bushels of Corn sent you by JAMES CUPID & BROCKLEBANK; To 1 1/2 bushel pease; To 1/2 gallon Rum to TODD; To 212 barrels of Corn by TODD 115 of it @ 9/6; The Credit Account shows payment of the Debit of 1170: 3: 6: By the Cr. of my accot. given in this day; By a bbl. of Sugar Nt. 316 unsold when the above acct. was given in; By 4 hhds. of Rum vizt. 2 hhds. sold EDMD. TAYLOR, By 1 do sold JNO: WEEDON; By 1 do to JAS: MARTIN; By 4 barrels of Sugar; By cash reced of ROBT. GILCHRIST; By cash reced of GEO: BLACK at times; By cash of do; By 10 pipes of Wine landed; By 8 do; By duty on 1 pipe of Wine; By 1 hhds. Rum after ullage; By 9 barrels of Sugar;

(p. 156). January 1, 1752. The Debit Account of Capt. PERRIN & SON; To 3/4 of a Pipe of Wine return'd being sour; To 300 barrels of Corn by Eeagle; To sundrys from H. TURNER's Store Book; The Credit Account shows January 1, 1752; By ballance due p Contra; By 1 Pipe of Wine Sour; (Account ballanced).

(p. 156). March 1, 1753. The Debit Account of DAVID BARTON of Prince William: (one entry): To 5 years Rent due last Christmas 10: 0. 0. The Credit Account shows: March 1, 1753; By Cash reced for 4 years Rent due last Christmas 8: 0: 0.

(p. 157). October 5, 1750. The Debit Account of the Estate of JOHN MORRISON deced; To yr. Account allowed by the Court Sept. 4, 1747; By do Augt. 5th 1748; By do Octr. 6th 1749; By do October 7th 1750; (total 253: 7: 12); To cash paid PARSON WILEY; To Cash pd. DODGINS his Taylors Account; To pd. DR. ALLISON his Accot; To Clerks & Secretarys fees on Administration allowed by the Court May 7th 1752; The Credit Account shows payment in full of 260: 5: 2: April 1749 By Cash reced of MILES THWEAT; By three crop notes; By cash reced of MR. DEWEY; Jany. 15, 1749/50: By Cash when you died; By your Brother, ALEXANDERs part of the Law Suit & charges &c; By your Sister, JANEs, do; By the amount of your Inventory in may hands 5: 3: 6; By your Brother, ALEXR. MORRISON;

(p. 157). October 1749. The Debit Account of JANE MORRISON; To yr. part of the Expences in the Law Suit brought agt. Mr. DEWEY; To Bills of Exchange to balla: reduced to Cash; Total debit of 100: 0: 0; The Credit Account shows: October 1749; By Cash reced of Mr. DEWEY 100: 0: 0.

(p. 157). October 1749. The Debit Account of ALEXR: MORRISON. To yr. part of the Expences in the Law suit against Mr. DEWEY; January 4, 1750/1; To paid WM. COUTTS for yr. Passage here; To a Silk Cap; To 4 months Board; To Bills of Exchange sent Mr. STRACHAN; To 30 per cent on do; To 3 shirts & 3 Necks yr. Brothers; To a pair of Boots, yr. Brothers; To Boarding two months; To the remaining part of yr. Brother's Cloaths as pr. Inventory in may hands, 3: 2: 0; To your Brother, JOHN's, ballance; To ballance due to ALEXR. MORRISON. This Account allowed by the Court May 7th 1752; May 12, 1752: To a Saddle Bridle & Crupper; May 19: To pd. for a Horse 4: 6: 0; May 21: To a pr. Saddle Baggs, The Credit Account shows: May 7, 1752: By ballance due as pr Contra: & sent the Cash by CAPT. HUNTER to JANE MORRISON, 24: 17: 6 1/2

(p. 158). April 27, 1752. The Debit Account of Mr. WILLIAM BOWLER. To Cash pd. you Febry. 22: last; 100: 0: 0: To yr. own debt to me: 75: 1: 10:, To my order on CAPT. JOHNSON, 324: 18: 2; for total Debit of 500: 0: 0; The Credit Account shows: April 27, 1752; By Mr. THOS: WILDS Excha: 400: 0: 0; By 25 pr. Cent on do: 100: 0: 0: for payment in full.

(p. 158). April 20, 1752. The Treasury: To 52 days wages attending the Assembly; To 6 do. going & coming; To Ferriages for total: 29: 13: 0; The Credit Account shows: August 1752; By duty on 12 Negroes bought of Colo. CHAMPE 25 pr. cent off; for Imported Cash 330: 0: 0:, By Duty on One Pipe of Wine pr. Mr. B. GRYMES; By cash reced of Collo. CHAMPE for ballance.

(p. 158). October 18, 1752. The Debit Account of OLIVER TOWLES. To pd. Mr. ROBT. GILCHRIST; To pd. Capt. DIXON; To pd. WM. GERRARD; To paid PATK. COUTTS; To paid Majr. VIVION; To pd. Mr. ROBT. GILCHRIST; To pd. JNO: STEPTOE; To pd. WM. FINNEY; Two cash entries; one dated May 23, 1754; the other July 24, 1755. The Credit Account shows payment in full of the Debit of 83: 17: 0 1/2; October 18, 1752; By yr. ballance; By deduct pt. of GERRARDs. Order.

(p. 159). April 18, 1752. The Debit Account of the Estate of HARRY TURNER; To cash pd. WM. HUNTER pr. Accot; To do pd. DR. GILMER; To pd. COLO: CHAMPE JNO: ROBINSONs Bill of Excha: for 116: 17: 4; To pd. Falmouth Inspectors; To pd. for 15 hhds. ship'd for WILCOX; To pd. Quit rents for Anno 1752; Janury 1, 1754: To paid duty of 21 Negroes; To paid MAJR. TUTT; To paid CHAS. DICKE for Servt. woman; (1755): To pd. for two Spinning wheels & pr. boys shoes; Sept. 4, 1756; To cash advanted MR. HUBBARD added in his

Bond; To my Account pd. C. LINDSEY towards Mill Work; The Credit Account shows a number of entries: April 1752: By Cash reced of Sundries for Salt; By Cash reced of MARTHA CATLETT; By SAML. WHARTON his Account on yr. Book; By WM. BOWLER for Salt; By JNO: GRAY for Salt; By Mr. ROBT. GILCHRIST for do; By JAMES MILLER; By Mr. JNO: MOORE for Salt; By MRS. SKINKER in part for a Chair; By JAMES BOWIE for goods at the Sale; By ROBT. GILCHRIST for do: By PATK. COUTTS for do; By do for 8000 Bricks; By JAMS: BOWIE; By CAPT. PERRIN for 300 barrels Corn; By SIMON DEGGE for do; By JAMS. BOWIE for Salt & Bricks; By JNO: ROBINSON of MIDDLESEX; By Collo: JNO: CORBIN; By Mr. WM. DAVIS. By JNO: GRAY; By JAMS: HUNTER; By WM. JOHNSTON; By PAT. COUTTS for JNO: KNIGHTON; By WM. GERRARD; By THO: HARPER; By FRAS: BURGES; By JNO: MILLER; Feby. 7, 1755: By PAUL SCOTT

(p. 160). My MATTAPONY PLANTATION October 1752. To paid COLO. MARTIN for the Land; October 1753: Paid one years Quit rents; To paid for Corn & Salt; To paid for Pork 2 years; To paid for Cattle, sheep & hogs; To paid for building Servants houses & nails; To paid for Houses; To Interest of 400 pds. for one year; To 18 Negroes; To paid for setting up 9 hhds; April 1754: Total shown: 1631: 1: 1; To clothing them to this day, 25: 0: 0; November 1754: To Clothing them to this day; To paid GATEWOOD for 22 Cattle; To Tools to this day; To Interest for one year. The Credit Account shows: April 1754: By 3444 pds. of Tobo: made in 1753; 21: 10: 6.

(p. 160). December 10, 1753. The Debit Account The Treasury: To 49 days attendance on the Assembly; 24: 10: 0; To 6 days going & coming & ferriages 3: 13: 0; February 24, 1754; To 8 days attendance 4: 0: 0; To 6 days going & coming & ferriages 3: 13: 0; August: To 12 days Attendance; To 6 days going coming & ferriages; November: To 19 days attendance 6 days going coming & ferriages; October 1755: To 5 days attendance 6 going & coming 5: 10: 0; To Ferriages 0: 9: 0. The Credit Account shows part payment of 45: 9: 0 By Cash received in November 1754 & May 1755; and payment of 19: 2: 0: the ballance, July 21, 1756; By my order payable to T: JETT.

(p. 161). November 10, 1755. The Debit Account of JOHN BELL of London, Merchant. To the Nett proceeds of 3 hhds. of tobo: as pr. Account of this date; October 26, 1756; To the proceeds of 4 hhds. of tobo: pr. *The SALLY,* as pr. Accot. of ye Date; 42: 5; 8. The Credit Account shows November 10, 1755: By amount of goods sent pr *The Sally,* 18: 13; 6; October 26, 1756: By amount of goods pr. *The Sally,*; By Insurance on do.

(p. 162). September 1, 1754. The Debit Account of Mr. WILLM. STEVENSON of LONDON; To 10 pr. ct. Commission for my trouble of collecting and remitting 11,784 lbs. tobacco; L 413..7..9 Sterling & L. 466..14..9 Currency; The above 11784 lbs. Tobo: 12/6; Deduct L 20..5..6 to make the Curt: money Sterling; The Sterling charge above; The dif: in Excha. paid for L 526 Sterl: Bills remitted you more then you allowed me in making the Debts Sterling in aforementioned Account: 52..12..0; To Colo. JOHN BAYLORs Bill on MR. LYDE remitted you; September 1, 1755; To CAPT. DIXONs Bill on MR. YOUNGER remitted you; Total Debit 393..18..0; The Credit Account shows full payment: September 1, 1751: By Balance of your Account of this date; By Interest on do. from the 1st day of September 1751 to the 1st day of September 1754; Balance in favor THOS: TURNER

(The foregoing is the end of this Account Book)

The Papers of
EDWARD DIXON
1748-1752

(The Index as found in the beginning of Book 3 (page numbers omitted). These names in this list are Indexed in our Book, only when they appear in an Account.)

(First two names water soaked)
ALLISON, William Doctr.
AIERS, Thomas
ALLON, Robt.
AIRS. saml.
ARNOLD, William
ASHTON, Charles
ALLCOCK, William
ARNOLD. James
BARBEE, Francis
BOUWLWARE, William
BATTALEY. John
BOWLWARE, John
BULLARD, George
BOWLWARE, James (Essex)
BURDON, Thomas
BURRISKILL, Richard
BODDINGTON, John
BELL, Esther
BROWN, Jere.
BERRY, Joseph (Capt.)
BOWLWARE, James Junr.
BUCKLEY, Randall
BERRYMAN, James
BURK, John
BURK, Henry
BUTTREY. Thomas
BOON, John
BULLARD, Ambrose
BARTLETT, Eliza:
BARWISE, Joseph
(Name faded) Elizabeth
BOWLWARE, John
BARKSDALE, William
BOWLWARE, James (Caroline)
BLACK. George
BURFORD. Luke
BENSON. Zachy.
BEASELY. Bennett
BENSON, Robt.
BROWN, John
BELL, Ann
BROWN, William
BLANTON, Richard
BRASFIELD, George
BERRY, Benja.
BEAZLEY, John
BERRY, Henry
BERRYMAN, William
BELL, William
BRASFIELD, Thomas
BEASLEY. Chas. Junr.
BALTHROPE, Fras:
BERNARD, Richard
BEASLEY, Mary
BAILEY. James
BENSON, John
BALTHROPE, John
BLANTON, John
BOWIE, James
BRASFIELD, George Senr.
BEASLEY, James
BULLARD, Elizabeth
BUTTLER, Thomas
BUTTLER, James
BUTTLER, William
BEASLEY, Charles Junr.
BERRY, Grace
BOWLWARE, Marke
BENSON, Charles
CHAMPE, John Majr.
CLATTERBUCK. Richard
COUTTS, Patrick
CROUCHER, Thomas
CALL, Robt.
CHAPMAN, Nathan
CALL, Isaac
CASH, James
CROUCHER, Hugh
CARTER, John
COPE, William
CASH, Stephen
COLQUIT. Jonah
CHASE, James
CHILTON, Sturman
COLQUIT, Jona: Junr.
COLQUIT, James
COLQUIT, John Junr.
COATON, William
CARTER, John (Porto:)
CARTER, Edward
CARTER, William
CRANAGE, Saml.
CHANDLER. Fras:
DIXON, Edward
DAWSON, Musgrove Revd.
DUVALL, Benja.
DILPECK, James
DUDLEY, Robert
DINGLE, Lucy
DEAN, Richard
DAVIS, William
DIXON, Edward Capt.
DOBYS, Thomas
DUDLEY, Christopher
DICK, William
DANIEL, William
DUFF, James
DISHMAN, James
DISHMAN, David
DICKINSON, William Capt.
DAVIS, John
DONOHOE, John
DODGIN, William
EVANS, Thomas
EVANS, John
EDWARDS, William
EDWARDS, George
EDWARDS, Simon
ELIOT, William
EWELL. Soloman
ELMS. Edward
EVANS, Richard
EVANS, Charles
FERRILL, John
FIDDLER, Francis
FURLONG, William
FLING, William
FOX, George

FOX, William
FRAZIER, Daniel
FAULCONER, Samuel
FLETCHER, James
FIDDLER, William
GILCHRIST, Robert
GREENWOOD, Eliza:
GRIFFIN, Eliza:
GRYMES, Benja:
GLANTON, John
GRUBBS, Benja:
GARROT, John
GRIFFITH, David
GRUBBS, Richard
GILLISON, John
GOUGE, James
GRAY, William
GIBSON, Elizabeth
GREEN, Isaac
GRIFFITH, Gabrl: Wt:haven
HOLLOWAY, John
HALL, Robt.
HIPKINS, Saml.
HOLLOWAY, John
HUDSON, William
HART. Charles
HARRISON, William
HILL, Leonard
HARRIS, William
HARRIS, Thomas
HURT. Moses
HOPSON, Richard
HENSHAW, Samuel
HAWS, Isaac
HOLMES, John
HARRISON, William (C)
HUNLEY, Robt.
HAWKINS, William
HARDICK, Aaron
HOARD, Ambrose
HUDSON, Lucy
HOLT, Richd.
HURT, James
HURT, Titus
HOARD, William
HILLIARD, Martha
HURT, Moses
JORDAN, William
JOHNSTON, Henry
JOHNSTON, Daniel
JETER, William
JOHNSTON, Saml.
JETER, John
JOHNSTON, Thomas Capt.
JAMISON, William
JAMES, Thomas
JOHNSTON, William PR:
JOHNSTON, Benja.
JOHNSTON, James
JAMES, Saml.
JETT, John
JONES, Esther
JOHNSTON, W. Capt. C. C.
JOHNSTON, William K. G.
LONG, John
LONG, Reubin
LEFOE, Dan:
LEWIS, James
LONG, Jeremiah
LAMPTON, Joshua
LONG, Gabrll. Junr.
LONG, Richard Junr.
LINDSEY, Joshua
LONG, John Junr.
LEWIS, Eliza.
LOMAX. Lunsford
LONG, Henry
LONG, Nicholas
LIGHTBOURN, Stafford
MURRY, Edward
MURDOCK, Jeremiah
MICOU, John
MARTIN, Abraham
MARSHALL, William
MOLEAR, John
MILLER, John
MARSHALL, William
MILLER, James
MERRYWEATHER, William
MARTIN, William
MINTOR, Anthony
MICKLEBURROW, Robert
MARTIN, Abraham Senr.
MOORE, John
MICHEL, John
MARTIN, Benja.
MARSHALL, Ann
MARTIN, Mary
MAJOR, Samuel
MASSY, Lovell
MITCHELL, Pattk:
MARSHALL, John
MORRIS, Griffen
MARSHALL, George
MARSHALL, Benjamin
MONROE, Andrew Colo.
MASSY. Thomas
MARSHALL, Edward
NALLE, Richard
NOEL, Edward
NALLE, Richard Junr.
NOEL, Sarah
OLDHAM, Samuel
PETROSS, Thomas
PARKER, William
POE. William
POWERS, Edward
POWEL, Mary
PEED, James
PITTS, John Senr.
POWELL, William
PROSSER, John
PRUETT, Hugh
PITTMAN, Moses
PITTMAN, William
POWELL, John
PITTS, John Junr.
PITTMAN, Thomas
PEAR, William
PRICE, John
PIN, William
ROYSTON. Thomas
ROY, Thomas
REYNOLDS, Cornelious
ROE, William
ROBERTS, James
RAWLINGS, John
ROBINSON, Benjamin Colo.
ROBERTS, Jonathan
ROBINSON, John
RANKINS, William
ROACH, John
RIGGONS, Charles
RATCLIFF, Thomas
RODGERS, Christopher
RIDING, George
RICE, Clemt.
RANKINS, George
REYNOLDS, James Junr.
REYNOLDS, Catherine

RANKINS, Eliza.
ROBINSON, Joseph
SKINKER, Samuell
SANDYS. Cuthbert
SAMUELL. Thomas Senr.
SETTLE, Benjamin
SETTLE, Eliza:
SANDERS, Silvs:
SMITH, Jere.
SETTLE, Issac
SANDERS, Robert
SAMUELL, Giles
STERN, Francis
SAMUELL, Thomas Junr.
STRAUGHN. Richd.
SHARMAN, William
SAMUEL, Foster
SLY, Daniel
SAMUEL, Peter
SHIP, Thos: Senr.
SAMUEL, Anthony
SAMUEL, James
SMITH, William
SULIVAN, John
SUMMERS, James
SHIP, Joseph
SAMUEL, Catherine
SIMPSON, Joseph
Ship Friendship, Capt. W. Dickinson
STROTHER, Joseph Junr.
SHIP, Thomas Junr.
STROTHER, John
STROTHER, Joseph Senr.
SMITH, Augustin
SMITH, Mary
SANDERS, John
SANDERS, Peter
SKINKER, Saml. Junr.
SNEED, John
STUERT, James
SAMUEL, William
SANDERS, Thomas
SHIP, Richard
STEVENS, Jeremiah
TURNER, Thos. Colo.
TALIAFERRO, William Capt.
TALIAFERRO, John Major
TANKERSLEY, Joseph
TANKERSLEY, George
THORNTON, Francis Capt.

TURNER, Thomas
THORPE, Marmaduke
TURNEY, Harry
TODD, George
TIBOE, John
TINSLEY, Philla:
TANKERSLEY, Richard Senr.
THATCHER, Thomas
TRIPLET, Daniel
TAYLOR, Edmund
TURNER, James
THORP, John
TINSLEY, David
TANKERSLEY, Dorcas
TILLER, Thomas
TURNER, James
THOMAS, William
TAYLOR, John Capt.
TERRILL, Henry
THORNLEY, John
TUTT, Joseph
WOODFORD, William Colo.
WREN, John Senr.
WARE, Henry
WARE, Edward
WALKER, Robert
WHITE, William
WALL, John
WREN, John Junr.
WILLARD, James
WHELER, William
WARDROPE, James
WATTSON, William Senr.
WREN, William
WRIGHT, Robt.
WILTSHIRE, Joseph
WILTSHIRE, Thomas
WHITE, Daniel Senr.
WHITE, James
WHITE, John
WHITE, Daniel Junr.
WHARTON, William
WHARTON, Charles
WALKER, William
WHARTON, Zachary
WHARTON, Samuel
WRIGHT. Charles
WILLSON, Abraham
WILEY, William
WHITE, James Potomack

WOOD, Joseph
WATTSON, Thomas
WATTSON, William Junr.
WEEDON, Elijah
WATKINS, William
WILLARD, Nicholas

YOUNG, Leonard
YOUNGER, John
ZACHARY, James

(Page numbers in Book 3 of the Edward Dixon Papers begin with number 129.)

(p. 129). June 1, 1749. The Debit Account of WILLIAM RANKINS. Various kinds and amounts of Cloth which make up the majority of entries in this account; To 1 pound Pepper; 2 handsaw files; 1 whip saw file; 1 large jugg; 1 brass cock; 1 large funnell; 9 yds. brown sheeting; powder & shott; 2 doz. large mettle buttons; 1 snaffle bridle, 1 m. 8d. nailes; 2 bushel Salt; 2 lb. powder, felt hatt for total Debit of 7: 6: 6; The Credit Account shows payment in full November 6, 1749: By your accot. in L. B.

(p. 130). May 26, 1749. The Debit Account of Mr. JOSEPH REYNOLDS. To ballance brot. from ( ); (a very long account mostly for various kinds and amounts of cloth); 3 Jews Harps; 1/2 doz. table knives; 1 pair best shoes; 1 pencil 2 1/2; a sett buckles; 1/2 doz. soap plates; 4 dishes; 1 Leghorn hatt; 2 1/2 yds. Fine Irish Linnen; thread, needles; pins; tape, 2 iron potts; pr. womans shoes 3/; 1/2 lb. allspice; 24 yds. Lace; 1 lb. Ginger; 6 doz. shirt buttons; 1 Tea pott; 2 yds. Ribbon; 3 thimbles; 1 Ink horn; 1 Carpenters Rule; 1 primmer; 1 clasp knife; 3 small cups; a mans fine felt; a boys felt; for total Debit of 26: 8: 4 1/2. The Credit Account shows payments June 16, 1749 by 4 hhds. on Roys Vizt. (numbers listed); By 1 ditto roys July 1, 1749, 1031; By 1 Ditto Conway 1067; July 6 by 1 pr. womens shoes 3/; 6 casks.

(p. 131). June 6, 1749. The Debit Account of JOHN GILLISON. To 1 dble. C. Pumps; To 5/8 Rum; To 1 qtsd. ditto; 5/8 ditto; To 1 1/2 Gall. Rum 4/6; 6 lbs. brown sugar; 2 3/4 lbs. refined Sugar; 1 pr. boys shoes; 1 pr. buckles; 2 gallons Rum; 1 bushell Salt. The Credit Account shows payment, 3: 2: 3 1/2, of the Debit August 16, 1749 By Roys Transfer 100 lbs. tobacco; November 6: By your accot. in L. B.

(p. 131). June 7, 1749. The Debit Account of Mr. WILLIAM DICK. To 1 womans cap; cloth, pins, pr. womans gloves; a womans saddle; a fine girth; thread, 3 yds. silk ferritt; 2 Bandine handkerchiefs; The Credit Account shows payment of the debit of 7: 9: 2 1/2 November 5, 1749: By 2 pr. mens fine pumps; By ballance to L. B.

(p. 132). June 1, 1749; The Debit Account of Mr. WILLIAM BERRYMAN. (A very long account including): various kinds and amounts of cloth; thread; 1 doz. table knives; 1 hair sifter; 2 lbs. bohea tea; pr. Callimanco shoes 4/; 2 loaves single sugar; pr. blanketts; 1 lb. Pepper; 1 doz. felt buttons; 7 3/4 yds. Gingham; 7 yds. Lace; 3 yds. Topsails; 2 pr. womans glas'd lamb; nails, a fine hatt; ribbon, needles, 1 1/2 doz. fine gold buttons; 1 hk. green silk, 1 glass can; 9 yds. Callico; 1 bottle Snuff; 2 pencils 3d; 1 whip 4/6; 1 tankard 4/6; pr. buckles; To Cr. WILLIAM PARKER; for total 32: 19: 9; The Credit Account shows payments June 1 & 12, 1749 By 1 hdd. tobacco; By 2 ditto; By Transfer; casks; By allowance on former tobo:, By transfer on Mattox;

(p. 133). June 8, 1749. The Debit Account of JOHN WREN JUNR. To your account from ( ); (a long account with various kinds and amount of cloth); pr. womans hose pr. WM. DICK; 1 Cream Jugg; 1/2 yds. lace; pr. sleeve buttons; razor strop; sugar; Cirb Bridle; 1 lb. Green Tea; pr. mens shoes 6/; 1 1/2 yds. french Ribon 2/; 1 pint bowle; 1 Qt. rum; 1 pint Rum; 2 m. 8d. nailes; bushel salt; 2 small ruggs; 1/2 oz. cloves; hair sifter; 1/2 lb. shoe thread; 2 small chisels, The Credit Account shows November 6, 1749; By your accot. in L. B. 26: 2: 5 1/2.

(p. 134). June 27, 1749; The Debit Account of Capt. SAML. OLDAM. one entry: To cash sent you to WESTMORELAND COURT; In the Credit Account the Debit of 16: 18: 7 1/2 is paid June 8: By 2 hhds. tobacco on Gibsons and six shillings in Cash.

(p. 134). June 8, 1749; The Debit Account of Mr. WILLIAM DANIEL. two entries: To 2 lbs. shott & To 1 flowerd. Quart. The Credit Account shows the payment of the debit of 4/1; June 23, 1749 By cash; September 18, 1749, by Cash.

(p. 135). June 8, 1749. The Debit Account of Mr. JOHN WREN SENR. To ballance from ( ); with additional entires for various kinds and amounts of cloth; powder & shot; 2 horn combs; pepper, nutmeg, cinamon; pr. womens white wash gloves; 100 needles; 1/2 m. large pins; thread; 3 yds. sacking; 1 hair sifter; 2 boys felts; yard of fine Cambrick; 59 lbs. brown sugar; 1 gross Corks; 2 quire paper; 1 lb. Chocolate; To ballance of Stg. Accot. L. B. The Credit Account shows payment of the Debit of 22: 7: 14; July 4, 1749: By 3 hhds. tobacco; By error in the weight of hhd. No. 6; By cask; November 6, 1749; By Gibsons inspection accot; By Ballancy Currcy; accot to L. B.

(p. 136). June 8, 1749; The Debit Account of SHIP, *FRIENDSHIP*, To 1 iron pott, 26 lb; ; To ditto 12 lb; July 18, 1749: To cash to Capt. DICKINSON; To Cr. Capt. DICKINSON; To 1 hhd. Rum qty. 107 galls 3/6; To 1 cask Beer 10/; To paid the freight of 22 hhds. Tobacco from Potowmack 5/. The Credit Account shows payment of the debit of 85: 6: 4 in 1749 by 1 Iron Pott return'd; By Mr. JOHN YOUNGER.

(p. 137). June 9, 1749. The Debit of DANIEL BARKSDALE. To your brought from ( ) To 1 purse 3/; pr. garters 6d; thread hose; 1 common Prayer Book 3/8; 2 yds. shipd. holland 2/, 1 fine hat 7/6; To 1 small bowle; To 1 womans hatt 10/10; 1 felt 3/6; 1 pair yarn hose, 2 oz. thread 2/; 1 fine felt 3/6; The Credit Account shows payment of the debit of 11: 5: 3 1/2 July 10, 1749 by your Account given in: By a yd. holland, By JOHN HOLLOWAY if allow'd; By 1 felt overcharg'd; By your ballance to L. B.

(p. 138). June 9, 1749. The Debit Account of JAMES DUFF. To 6 1/2 yds. German serge; 2 1/2 doz. buttons; blue thread; 2 hanks silk, 5 yds. shallow; 2 yds. Irish Linen; 1 silk handkerchief 3/; 2 lbs. shott 5d; 1 mans fine hatt No. 1 4/; The Credit Account shows one entry for June 9, 1749: By JOSEPH STROTHER; the account of 3: 4: 2 1/2 and 3: 16: 10 is paid.

(p. 138). August 23, 1749; The Debit Account of Mr. ENOCH BERRY. To 1 snaffle bridle; 1 1/2 yds. narrow cloth; buttons, hank of silk; 2 glass cans; 1/2 yd. China Taffaty 29/6; 2 oz. silk 4/; 1 Cruett 4d; 2 oz. fine thread @ 8d; lb. Ginger; a fine candlestick; 50 needles; ribbon, 19 yds. fine Irish Linnen 3/2; a quire of paper; 1/4 m. nailes; 2 dram glasses; 3 1/2 gallons Rum; 1 Auger; To ballance of Curr: Accot. L. B. The Credit Account shows payments August 23, 1749 by 2 hhds. tobacco on Gibsons; by 4/ cash; November 6, By your ballance to L. B.

(p. 139). June 10, 1749. The Debit Account of Mr. JOSEPH STROTHER JUNR. To 1/2 yd. fine Chintz 27/; Irish Linen No. 29, 25 yds; 2/10; a dozen plates 10/; 1 dozen table knives 3/6; 2 1/2 yds. serge; a dozen small & 2 big buttons fine; 1 silk fine twist; 2 oz. red thread; 1 oz. cloves 11d; 1 oz. Mace 11d; 1 loaf single sugar 5/10; 2 yds. muslin 5/; 1 hk. silk 4d; 1/2 yd. buckram 6d; 1/2 m. pins; 1 French Necklace 1/3; 200 needles 1/; 4 yds. fine Jeans; 1 Watch seal & 2 lbs. bohea Tea; To 1 shammy skin; 1 fountain pin; ribbon;

15 yds. Cotton, 20 yds. Plaid; 1 pr. womens Lamb gloves, 1/4 hundred needles; The Credit Account shows: June 10: By 5 hhds. of Crops tobacco on Gibsons; (gives numbers: JAMES DUFFs Share; Cash. November 6, 1749; To your accot. in L. B. 1: 18: 8 1/2; 0: 5: 0.

(p. 140). June 10, 1749. The Debit Account of JOHN MITCHELL. To 1 ivory comb 9d; To 1 m. pins 10d; To 8 ells Ozna:, pr. womans shoes 19 1/2d; pr. womans fine shoes 4/7; 7 yds. Irish Linen 2/8; 1 yd. fine Irish Linen 5/; 10 oz. white thread; 800 20d. nailes; 1 pr. blanketts 10/9; 1 boys hatt 9d; 1 womans Rain Hatt 6/9; 2 small pin knives; 1.2 oz. of fine thread; 1 mortar & pestle 3/9; 1 lb. Giner 1/2; a thimble; 1 mans fine hatt 4/; 1/2 doz. small buttons; 1 hk. hair & 1 pr. buckles; 1 bushel Salt 1/6; 12 lbs. brown sugar; 2 primmer; The Credit Account shows payment June 10, 1749: By Roys Crop 2hhd. tobo: Ded'd for WILL ARNOLD; Cash 2/. Debit of 6: 19: 11 & 1: 13: 4 paid.

(p. 141). June 10, 1749. The Debit Account of WILLIAM ARNOLD. To 2 small ruggs; 20 ells ozna; 2 basons; 1/2 doz. spoons 1/2 1/2; 10 yds. white sheeting 10/10; 1 bridle 1/11; 1 pr. cotton crds 2/; 21 yds. Irish Linnen 21/10 1/2; To Drisdale Collector 84 lbs. tobacco; 2 lbs. sugar 2/; 3 oz. thread 1/3; 4 laces; June 20: 4 1/2 yds. topsails; 6 yds. check; 1 m. large pins; 1 Ship Silk Gown 22/6; 1 womans hatt 6/6; 1 mans ditto 5/6; 1 hair sifter 1/2; 3 yds. ribbon 1/2; 15 lbs brown sugar 5/; 7 oz. fine thread; pr. buckles; The Credit Account shows payment of debit June 10, 1749: By JOHN MITCHELL tobacco & cash; By 2 hhds. tobacco; By 54 lbs. paid WOOD included in the charges above.

(p. 142). June 10, 1749. The Debit Account of BENJA. MARTIN. To 1 mans saddle 15/; 1 plain hatt 6/9; 7 yds. brown linen 3/9 1/2; 1/2 dozen plates 1/8; 2 yds. Irish linen 3/4; 1/2 dozen table knives 2/8; 2 oz. thread; 1 pepper box; powder & shott; ribon, broad hoe; bed cord; October 4: 1 pr. blanketts 10/; 1 yard shaloon; 1 1/2 bushel salt. The Credit Account shows payment in full June 10, 1749: By Roys Crop hhds. BM & cask; November 6: By your Accot. in L. B.

(p. 142). September 19, 1749: The Debit Account of RICHARD SHIP. To 1 gun 19/; or 35/ currency; The Credit Account shows: November 6, 1749: To your Accot. in L. B., 0: 19: 0.Sttg.

(p. 143). June 11, 1749. The Debit Account of EDWARD DIXON. To your accot. from ( ); 1 razor strop; pr. womens gloves; 1/2 lb. powder; 1 1/2 yds wadding; 2 hanks silk; 2 oz. thread; 1 bottle snuff 1/6; 2 bushels Salt to MRS. BERRY in curry; Accot; 1 single 10 lb; pair mens cotton hose; 1 coffee mill; 1 womans whip; 1 dozen small gilt buttons; To paid for Chickens 4/8; 1 hank silk; 1 pr. cotton cards 1/8; 6 yds Diaper 1/2; 1 lb. Green Tea; 1 tin pan; 1 Velvett Cap; The Credit Account shows: July 8 1749: By Velvett Cap return'd: Ballance carried to: 281: 25: 19: 10.

(p. 144). June 12, 1749; The Debit Account of Mr. JOHN MOORE. To 4 tin pans; various kinds and amounts of cloth; 1 hk. silk; 1 hund: needles; 9 lbs. single sugar; 2 fine hatts; 1 dish cover; 1 1/2 m. small pins; 1 pr. fine Callimanco shoes 5/; 9 1/2 yds. flannell 1/9; 3 tin pans; 1/4 m. 20d. nailes; gallon Rum; 1 m 8d. nailes; 1 m. 10d nailes; 1/2 doz. Table Ivory knives & forks 12/; 1 oz. of thread; the Credit Account shows (undated) By 1 fine Patch return'd 50/; November 6: By your accot. in L. B. 9..9..0 3/4; 0..6..0.

(p. 145). June 12, 1749. The Debit Account of ANTHONY SAMUEL. To your debt brought from ( ); 3 1/2 ells Ozna; 21 ells Wrapper 4d; 10 yds. Irish Linen 20d; buttons, silk, thread; 1 lb. Ginger 4/6; 2 prs .mens shoes 3/6; 1 fine hatt 5/6; 7 yds. Irish Linen 1/4; a broad hoe 1/9; a pen knife 4d; 2 pr. knee buckles 9d; 50 needles 3d; 2 yds. ribbon; 1 box iron & heaters; 6 yds. cotton 6/; 1 butcher knife; 2 combs 1/1; 1 fine hatt 2/3; Exchange in pr. womens hose; To PETER SAMUEL; To MARY MARTIN; 1 tin pan; The Credit account shows payment June 12, 1749: By your Credit brot. from ( ); By allowance of Callico 6/; Linen 2/6; By 1 hhd. tobacco on Laytons; By Cash 2/.

(p. 146). June 12, 1749; The Debit Account of Majr. JERE: MURDOCK. To 2 pr. silk hose 16/; pr. fine worsd. do 4/; 3 horse comb 9d; 4 yds. muslim 11/; 3 yds. China Taffaty 4/6; 14 yds. fine Jeans; 10 gross Corks; 2 doz. coat buttons; 1 curry comb; 1 brush; 1 razor strop; 3 yds. fine ribbon; pr. womens lamb gloves 1/4; 2 hair sifter 2/4; 2 fine hatts 16/; 1 glass can; pr. falls 1/8; 1 pen knife 8d; 6 single loaves 61 lbs 9d; 3 lbs. Green Tea 8/; July 4; thread, Kendall Cotton; tape, 1 broom 1/8; 207 ells Oznaburg; 12 quire paper 8/; 20 lbs. pepper 1/4; 2 oz. Cinamon 1/4; 2 oz. Cloves 1/8; 1 oz. nutts 9d; 2 oz. Mace 1/; 1 pr. fine candlesticks 6/6; 1 best rugg 18/6; 1 lb. Ginger 1/2; doz. mens fine hatts 4/6; 12 lbs. powser 12/; 56 lbs. shott 2d; 1 doz. large pins 11/; 10 doz. shirt buttons 2/1; 6 padlocks 6d; 6 yds. fine check 1/6; 11 yds. Damask 23d; 3/4 yds. China Taffety. The Credit Account shows payment June 12, 1749: By 2 hhds. tobacco on Gibsons, By 1 ditto Brays; By casks. July 4: By ballance this day; By ballance to 223. 33..11..4.

(p. 147). June 13, 1749. The Debit Account of JOHN ROACH. To 1 mans hatt 6/; 1 ivory comb; 5 yds. Irish linen; 5 ells Ozna; thread, nails, buttons, 2 glasses; 2 pr. womens gloves 2/; 5 yds. fine pink shalloon 10/; oz. of thread; 7 yds. check; 1 glass can; The Credit Account shows payment June 13, 1749: By 1 hhd. toacco; Cask, 2/.

(p. 147). August 23, 1749. The Debit Account of AUGUS: WEEDEN. To 1 hhd. Rum 106 1/2 galls. 3/4; September 11: To 1 snaffle bridle; 1 lb. tea; 1 tea pott; 1 hhd. Rum 104 1/2 gallons 3/4; To 1 cask sugar 242 nt. 4...4...6. The Credit Account shows payment on August 23, September 11 & October 3 cash payments; By JOHN BALTHROP; By Ballance to L. B.

(p. 148). June 13, 1749. The Debit Account of JOHN COLQUIT. To 25 ells Ozna: 1 bed cord 1/4; 1 Jackett 1/; 1 pen knife 3d; 10 yds. sheeting 10/; 1 pr. pumps 3/6; 2 broad hoes 3/; powder & shott; 1 lb. Giner 1/1; 1 lb. Peper 1/4; 1 oz. nutts 9d; 1 bed Bunt 10/6; 1 Prayer Book 2/8; 1 Brass Cock 1/6; 2 plain hatts 13/6; thread, nails, 2 combs 1/4; 1 horn comb 2d; 1 pr. buckles 9d; 4 pockett bottles 1/; September 16: To 1 single loaf 9 3/4 lbs; October 16; 3 yds. shaloon; pr. mens hoes 3/3; 1/2 lb. allspice; 1 pr. Compasses 3d; 16 yds. Linnen; 1 lock 11d; 2 felts, 3/6; The Credit Account shows payment June 13, 1749: By allowance on former hhd: By Laytons 1 hhd. 1052; By cask; November 6: By your Accot. in L. B.

(p. 149). June 13, 1749; The Debit Account of WILLIAM AYLE. To your Sttg. ballance: To 1 wrapper; 1 lb pepper; July 25; To advance on the Sttg. 75 p. cent; 10d, 8d. & 2d. nails; pr cards 2/4; September 8: gallon Rum 4/6; 1/2 hund. needles; 1 razor 1/; 2 lb. Sugar; The Credit Account shows July 27, 1749: By cash: 1..1..8; November 6; By your Accot to L. B.

(p. 149). August 21, 1749. The Debit Account of Capt. JOS: BERRY. To 4 yds. Cambt; 2/4; 1 1/2 yds. shaloon 2/; 1 doz. small buttons; hk. silk, 3 yds. linnen 4/6; pr. mens shoes 5/; The Credit Account shows November 6, 1749: By your Accot in L. B. 1..4..5 Curry.

(p. 150). June 13, 1749; The Debit Account of THOS: SAMUEL SENR. To 3 doz. coat buttons 1/6; 3 oz. fine Taylors thread; 2 prs. boys hose 5/; 2 prs. womens do 5/8; 75 needles 5d; 10 1/2 yds. Irish linen 1/9; pr womens gloves 1/; 1 lb. Tea 5/; 2 mens fine hatts @ 4/6; 100 3d. nails; 1 large sifter; 2 bowles; 1 snaffle bridle 2/; 7 lbs. Dble. Sugar; The Credit account shows payment June 13, 1749: By your ballance brot. from ( ); November 6: By your accot. in L. B.

(p. 151). June 13, 1749. The Debit Account of WILLI: HAWKINGS. To 60 ells Ozna; pr. dble. C. Pumps; 1 bridle 1/10; 12 yds. Camblett 1/8; 2 1/2 yds. lace 3/6; 2 womens plain hatts 6/9; 8 yds. Callico 3/; pr thread hose 3/; 1 Counterpaine 25/; 4 silk laces 1/10; 1 drawing knife 1/3; To Cr. THOS: TILLER 367 lbs. tobacco; 1 lb. pepper 1/4; 1 fine hat 13/6; 3 necklaces 6d; 1 felt 1/9; 1 iron pott 1/10: 1 small jugg 6d; 3 Broad hoes No. 3 1 do No. 4; 9/1; 3 1/2 yds. german serge 4/; 4 small ruggs 4/6; To sundrys paid DAVID PITTS for 196 lbs. tobacco; To 1 loaf sugar omitted, 1 felt, 2 oz. red thread; The Credit Account shows payments June 13, 1749 By 7 hhds. tobacco: (numbers given); by casks; November 6: By your accot. in L. B. 0..9..11 Sttg.

(p. 152). June 13, 1749. The Debit Account of GEO: BRASFIELD SENR. To your ballance from (65): various kinds and amounts of cloth; pr. knee buckles 2/; 1 small necklace 3d; 1/2 dozen plates 5/6; nails, 1 small cup 2d; 6 loaf sugar 5/1; 2 basons 2/; 1/2 gallon Rum 2/6; pr. shoe buckles; 1 small cup 2d; 4 yds. bro. linnen 7 1/2; October 6: paid ELIZA: JACKSON 10/ Curry. The Credit Account shows November 6, 1749: By your Accot in L. B. 14..13..4; 1..5..7 1/2.

(p. 153). June 13, 1749. The Debit Account of ELIZA: BULLARD. To 1 womans saddle; To 1 linen handkerchief 1/6; 1 1/2 yds fine linen 3/8; To THOMAS SHIP SENR. 144 lbs. tobacco 18/6; 5 yds. fine Linnen; pins, lace, ribbons, pr. womens gloves 1/4; 1/2 lb. pepper 8d; 1 primmer 3/; 1 boys felt 9d; 4 oz. blue thread, 1 pocket knife 7 1/2; 1 Butcher 3 1/2; 2 1/2 yds. Cotton 2/11; 1 lb. powder; 4 lbs. shott; To 1 womans Ruff'd hatt 14/ curry; The Credit Account shows June 13, 1749: By 1 hhd. Tobacco 1226; Cask; November 6; By your account in L. B.

(p. 154). June 13, 1749. The Debit Account of THOS: TILLER. By 3 1/2 yds. Cloth 6/6; 5 1/2 yds. shalloon; 2 doz. coat buttons; 1 doz. small; Oznaburg, Linnen, Check, hank silk, 1 drawing knife 1/3; 1/2 m. pins. The Credit Account shows payment June 13, 1749: By WILLIAM HAWKINGS 367 lbs. tobacco:

(p. 154). June 13, 1749. The Debit Account of THOS: SHIP JUNR. To 4 ells Ozna:, 1 broad hoe No. 4, 2/1; 1 boys felt 9d; 1 box iron & heaters 5/6; 6 yds. Check 1/4; 6 ells Dowlass 5/6; 5 yds. bro: sheeting; 1 pr. cotton cards 2/; 1 pr. large scizors 4 1/2; 1 thimble; pins, needles, womens hose 2/10; mans hatt 4/6; womans hatt 9/; 1/2 lb. pepper 8d; 1 Silk cap 4/6; 1 lb. Power & 4 lb. Shott 1/7; September 16; To 1 pr. wool cards 1/4; 1 yard Cotton 1/2; 1/4 m. 6d. nails. The Credit Account shows June 13, 1749: By 1 hhd. tobacco Roys 1451; Ded'd for THOMAS SHIPs Son, Cask; November 6, By your accot. in L. B.

(p. 155). June 14, 1749. The Debit Account of Mr. JOHN PITTS. To 1 gallon pott 7/8; 1 dble. loaf 7 1/2 lbs. 1/2; To your accot. from (88); The Credit Account shows: undated: By allowance on your tobacco: 3..6..9.

(p. 155). August 14, 1749. The Debit Account of THOS: PITTMAN. To 1 pr. single chaneled pumps; 1 ivory comb; 2 bowles; October 27; 1 pr. womans hose; The Credit Account shows: November 6, 1749: By your accot. in L. B., 1..12..8 Sttg.

(p. 156). June 14, 1749. The Debit Account of WILLIAM MARSHALL. To your ballance brot. from (56). To 1 womans plain saddle & furniture 2/8/0; 1/2 lb. allspice 7d; 20 ells Ozna: 2 oz. Indico; pr. garters 4d; 1 womans ruff'd hatt 9/; 1 card sleeve buttons 6d; 1 lb. pepper 1/4; 3 lbs.single sugar 10d; June 19: To sundry paid your Brother; To 1 platter & 1 primmer, 2 oz. thread; 1 felt 1/9; 1/2 oz. Cinamon 3d; 1 bridle 2/4; 1 pr. cotton cards 2/; The Credit Account shows payments June 14, 1749: By 1 pr. womans shoes return'd; By Gibsons 1 hhd. 1025; By ditto 948; By allowance on former hhd.; casks; November 6, By your ballance to L. B.

(p. 157). June 14, 1749; The Debit Account of JOHN STROTHER. To 1 spring Knife 5d; To 1 pockett Bottle 1d; To 4 prs. mens buckles 1/8; 6 yds. fine check; 1 pr. knee buckles; The Credit Account shows: November 6, 1749: To your accot. in L. B. 1..0..1 curry.

(p. 157). July 31, 1749. The Debit Account of JOHN DAVIS. To 1 mans fine hatt 7/6; To 3 1/2 yards Check; 1/2 lb. pepper; 1 oz. thread; 2 black potts; 5 pints Rum; 1/2 gall. Rum & 2 lbs. Sugar; To 1 qt. Rum; 1 bason 3/10; 1 Bridle 2/4; 1 girth 10d; 1 pr. womans hose 2/; 1 pr. girls hose 1/2; 5 yds. serge; 3 yds. Bolster ends 3/6; 11 1/4 yds. duck; The Credit Account shows: November 6, 1749: By your accot. in L. B. 2..14..5 & 0..6..10 1/2.

(p. 158). June 14, 1749. The Debit Account of Mr. JOHN JETT. To 1 silk Cap 4/6; 1 lb. peper 1/4; 1 Japand. Quart 2/; 1 small ditto 1/; 2 augers 11d; pr. cards 1/4; 1 felt No. 2 1/; 2 pr. mens hose 2/3; 25 ells Ozna: pr. womans shoes 3/; 12 3/4 yds. fine Check 17/; 100 needles 7d; 1 peper box, 1 small porringer 2d; 1 pr. pumps 5/; 1 1/2 yds. Muzlin 3/6; 2 razors @ 8, 1 Leghorn hatt 1/6; pr. womens gloves 1/4; ivory comb 9d; 3 thimbles 7/; pr.sleeve buttons; 2 yds. ribon; 3 3/4 yds. lace 7/9 1/2; 4 yds. Check 2/9; 1 felt 1/9; 1 iron pott 31 lbs. 5/2; , 8d, 10d, 20d, 3d, nails; 1 ax, 1 drawing knife 1/3; 1 mans fine hatt 4/; 2 oz. Indico @ 4 1/2; 1 square steel tobacco box 1/10; 1 spring knife 3d; pr.mens hose 2/4; quire paper; 1 pr. stirrups leather 1/6; 1 doz. fish hooks, 1 best silk purse 2/10; The Credit account shows: June 14, 1749: By 2 hhds. tobacco on Gibsons; By do on Mattox; casks; July 1; By 1 ditto on Mattox; cask; (See folio 231).

(p. 159). June 14, 1749; The Debit Account of CHARLES WRIGHT. Various kinds and amounts of cloth; small buttons; 2 potts; a mans fine hatt 5/6; a womans hatt 8/; 1 broad hoe 1/6; a bed cord 1/4; 2 pr. buckles 1/6; pr. womans gloves 1/4; a bridle 2/4; a silk cap 4/6; yd. fine shalloon 1/5; 2 silk handkerchiefs 6/9; 1 curry comb 7 1/2; 2 Necklaces & 1 oz. thread 6d; To ballance as p. Contra: Coppy given The Credit Account shows June 14, 1749: By 1 hhd. tobacco on Gibsons 1036, Cask; July 19: By ballance due this day; November 6: By your accot. in L. B. 2..0..1 Sttg.

(p. 160). June 14, 1749. The Debit Account of ANN MARSHALL. To 10 yds. Irish linen; (other amounts and kinds of cloth); 1 oz. fine thread 1/6; pr. womans white gloves; 1 Japand. Quart 1/8; 1 pen knife 10d; 4 lbs. single sugar 10d; To cash; paid a man; 1/2 lb. allspice; 1 oz. nutts; 1 oz. Cinamon; 2 doz. small buttons; oz. of thread; 2 tin pans; pr. buckles, a fine hatt 6/2, this charged to GEO: MARSHALL; To 1 Bible 3/4; To pd. your Note favor of OWEN CAMPBELL; 2 bushels Salt 3/; pr. womans shoes 2/4; powder & shot; The Credit Account shows: June 16, 1749 By 2 hhds. at Gibsons, Casks; November 6: By 1 pr. womens gloves return'd; By ballance to L. B.

(p. 161). June 14, 1749: The Debit Account of JAMS: TURNER. To 1 oz. Cinamon 9d; 1 oz.Cloves 9d; 1 oz. nutts 9d; 2 lbs. peper 9/8; 1/2 lb. Ginger 1/2; 1 lb Allum 4d; 2 doz. laces; 1/2 m. small nails; 40 needles; pr. buckles 1/3; an ax 2/4 1/2; 2 cups 5d; 12 ells Ozna; mortar & pestle 3/5; oz. of thread 1/6; a green rugg 18/6; 2 small ditto @ 4/6; 1 felt 1/9; 2 Leghorn ditto 5/; 1 Leghorn hatt 3/9; 2 yds. Callico 3/8; 11 1/2 yds. Kersey 15/; 4 doz. small buttons 1/2; July 14: 10 yds. linnen 10/; 1 m. 10d. nails; 2 pr. hose 2/; 3 pr. hose 2/; 1 Padlock 11d; 1 bottle beer, 3 pewter plates 3/3; 1 silk handkerchief 3/6; 2 oz. Indico 9 1/2; The Credit Account shows: June 14, 1749, By your ballance brot. from (95); 12..11..6 1/2 & 8..0..0. Sttg.

(p. 162). June 15, 1749. The Debit Account of Mr. GEO: TANKERSLEY. To your ballance brot. from (35); To 12 yds. blue damask; 10 yds. check, hank of Silk, 6 yds. Irish linnen; (various other kinds and amount of cloth); 1 razor strop; 1 oz. thread; 1 oz. cinamon; 1 oz nutts; 1 lb. peper; 2 Ells Ozna; 1 pr. small sizors; 1 silk lace; 1 womans furr'd hatt 6/; July 6: 1 m. 10d. nails 4/4; 1 m. 8d. nails 3/4; 1 felt No. 5 1/6; 1 worsted cap 6d; 1 large spring knife 6d; 50 lbs. bro: sugar; 4 1/2 gallons Rum; 1 m. 4d. nails; 2 boys felts 1/4; The Credit Account shows: July 10, 1749: By ADAM LINDSEY 0..18..3; By 4 hhds. tobacco 4059 lbs; @ 13/ 26..7..8; cask; By ballance to (279). 0...11..0; 5..1..4.

(163). June 15, 1749. The Debit Account of THOS: BUTLER. To 1 mans hatt 5/6; 1 womans ditto 9/; 1 m. pins 9d; 5 yds. shalloon 1/1; 1 rugg 18/6; pr sizors & comb 1/4 1/2; 4 oz. blue thread; 2 yds. ribon; 1 bed cord; 6 yds. chequе; 1 pewter pott 5d; 1 mortar & pestle 4/10; 8 yds. Irish Linen and various other kinds and amounts of cloth; 1/2 lb. peper; 1 oz. nutts 9d; 3 spring knives 1/2. The Credit Account shows: June 15, 1749: By 2 hhds. at Mattox; 2078 lbs; By casks; 6..11..0; & 9...3...4.

(p. 163). August 16, 1749. The Debit Account of STAFFORD LIGHTBURNE. To 1 sauce pan 1/3; To a Tea pott 1/3; 2 yds. bro: linen 2/1; 1/2 gallon Rum 2/3; 2 oz. blue thread; pr. garters to WILL:, To 1 lb. shoe thread; 1 bottle Mustard 2/; 2 lbs. sugar, 1 doz. pipes; pr. wool cards 2/4; The Credit Account shows: November 6, 1749: By your accot. in L. B. 1..4..9 Curry.

(p. 164). June 13, 1749. The Debit Account of AARON HARDITCH. To 4 1/2 yds. Serge 4/6; 2 1/2 dozen buttons 6d; 2 hks. silk; 4 yds. shalloon; 1 mans hatt 5/6; 1 rugg 18/6; 1 womans hatt 6/9; pr. buckles 9d; 75 needles 5d; pr. gloves 1/4; 1 pott 1/6; 3 3/4 Ells Dowlass 3/5; 2 oz. blue thread 4d; 1 yd. ribon, 1 lb. Peper 1/4; 7 yds. Irish linen 1/8; 3 doz. pipes; 1 silk cap 7/6; 1 1/2 bushell salt 3/; November 6: To Ballance of Curry: to L. B. The Credit Account shows: June 15,1749: By 2 hhds. tobacco Mattox; 1940 lbs; cask. 6...10...1; & 8...1...8.

(p. 164). July 22, 1749. The Debit Account of CHRISTO: RODGERS. To 1/2 yd. fine Linen 2/9; 1/2 yd. muzlin 1/6; 1 oz. of thread 8d; August 15: To 1/4 Rum 1/3; Sept. 29. 1/4 Rum 1/3; 3 yds. Linen 1/10. The Credit Account shows: November 6, 1749; By your accot. in L. B. 0..14..2 Curry.

(p. 165). June 15, 1749. The Debit Account of JAMS: BUTLER. (Many entires of various kinds and amounts of cloth buckram, check, oznabrig; chamblett, muslin; dowlass; bolster ends); 2 hks. silk, womans hatt 9/; 1 pr. Call: shoes 4/6; pr. cotton cards 2/; 1 scarlett cloak 11/6; 1 lb. peper 1/4; 1 lb. allspice, 1 hair sifter 1/2; 1 oz. nutts 9d; 1 cloves 1/; ribbon, necklace; pr. womans gloves 1/4; 4 spring knives 1/6; 4 oz. white thread 1/6; 4 dishes 10/8; 1 doz. plates 11/; 2 basons 2/4; 1 m. pins; 1 pen knife 9d; 2 felts 2/; 2 iron potts 42 lbs. 1 rugg 11/4; broad hoe 2/1. The Credit Account shows June 15, 1749: By 3 hhds. tobo: on Mattox 2901 lbs; cask. (This account is not totalled)

(p. 166). June 15, 1749. The Debit Account of WILLIAM BUTLER. To 1 mans hatt 3/6; 2 silk caps 9/; 1 best pen knife 9d; (cloth: check, Irish linen, holland oznabrig); thread; 1 mans hatt 4/6; pr. buckles 9d; 1 felt 9d; pr. womans gloves 2/8; 1 half curb bridle 2/6; 1 sett buckles 1/2; 3..19..2; Cash 4..3..4. The Credit Account shows payment for the goods and the cash June 15, 1749 by 1 hhd. tobacco on Mattox 1594 @ 16/8 for the 4..3..4; 594 @ 13/ and cask for the 3..19..2.

(p. 166). July 22, 1749. The Debit Account of JAMES FLETCHER. To 1/4 yd. fine Irish Linnen 14, 4 lbs. Shott 1/4; August 3: To 1 oz. Indico 7 1/2; 1 lb. alum 7 1/2; 4 lbs. Sugar 2/; October 8: To 1/2 lb. powder 6/; 2 lbs. shott 8 1/2; 1/2 m. Pins 8; The Credit Account shows November 6, 1749 By your account to L. B. 0..8..3 Curry.

(p. 167). June 15, 1749. The Debit Account of ELIZA LEWIS. (Various kinds and amounts of cloth; oznabrig; Irish linnen; callico); pr. wool cards 1/4; pr. cotton cards 2/; a bed cord 1/4; pewter chamber pott 2/8; 3 felts 2/3; thread; 2 ruggs 22/8; a womans saddle 60/; 1 Leghorn hatt 2/6; pr. gloves 1/4; 1 m. pins 10d; 2 hatters 3/; 1 lb. powder 1/; 4 lbs. Shott 8d; 1 hair sifter 1/2; 1 felt 9d; 1 ditto 1/4; 2 pounds in Cash. The Credit Account shows June 15, 1749: By 1 hhd. tobacco on Mattox 1112 @ 13/, cask 2/; June 19, 1749: By 1 ditto Boyds 240 @ 16/8; 762 @ 13/ & cask. Debit of 12..7..6 and the cash paid.

(p. 168). June 16, 1749. The Debit Account of WILL: POWELL. To your brot. from 89; (various kinds and amounts of cloth; tammy, linnen, muslim, callico; dowlass, buckram, Irish linnen); pr. womens gloves 1/4; 1 3/4 yds ribon 2/7 1/2; 1 womans furr'd hatt 9/; 1 Cloak 13/6; 1/2 doz. table knives 4/4; 1 silk lace 5d; 2 oz. Indico; 1 lb. shott 1/; 2 felts 1/6; mans fine hatt 4/; 6 chissels 2/; 4 mortiss Chisells 1/8; 1 paring ditto 8; 1 Carpenters rule 8; 2 compasses, a pewter bayson 2/6; Cash of 3/1 1/2; Cash 3..2..4; ivory comb; bushel salt, a fine hatt 6/2; 1/2 m. pins 4 1/2; 2 pencils 6d; The Credit Account shows June 16, 1749: By 1 hhd. tobacco 240 @ 16/8; 912 @ 13/; cash @ 2/; November 6, 1749: By your accot. in L. B.

(p. 169). June 16, 1749. The Debit Account of ABRA: WILLSON. To pr. cards 2/; 1 doz. table knives 4/2; 1 pr. Callimanco shoes 4/6; 4 oz. thread 1/4; 1 small fine hat 4/; 1 mans hatt 4/6; quire of paper 8; 6 yds. Callico 18; 2 yds. muslim 1/ 4 1/2; pr. linen hose 2/9; 1 necklace 11d, 4 yds. cotton 11d; pr. womans gloves 1/4; To 1 razor strop. The Credit Account shows: June 16, 1749: By 1 hhd. tobacco on Roys 1142, cask. November 6, By your accot in L. B. 0..5..6 Sttg.

(p. 170). June 16, 1749. The Debit Account of CHAS. BEASLEY JUNR. To 1 yd. fine Linnen 3/8; 20 ells oznabrig 14/2; 9 yds. Irish Linne 1/4; 1 fine hatt 6/2; 1 pair best pumps 5/; 2 yds. check 2/ 0/4; powder & shott; 1/2 lb. Peper, 7 yds. cotton 7/4 1/2; 2 barrels of Tarr 18/; 1 felt 1/2; To Cash 4..0..9. The Credit Account shows payment June 16, 1749: By 1 hhds tobacco on Roys 600 @ 16/8; 495 @ 13/, cask. Debit 3..6..1; Cash 5..0..0.

(p. 170). August 10, 1749. The Debit Account of JEREMH: BROWN. To 2 broaches 4/; 5 ells ozna: 1 felt 1/4; 1/2 lb. powder 6d; 2 lbs. shott 4; pr blanketts 11/; 2 pr. yarn hose 1/; 3 yds. sacking 1/6; bro. thread; tape. 12 yds. plaid 8/; 1 1/4 yds. check 1/6; The Credit Account of November 6, 1749 shows: By your accot in L. B. 2..13..11 1/2 sttg.

(p. 171). June 16, 1749. The Debit Account of WILLIAM EDWARDS. To 15 ells Ozna: 8 1/2; 6 1/2 yds. Irish Linnen 1/8; 1 1 mans felt hat 5/6; 1 bed cord 1/4; pr. mens hose 3/8; (various other kinds and amounts of cloth: kersey, bro. linnen, buckram; check, shalloon); quire of paper 8; pr. womans gloves 1/4; 2 doz. mettle coat buttons; 1 rugg 9/7; 1 curry comb 7 1/2d; To cash 0..19..8; 1 stock lock; 200 small nails; pr. womans shoes 2/6; 1/2 bushel salt 9d; The Credit Account shows June 16, 1749: By 2 hhds. tobacco on Gibson 953 @ 13/ and cask; By allowance off bed tyck; November 6, 1749: By your accot. in L. B. 1..5..2 sttg.

(p. 172). June 17, 1749. The Debit Account of WILL: SPEED. To 1 mans fine hatt 13/9; 25 needles; 2 knives & forks 1/3; September 22: 1 3/4 yds. Linnen; pr. mens shoes 6/1; 4 lbs. Bro. sugar 1/4. The Credit Account shows: November 6, 1749; By your Accot. in L. B. 0..16..8.

(p. 172). June 17, 1749. The Debit Account of MARY MARTIN. To 1 felt No. 1, 9d; July 13, 1749: To 1 mans fine hatt 6/; 1 pr. womens shoes 2/4; 1 funnell 4d; 3 1/2 yds. bolster ends 3/6; 3 yds. kersey 4/; 3 small knives 1/3; 1/2 m. large pins 5d; 7 yds. linnen 7d; nails, 1 bason 2/; yd. ribon 6d; a linen handkercheif 6d; 3 1/2 yds. check 2/5 1/2; 4 oz. blue thread 8d; 1 felt 9d; 1 horn comb 2d; 1 broad ax 2/10; 1 narrow hoe 1/6; The Credit Account shows July 13, 1749: By ANTHONY SAMUEL 300; 1..19..0; November 6, 1749: By your accot. in L. B. 0..12..11 sttg.

(p. 173). June 17, 1749. The Debit Account of AMBROSE HOWARD. To 1 flowered can 1/8; 1 pint ditto 1/; 1 womans hatt 9/; 1 cruett 4 1/2; 1 leghorn hatt; pr gloves 1/4; 1 glass 1/; 5 m. 4d. nailes, 300 2d. ditto; 7 1/2 yds. Irish linnen 1/3; a large tin pan 1/2; 1 glass salt 10d; pr. womans hose 2/; 2 gimbletts 2d; To cash 3..0..0; 1 mortar & pestle 6/6; August 3, 1749: To 4 1/2 lbs. single sugar 3/9. The Credit Account shows July 8, 1749: By 1 hhds. tobacco on Roys 360 @ 16/8; 748 @ 13/; Cask 2/; payment in full of 7..19..2.

(p. 174). June 17, 1749. the Debit Account of JAMS: GOUGE. To 1 mans hatt 5/6; 1 felt 9d; 1 quire paper 8d; 1 rugg 4/6; pr. cards 2/; 2 broad hoes 3/10; pr. womans shoes 2/9; (various kinds and amounts of cloth: bro. linnen, Irish linen; muzlim, dowlass, oznabrig); pr. womans gloves 1/4; 1 dish 3/1; 1 pen knife 10 1/2 d; 2 small knives 6d; pins, thread; 1/4 m. 6d. nails; To cash: 0..16..8; August 22: To paid Mr. BOWLWARE 58 lbs. tobacco 0..7..6; 1 grubbing hoe 2/5 1/2; The Credit Account shows June 17, 1749: By Roys Crop 1 hhd. marked J: G: to pay 5..8..2; and the cash amount of 0..16..8; November 6, 1749; By your accot. in L. B. 0..15..6 Sttg.

(p. 175). June 17, 1749. The Debit Account of ROBT. BENSON. To 12 ells Dowlass 12/ 1 blankett 6/6; 7 1/2 yds. linnen 1/3; 1 1/2 yds. flannel 1/7; 9 ells Oznabrig 7 1/2d; a velvett cap 1/4; 1/2 lb. Cinamon 9d; 1 oz. mace 1/; 2 oz. ginger 7d; Allspice 7d; 4 lbs. brown sugar; a linen handkerchief; 2 hks. silk, blue thread; 1 1/2 doz. buttons; 2 1/2 yds. sheeting; a curry comb; a great Coat 13/6; 2 pr. yarn hose, a worsted cap 8d. The Credit Account shows: June 17, 1749: By ballance brot. from 45; 7..11..2; November 6, 1749; By your accompt. in L. B. 89; 1..18..9 1/2; and 0..1..0.

(p. 176). June 17, 1749; The Debit Account of Mr. WILLIAM WILEY. To 3 1/2 yds. Ribon 4d; 1 curb Bridle 2/10; 1 small snuff box 1/; 1 bottle Scotch Snuff 2/12. The Credit Account shows payment of the 16/ debit July 22, 1749; By Cash

(p. 176). July 22, 1749. The Debit Account of HENRY LONG. To 1 silk hatt 11/. The Credit Account shows November 6, 1749; By your accot. in L. B., 0...11...0 sttg.

(p. 177). June 17, 1749; The Debit Account of GRACE BERRY. To 100 needles 7d; 17 1/4 yds. fine Check 1/4; 21 yds. Irish Linen 1/8; 2 pr. cotton cards 6d; 3 Pinons shoes 10/6; 66 yds. bro. linen 6 1/2; 1 bed cord 1/4; 1 flowered quart 1/8; 1 small ditto 1/4; 1 bowle 6d; 2 chamber potts 1/2; 1 felt 1/3; 1 pint mugg 3 1/2; 1 m. 8d. nails 3/9; 1 hair sifter 10d; 1 stock lock 2/4; 1 pr. blanketts 13/10; July 13. To Cash 4...0...0. The Credit Account shows June 7, 1749; By 2 hhds. tobacco Gibsons viz. 480 @ 15/8; 1487 @ 13/; casks 0...4...0; Debiut of 9...17...3 and 4..0..0 paid

(p. 177). August 15, 1749. The Debit Account of JOHN YOUNG. To ballance brot. from 58; To 1 sett buckles 1/2; 1 doz. hooks 3d; To Cash 0...8...8; dozen mettle buttons; 2 oz. taylors thread 4d; 1 Crupper 8d; September 13: 1 lb. Powder 1/; 5 lbs. Shott 10d; 1/4 Rum; 1 m. 8d. nailes 3/8; 1 bowle 8d; oz. of nutts 9d; 5/8 Rum 1 wine glass; 1 doz pipes & 1 lb. Sugar; 1 bowl 9d; 2 bushel Salt 3/; 1 gall. Rum 4/6 curry; 1 worsted cap 8d; Cash 1/3. The Credit Account shows (undated) By 1 pr. shoes return'd, 0..2..4; ; November 6, 1749 By ballance to L. B. 4...2..o and 1..14..9.

(p. 178). June 17, 1749. The Debit Account of JOSEPH STROTHER. To 2 pr. Spectacles @ 10d; 2 quart muggs 1/; 1 mans fine hatt 4/6; 1 mans fine hatt 6/6; 2 broad hoes 3/8; 2 flowered quarts 4/; 1 Leather Ink Pott 2d; 1 pr. Ink Powder 4 1/2; 1 pr. stays 16/; 1 yd. Irish Linnen; 10 yds. bro: Linnen 7 1/2; July 13: 1 Cotto: Turner 4..0..0; To cash 0...3...1; 1/2 dozen buttons @ 5d; September 1, a quire of paper 8d; powder & shot; hair sifter 1/4; 2 oz Indico. The Credit Account shows June 17, 1749: By 1 hhd. tobacco on Gibsons; 420 @ 13/8; 512 @ 13/, casks 0..2..0; November 6: By ballance to L. B. 0...9...7 sttg.

(p. 178). October 31, 1749; The Debit Account of WILLIAM MARSHALL. To ballance brot. from 71; To 1/2 yds. China Taffety; 2/3; 1 yd. Linnen 1/; November 4: To 1 pr. small shoes; The Credit Account shows November 6, 1749: By your accot. in Lb. 4..9..1 and 0...16..0

(p. 179). June 17, 1749. The Debit Account of MARK BOULWARE. To 18 yds. Ticking 1/7; 11 1/2 ells dowlass 10 1/2; brown thread; white thread; pr. womans shoes 2/8; 3 yds. fine ribon 3/; 2 womans furr'd hatts 18/; 2 broad hoes 4/2; 4 1/4 lbs. sugar 3/5; To Cash 0...11...8. The Credit Account shows: June 17, 1749; By 1 hhd. tobacco on Laytons; 70 @ 16/8; 986 @ 13/6; Casks 0..2..0.

(p. 179. July 19, 1749. The Debit Account of THOS: RATCLIFF. (various kinds and amounts of cloth as Irish linen, check; chamblett, buckram, sheeting); a mans fine hatt 5/; 1 oz thread 5d; pr. womans shoes 3/; 2 dozen buttons; 2 hks. hair; a pencil 2/2; 1 silk handkerchief 3/; The Credit Account November 6, 1749, CHAS. WRIGHT, security, By your accot. L. B. 2..0..11 1/2 sttg.

(p. 180). June 17, 1749. The Debit Account of WILLM. THOMAS. To 2 yds. Muslim; 2 prs. sheep shears 1/8; 9 yds. shalloon; pr. buckles 6d; mans furr'd hatt 5/6; 2 womens furr'd hatts 18/; 2 plain ditto 13/6; 1 rugg 11/4; 1 oz. fine thread 1/; 11 yds. bro. linnen to ballance; July 24: To Cash 6...0...0. The Credit Account shows June 18, 1749: By Boyds 2 hhds. 120 @ 16/8; 1240 @ 13/; casks 0..4..0;

(p. 180). August 25, 1749. The Debit Account of WILLM. PEAR. To 1 qt. Rum 1/3; 2 sugar 1/; 2 butcher knives 8d; 2 muggs 1/2; 1/4 Rum 1/3; September 4: 1 qt. Rum 1/3; 1 funnell 7 1/2; September 26: 1/4 Rum 1/3. The Credit Account shows November 6, 1749: To your accot. in L. B. 0...9...5 Curry;

(p. 181). June 17, 1749. The Debit Account of LUCY HUDSON. To 6 yds. Callico 18/; 6 1/2 yds. top sails 1/6; 2 womens ruff'd hatts 18/; 1/4 bushel Salt 1/6; pr. large blanketts 14/9; a large bason 3/10; an ax 2/9; a broad hoe 1/9; a candlestick 2/9; pins, needs, buckles, white thread, 6 yds. bro. linen, 1/2 doz. table knives 2/9; pr. womans gloves 2/; To Cash 1...11...4; The Credit Account shows June 17, 1749: By Gibsons hhd. 200 @ 16/8; 808 @ 13/; Cask 0..2..0;

(p. 181). October 27, 1749. The Debit Account of JAMS: BEASLEY. To your acct. brot. from 122; To 1/2 lb. shoe thread 1/ curry; ! lb. powder 1/. The Credit Account shows November 6, 1749: By your Accot. in L. B. 3...5...4; 1...13..1.

(p. 182).June 17, 1749. The Debit Account of Mrs. FRANS: BALTHROP. To 20 1/2 yds. serge 1/6; 40 yds. check 8 1/4; 9 mens fine hatts 4/; 6 lbs. thread; 6 Curry combs 6/3; 6 spelling books 5/2; 2 pr. gartering 1/4; 1 dozen table knives 2/6; 1 1/2 dozen Bath Thimbles 1/10 1/2; 3 womans ruff'd hatts 24/; 3 ditto plain 18/; 5 silk pursesllll No. 1 7/6; pr. mens best silk hose 14/6; 1 doz. horn combs 2/; 9 ivory combs 6/; buttons, cloth, 21 boys felts No. 1 14/; 9 do No. 3 10/6; 12 do. No. 4 16/; 3 ditto No. 5 4/6; 1 1/2 dozen hair sifters 21/; 1/2 doz. bed cords 8/; 6 yds. French ribond 3/6; 1 1/2 dozen large pins 12/9; 8 large pocket bottles 5/4; 22 small do. 3/8; 6 wine glasses 4/6 1/2; 3 oz. cinnamon 1/6; 2 cotton gowns at 12/ 9 yds. fine James 18/9; pr. womens shoes 6/; 1 doz. Ink potts 1/; 1 dozen pen knives 4/6; 1 dozen silk lace 4/6; 1 dozen cotton cards 21/; June 29: 6 Testaments 5/6; 1 doz. jews harps 6d; 6 curry combs 7/6; 1 lathing hammer 1/; July 6: To JAMES WHITE 0...3...0; 1 1/2 doz. sizors; 150 needles @ 6d; 3 pr. mens pumps 3/6; To ballance carried to 224: The Credit Account shows June 17, 1749: By 6 hhds. crop tobacco Nt. wts. (viz) (total 6215); June 19: By 3 hhds. tobacco (total 3190); 3 casks; By Allowance on Sheeting; By 1 handkercheif wanting; July 6: By 2 hhds. on Brays 2234; Transfer note on Boyds 32; 11 casks; 53...2...11; 22...10...0.

(p. 183). June 17, 1749. The Debit Account of JOHN CARTER. To yr. Debt brot. from 62: 2 one curry comb & 2 glasses @ 4 1/2; To ballance as p. Contra; October 4: To 1/2 lbs. powder & 2 lbs. shott. The Credit Account shows (undated) By your Credit brot. from 62; By ballance as pr. Accot. given in; November 6: By your accot in L. B. 0...2...10 sttg.

(p. 183). June 17, 1749; The Debit Account of WILLIAM CARTER. To 1 pr. buckles 1/6; 1 pr. thread hose, 1 handkerchief. The Credit Account shows November 6, 1749: By your accot. in L. B. 0...5...0 sttg.

(p. 184). June 17, 1749. The Debit Account of SAML. MAJOR. To sundrys; To 1 hatt 8/; 1 flower'd quart 2/; 4 reap hooks 1/6; 1 felt, 3 knives; quire paper, whip saw file, bed cord 1/4; pr. blanketts, 1 lbs. Sugar 8d; September 26: To one pair shoes from Mr. GRAYs; October 14: To 1 lb. shoe thread; 1 pr. plad. hose; pr. garters; The Credit Account shows November 6, 1749: By your accot. to L. B. 4...2...3; 0...14...4.

(p. 184). August 15, 1749. The Debit Account of RICHARD CLATTERBUCK. To ballance brot. from 16; To 1 mans fine hatt; To Cash 0...5...0; September 1: 3 yds. Cotton 4/6; 3 yds. bro: linen 3/; 2 spring knives, 4 lbs. shott. The Credit Account shows: November 6, 1749: By your accompt. in L. B. 7...9...5 Curry.

(p. 185). June 17, 1749. The Debit Account of WILLIAM BANISTER. To your ballance brot. from 19. (various kinds and amounts of cloth: Tammy, collo. check; Irish linen; bro. linnen); pr. womans hose 2/; 2 1/2 m. nailes; The Credit Account shows: October 16, 1749: By JAMES BEASLEY 0...7...0; November 6, 1749: By your accot. in L. B. 3..2..7 1/2; 0...15...0.

(p. 185). October 25, 1749: The Debit Account of MARY BEASLEY. To ballance brot. from 201; To 2 pr. plad. hose; October 27: 1/2 lb. shoe thread; 1/; Cr. MR. GILCHRIST for 37 buttons. The Credit Account shows November 6, 1749: By your accot. in L. B. 6...14...2; 1...19...0.

(p. 186). June 17, 1749: The Debit Account of CHARS. BENSON. To 1 m. large pins 9d; 1 m. small ditto 1 1/2; 5 ells dowlass 10 1/2; 1 ivory comb 10d; 1 Bath Thimble 2d; pr. buckles 1/; 1 bell mettle skillett 10/; 3 single girths 1/3; 1 womans furr'd hatt 6/; To Cash 0..1..6; The Credit Account shows: November 6, 1749: By ballance to L. B. 1..13..5 1/2; 0..2..6.

(p. 186). October 6, 1749: To ballance brot. from 97; October 9: To 1 1/2 lbs. powder 1/6; 6 lbs. shott 1/; To cash 0..4..4; 1 fine felt 2/3; 2 hks. silk 8; 10 yds. check 6/8; thread, bro. linen, sacking, 1 Stick Sealing Wax 3d; October 17: ToCr. Majr. SAML. SKINKER. The Credit Account shows November 6, 1749: By your accot. in L. B. 1..2..7 1/2; 1..2..6 1/2.

(p. 187). June 10, 1749. The Debit Account of SAML. CRANAGE. To WILLIAM HARRISON the whole accot: 9..0..10. The Credit Account shows June 18, 1749: By 1 hhd. tobacco on Gibsons Nt. 1061 16/8; cask 0..3..0.

(p. 187). September 2, 1749: The Debit Account of THOMS. MASSEY. To 1 lb. powder 1/; To 4 lbs. shott 8; 8 Ells. Oz. 5/1; To Cash 4..4..2. The Credit Account shows September 2, 1749: By hhds. tobacco on Gibsons 814 nt., September 6: By paid SARAH WILLIAMS 200; 54 @ 12/6; 560 @ 14/6; cask.

(p. 187). September 2, 1749. The Debit Account of GEORGE RANKINS. To 10 1/2 yds. Check 8; 1 oz. thread 5; 2 1/2 yds. narro. cloth 3/6; 1 doz. buttons; 1 oz. thread; 1 hanks silk; 1 1/2 yds. shalloon; 1 yd. bro: linen; 1 mans fine hatt 4/. The Credit Account shows November 6, 1749: By your accot. in L. B. 1..7..3 sttg.

(p. 187). June 17, 1749. The Debit Account of JAMES CASH. To 1 mortar & pestle 5/10; 1 candle stick 1/3; (various kinds and amount of cloth: Irish linnen, callico; check; ticking; serge); 1/2 doz. plates 7/6; 2 tin panns 2/4; pr. womans gloves 1/4; ivory comb 11d; horn comb 2d; 2 thimbles 3d; 1 leghorn hatt 1/10; 2 yds. ribon 1/; 3 felt hatts @ 9d; powder & shott; 1 oz. nutts & 1/2 lb. Allspice 1/4; 1 pr. sizors 8/; bed cord 1/4; 4 bushel salt 6/; 1 silk handkerchief 3/6; To cash 3..0..0; To ballance from 57: September 26: To 1 bridle 2/4; 4 pr. plad. hose 2/10; 1 bowle 4/; 1 glass 4d; 5 lbs. sugar 1/8; The Credit Account shows June 17, 1749: By 2 hhds. tobacco 360 @ 16/8; 1847 @ 13/.

(p. 189). June 18, 1749. The Debit Account of JAMES WHITE. To 6 yds. callico 2/8; 12 yds. check 8/3; 1 m. 10d. nails 4/9; peper. allspice, nutts; a broad hoe 2/1; pr. mens shoes 3/6; 1 rugg 9/7; To Cash 2..10..0. pr. womans gloves 4/6; 1 common Prayer Book 2/8; butcher knife 2 1/2; August 10: To Exchange in Callico; To 2 yds. damask 1/11; The Credit Account shows: June 18, 1749; By 1 hhd. tobacco on Gibsons 300 @ 16/8; 768 @ 13/; July 1: By 2 Transfer notes; By Cash; By FRANS: BALTHROP, By JOHN BALTHROP; November 6, 1749: By your accot. in L. B. 0...6...10 sttg.

(p. 190). June 19, 1749. The Debit Account of CHAS. RIGGENS. To cloth, buttons, hk. silk, 12 1/2 yds. check; 1 saddle & bridle 21/; 1 fine hatt; To cash 2..12..0; The Credit Account shows June 19, 1749: By Gibsons 1 hhd. 360 @ 16/8; 618 @ 13/. Cask.

(p. 190). July 25, 1749. The Debit Account of MARTHA HILLIARD. To 2 oz. Indico 1/3; 1 Linen handkerchief 2/4; 1/2 m. pins 8; The Credit Account shows November 6, 1749; By your accot. in L. B. 0..4..2 Curry.

(p. 191). June 18, 1749); The Debit Account of ROBT. JOHNSTON. (various kinds and amounts of cloth: camblett, shalloon, bro. linnen; kersey; sheeting; check, buckram); 1 boys felt 9d; thread; 2 tin pans 2/4; 2 qt. Rum 2/; 1 oz. indico; 1 worsted cap; pr. yarn hose; bushel salt 3/; The Credit Account shows September 25, 1749: By ballance as pr. Accot. given in: November 6, 1749: By your accot. in L. B. 3..0..0 1/2; 0..5..6.

(p. 192). June 19, 1749. The Debit Account of Mr. CHAS. ASHTON. To 1 pr. womens shoes 2/9; pr. sizors 1d; (various kinds of cloth & amounts bro. linnen, check; irish linen; callico); 50 needles 4d; 2 tin panns 2/; 2 pr. womans hose 6/; 1 pr. youths shoes 3/6; 1 thimble 1d; To cash 3..0..0; pr. small pumps 1/3; quire paper 8; The Credit Account shows June 19, 1749: By 1 hhd. tobacco on Gibson 360 @ 16/8; 614 @ 13/; November 6, 1749: By ballance to L. B. 0..3..2 1/2 sttg.

(p. 192). October 21, 1749. The Debit Account of EDWD. MARSHALL. cloth; buttons, white linnen thread; 2 pr.yarn hose; 4 lbs. sugar; 1/4 Rum; bushel salt. The Credit account shows November 6, 1749: By your Accot. in L. B. 2..16..6 curry.

(p. 193). June 19, 1749. The Debit Account of JAMS: DISHMAN. To 1 pr. sizors 7d; ivory comb 11d; pr. mens best shoes 5/; powder and shott; 1 barrel Sugar No. 17 272 nt. 35/; The Credit Account shows June 19, 1749: By 1 hhd. tobacco on Gibsons 360 @ 16/8; Deducted for a Transfer Note 116; 445 @ 13/; cask. July 29, 1749: By cash: 1..15..2.

(p. 193). August 28, 1749. The Debit Account of JOHN DONOHOE. To 1 Pinons hose 3/; powder & shott; linen handkerchief 9; 2 hanks silk 1/1; 1 curb bridle 4/10; brown sugar, rum; 7 pints Rum; 1 best glass 6d; 2 quash Rum; The Credit Account shows November 6, 1749: By your accot. in L. B. 3..16..10 1/2 sttg.

(p. 194). June 19, 1749. The Debit Account of DANL. DISHMAN. (various kinds and amount of cloth: ticking, check, cotton, oznabrig; dowlass; chamblett; fine linnen; shalloon, Irish linnen); a broad hoe 1/10; 4 reap hooks 1/6; 250 8d. nails 11d; mans fine hatt 5/6; pr. womans gloves 3/; pr. mans hose 2/; ivory comb 5d; 1 lb. Chocolate 1/8; 1 flower'd quart 1/9; 1 tin quart 8d; To Cash 3..0..0; boys felt 9d; best rugg 18/6; a small ax 1/10; a chamber pott 7d; pr garters 5d; sugar, shoe thread, shott. The Credit Account shows June 19, 1749: By 1 hhd. Tobacco on Laytons; Deducted for notes paid 147; 360 @

16/8; 600 @ 13/. Cask. By DANIEL FRAZIER 0..15..0; November 6, 1749: By ballance to L. B. 3...7...4 1/2.

(p. 195). June 19, 1749. The Debit Account of DANL. FRAZIER. Brown linnen, Irish linnen, checque; fine linnen; pr. mens gloves 1/4; 1 mans hatt 5/6; pr. buckles 6d; linen handkerchief 1/1; 2 clasp knives 6d; To Cr. DAVID DISHMAN 0..15..0; 1 pr. best dble. Channel'd pumps 8/; 1 razor 8; 1 oz. indico; 1 leghorn hatt 1/7 1/2; To CORNL. REYNOLDS 0..4..6; To Cash 3..0..0; The Credit Account shows June 19, 1749: By 1 hhd. Tobacco on Laytons 360 @ 16/8; 599 @ 13/. By Linnen return'd; November 6, 1749; By your accot. in L. B. 0..2..5 1/2; 0..4..6.

(p. 195). June 21, 1749. The Debit Account of SAML. FAULCONER. To 2 oz. fine thread; 2 yds. Irish Linnen, 7 yds. Holland; 1 1/2 yds. Muzlins 5/3; 1 pinons hose 3/; 2 yds. ribon 1/; 1 pen knife 8; To cash 6..1..2. The Credit Account shows June 21, 1749; By 1 hhd. tobacco on Laytons 300@ 13/; 715 @ 16/8; Cask 0..2..0.

(p. 196). June 21, 1749. The Debit Account of Collo. LUNSFORD LOMAX. To 1 fine silk handkerchief; To 2 oz. stone blue; August 10: To 6 garden spades 5/. The Credit Account shows July 6, 1749: By Cash 0..19..8; By your accot. in L. B. 1..10..0 Curry.

(p. 196). June 21, 1749. The Debit Account of WILLIAM PULLIAM. To 1/2 m. pins 4d; 3 3/4 yds Irish linnen 12/6; 3 yds. bro: linnen 1/10 1/2; To 1 bason & 6 laces; July 13: To Cash. The Credit Account shows June 21, 1749: By 1 hhd. tobacco on Roys 1300 @ 15/; By transfer 248;

(p. 197). June 21, 1749. The Debit Account of LOVETT MASSEY. To 1 leghorn hatt 1/9; 1 oz. nutts 9d; 1 lb. peper 1/4; 1 lb. allspice 1/4; 1 oz. cinamon 9d; 1 lb. ginger 1/2; (various kinds and amounts of cloth: oznabrig; sheeting, ticking, jeans, shalloon, check, linen), 2 dishes 5/11 1/2; pr. buckles, 1 knife & fork; To cash 1..10...6. The Credit Account shows: June 2, 1749: By 1 hhd. tobacco on Mattox. 829 @ 13/; 165 @ 16/8; Cask.

(p. 197). September 13, 1749. The Debit Account of THOMAS HARRIS. (one entry) To ballance brought from 90; 7..2..11 1/2 Curry. The Credit Account shows September 13, 1749; By Muzlin return'd 0..0..10; By an accot. in 284: 7..2..1 1/2.

(p. 198). June 22, 1749; The Debit Account of Mrs. ESTHER JONES. To 1 single loaf 9 lbs. 6 oz; 1/6; powder & shott; 1 velvett cap 1/8/0; 1 bushel Salt 2/4; July 3: To 1 cask Beer 11 doz. & 8 bottles @ 11/1; September 13: To 7 yds. China Taffety 76; 1 hk. silk 8; The Credit Account shows November 6, 1749: By your accot: in L. B. 11..9..9 Curry.

(p. 198). August 25, 1749. The Debit Account of WILLIAM WATTKINS. To Cr. RICHARD HOLT 420 lbs. tobacco; To 12 yds. cotton; 1 blankett 7/; 9 ells ozna: 5 yds. linen; 1 oz. fine thread; 1 1/4 yds. sheeting 1/3; a small knife; 2 pr. plad. hose; 1 girth 9; The Credit Account shows August 25, 1749: By sundry notes amotg. to 992 10/; to pay Debit of 4..19..2.

(p. 199). June 22, 1749. The Debit Account of AUGUSTINE SMITH. (various kinds and amounts of cloth; linnen, check, oznabrig, white linnen); 1 mans hatt 4/; linnen handkerchief 8; pr. womens shoes 3/; 1 tea pott 8d; powder & shot, quire paper; To Cash 2..10..4; The Credit Account shows June 22, 1749: By 1 hhd. tobacco on Mattox: 698 @ 13/; 284 @ 16/8; Cask. 4..10..8 and 2..10..4 paid.

(p. 199). September 28, 1749. The Debit Account of RICHARD EVANS. To 1 pr. blanketts 14/8; 1/2 m. 6d nailes 1/2; 1 oz. indico; 3 1/2 yds. Linnen 7/; 1 felt 1/4; powder & shott; 2 yds. cotton. The Credit Account shows November 6, 1749: By your Accot. in L. B. 1..9..6 Sttg.

(p. 200). June 22, 1749. The Debit Account of MARY SMITH. To 1 Fan 10d; 1 leghorn hatt 1/4; 2 furr'd hatts 12/; 3 felts 4/; 40 ells Oz; 1 brush 10d; 4 yds. check 2/9; thread, pins, white linen; 4 bowles 2/8; July 27: To Cash 2..9..0. The Credit Account shows June 22, 1749: By 1 hhd. tobacco on Mattox 768 @ 13/; 276 @ 16/8; cask. for payment of Debit 4..19..9 1.2 and 2..9..0.

(p. 200). September 28, 1749. The Debit Account of FRAS. FIDLER. To your accompt brot. from 75; To 1 pinon shoes 5/; 1 oz. thread 9d; 1/2 yd. muzlin 1/6; 1 linen handkerchief 1/3; October 24: 1 pr. plad. hose 1/4; 1 lb. powder & 4 lbs. shott 3/4. The Credit Account shows November 6, 1749: By your account in L. B. 7..15..8 Curry.

(p. 201). June 22, 1749. The Debit Account of JOHN SANDERS. To 6 yds. of Callico 18/; 1 Mouse Trap 4d; 20 yds. bro. linen 12/4; 4 1/2 yds. fine shalloon 8/9; 2 hanks silk 1/4; pr. wool cards 2/6. The Credit Account shows June 22, 1749: By JAMES BOULWARE 410 lbs. @ 13/; November 6, By your accot. in L. B. 0..3..10 Curry.

(p. 201). June 22, 1749; The Debit Account of ROBT. CALL. To your accot brot. from 75; (various cloth: check, sacking, camblett, bro. linnen; Irish linnen; kersey); quire paper 8; pr. womens shoes 3/; bushel Salt 1/6; 1/2 lb. peper 8; 6 lbs. brown sugar 2/; 1 fine felt 2/4; buttons, thread; To Cash 0..7..9. The Credit Account shows (undated) By allowance on your tobacco 2..8..6; November 6, 1749: By your accot in L. B.

(p. 202). June 23, 1749. The Debit Account of PETER SANDERS. To pr. shoes 6/; 1 iron pott 17 lbs., 3 1/2; The Credit Account shows November 6, 1749: By your accot. to L. B. 0..10..11 Curry.

(p. 202).July 10, 1749. The Debit Account of CHARLES HART. To ballance from 53; To 1 Testament 2/6; 1/4 m. 4d. nails 10 1/2; To Cash 0..1..3; To ditto paid Mrs. TALIAFERRO; 2 small spring knives 1/; powder & shott; 1/2 lb. glew 7 1/2; 1 single girth 9d; quart rum 1/3; 2 earthen plates 4d; To Cash 0..1..3; To ditto 0..2..6; 2 oz. indico; bushel salt 2/6; mettle buttons, linnen, thread; check; The Credit Account shows November 6, 1749; By your account in L. B. 6..19..4 1/2 curry.

(p. 203). June 26, 1749. The Debit Account of PETER DISHMAN. (various kinds and amounts of cloth: kersey, ticking, check; oznabrig; bro. linnen, white linnen); thread, powder & shott; nails; linen handkerchief; pr. mens hose 2/4; To Cash 1..13..4; pr. womans shoes; pr. garters 4 1/2; 25 needles, 2 ivory combs @ 5d; 1 horn comb 1 1/2d; 1/4 lb. Ginger 3 1/2; a broad ax 2/; 10 lbs. sugar 3/4; 1/2 lb. shoe thread 8; The Credit Account shows June 26, 1749; By 1 hhd. tobacco on Roys 200 @ 16/8; 829 @ 13/; cask; November 6, 1749: By your accot. in L. B. 3..1..0 sttg.

(p. 204). June 26, 1749. The Debit Account of RICHARD HOLT. To 2 single girths 5d; 2 1/2 yds. cloth d7/6; small buttons, thread, lace; pr. womens shoes; (cloth: kersey, irish linnen; gingham; irish linnen; oznabrig; a fine comb 11d; 50 needles 4d; 2 small knives; 1 furr'd hatt, 1 yd. ribon; The Credit Account shows June 26, 1749: By 1 hhd. tobacco on Laytons; By MARY BEASLEY, By JAMES BEASLEY; 1165 lbs. tobo: @ 13/; cask;

(p. 204). June 26, 1749. The Debit Account of JOHN POWELL. To 1 pinons shoes 7/6; To 1 mans fine hatt 8/. The Credit Account shows November 6, 1749: By your account in L. B. 0..15..6 curry.

(p. 205). June 26, 1749. The Debit Account of FRAS; BARBEE. To 4 yds. serge; 1 1/2 doz. buttons. 1 hank silk blue thread; small buttons; irish linnen; carpenders Rule 8; pr. dble pumps 5/6; 1 faddle &c; 21/; To Cr. JNO: PITTS JUNR. 172 lbs. tobo: 13/; The Credit Account shows June 26, 1749: By 1 hhd. tobacco on Laytons 894 Nt. 13/; cask.

(p. 205). June 26, 1749. The Debit Account of JOHN PITTS JUNR. To 1 mans fine hatt 5/; womans furr'd hat 8/; pr. womens shoes; To cash 0..1..3; 1 mans hatt 1/4; (various cloth: bro. linnen, fine shalloon; check; linnen). The Credit Account shows June 26, 1749: By FRAS: BARBEE 172 lbs. tobo: November 6, 1749: By your accot in L. B.

(p. 206). June 26, 1749; The Debit Account of Mr. WILLIAM BOWLWARE. To 1 bottle scotch snuff 3/; July 14: To Cr. Collo. TURNER by Collo. ROBINSON order on you 600 lbs. tobo: The Credit Account shows August 22, 1749 By Cash; By Collo. TURNER for order ret'd 600.

(p. 206). August 28, 1749. The Debit Account of BENJA: MARSHALL. To buttons, cloth, thread, shott, 1 oz. fine thread; boys hatt 9d; mans do 5/; nails, powder, pr. garters, bro. linen, 1 silk handkerchief 2/6; The Credit Account shows September 12, 1749: By 4 1/2 yds. Shalloon return'd; November 6, 1749: By your accot. in L. B. 3..13..2 1/2 sttg.

(p. 20). June 27, 1749. The Debit Account of Mr. PATRICK MITCHELL. To 9 1/2 fine jeans; 1 hank silk 4d; 2 oz. fine thread 4d; The Credit Account shows October 6, 1749; By your account in L. B. 1..0..3 1/2.

(p. 207). September 6, 1749; The Debit Account of JAMES ZACHARY. To 4 lbs. sugar 1/4; 1 Qt. Rum 10 1/2; 1/2 m. pins 4 1/2; 1 carpenders rule 9d; powder & shott; October 4; 1 pr. blanketts 12/; 2 prs. women shoes 4/8; 10 yds. bro. linen 6/3; 3 yds. white linen 3/1 1/2; The Credit Account shows November 6, 1749; By your accot. in L. B. 1..6..7 1/2 sttg.

(p. 208). June 26, 1749. CASH. To Debt brought forward from 43: 225..14..8; June 28: To RICHARD STRAUGHN; To PATRICK WHITE; July 6: To Collo. LUNSFORD LOMAX; July 9: To EDWARD DIXON; July 10: To Doct: JAMES DELPEACH; July 13: To EDWARD DIXON; To ROBT. GILCHRIST; To EDWARD DIXON totals: 513..19..4. The Credit Account shows June 26, 1749: The Credit brought from 43; 447..3..5. By FOSTER SAMUEL; By LOVET MASSEY; By SAMUEL ADAM; July 28: By WILLIAM EDWARDS; By ISSAC SETTLE; By Doctr: DELPEACH; By CHARLES BENSON; By LEONARD YOUNG; June 30: By JOS: SHIP; By JOSEPH REYNOLDS; July 3; By Capt. DICKINSON of the *FRIENDSHIP*, By EDWARD DIXON; By RICHD. HOLT; July 5: By ANN BELL; By Majr. JEREMIAH MURCOCK; July 6: By JOHN BALTHROP, By JAMES BEASLEY; July 8: By JOSEPH WOOD; By Capt. WILLIAM DICKINSON; By AMBROSE HOWARD; By WILLIAM MARSHALL; By CHARLES BEASLEY; By CORNL. REYNOLDS; July 10: By JAMES BOWLWARE (Essex), By TITUS HURT; By FRANCIS FIDLER, By THOS: CROUCHER, By CHARLES HART; By WILLIAM HARRISON; By JOHN PRINCE; July 12: By ANN MARSHALL; By GABL. LONG; By MOSES HURT; By JAMES SAMUELL; July 13: By ANTHONY SAMUEL; By CATHERINE SAMUEL; By EDWARD ELMES; By SAML. FAULCONER; By DAVID DISHMAN; By DANIEL FRAZIER; By GILES SAMUEL; By JOHN BOWTWELL; By MOSES PITTMAN. Carried Forward 606..19..9 1/2.

(p. 209). July 13, 1749. CASH. To brought forward from 208; July 17: Collo. TURNER; To EDWARD POWERS; July 19: To EDWARD DIXON; To DANIEL WHITE SENR., July 22; To JOHN GRIFFIN; to WILLIAM WILEY; To THOMAS HARRISS; July 24: To EDWARD DIXON, July 27: To Doctr. DELPEACH; To WILLIAM AYLE; July 29: To Collo. THOMAS TURNER; To JAMES DISHMAN. The Credit account July 13, 1749 Brought forward from 208: By DANIEL BARKSDALE, By THOMAS ROY; By ROBERT HUNLEY, By WILLIAM PULLIAM, By JOS: WOOD; By THOMAS HARRIS; July 14: By WILLIAM ARNOLD; By JOHN SWILLIVAN; By GRACE BERRY; By JOS: STROTHER; July 15: By GABL. LONG; By THOMAS EVANS; July 17: By JAMES BEASLEY; By WILLIAM BERRYMAN; July 20: By Capt. WILLIAM DICKINSON; By Ship *FRIENDSHIP*, July 21: By JOHN HOLLOWAY; By LEO: HILL; July 22; By JOHN PRINCE, By DANIEL WHITE JUNR., July 24: By WILLIAM POWELL; By JOHN FERRILL; By MARY POWELL; By WILLIAM THOMAS; By MARY POWELL; July 25: By JOHN HART; By CHAS. HART; July 26: By RICHD. CLATTERBUCK; By MARY SMITH; By JOHN SNEED; By AUGUS: SMITH; By JOHN YOUNG; July 27: By JOHN ASTON; July 28: By JOS: WILTSHIRE; By REVD. MR. DAWSON; By GRIFFIN MORRIS; By WILLIAM FOX; By JOHN PRINCE; By EDWARD DIXON; By CHARLES ASHTON (carried to 210.)

(p. 210). August 1, 1749; Brot. forward. To MARY POWELL; August 3: To HENRY TERRILL; To WILLIAM HARRISON; To EDWARD DIXON; August 10: To Capt. WILLIAM JOHNSTON; August 15: To SAML. JAMES; To GEO: FOX; To Capt. THOMAS BURDON; To WILLIAM HARRIS; August 22: To WILLIAM BOWLWARE; August 25; To AUGUS: WEEDEN; August 26: To EDWARD DIXON; To WILLIAM SHARMAN. Carried to 273. The Credit Account: Brot. forward from 210: July 1: To MARY POWELL; July 3: By paid for 6 doz. Linnen handkerchiefs; July 10: By CONWAYS INSPECTION for 10 hhds; July 22; By paid for 10 lb. Indico; By HARRY TURNER; July 31; By JAMES WHITE; By STURMAN CHILTON; August 1: By JOHN BALTHROP; By WILLIAM BERRYMAN; August 6: By JAMES BEASLEY; By JOHN HART; By MARMADUKE THORP; August 7: By JAS. ROBTS. August 8: By JAMES WILLARD, By ANN BELL; August 10: By DANL. WHITE; By MAJR. MURDOCK; By JOHN PRINCE; By PATTK. COUTTS; By RICHARD STRAUGHN; August 14: By JOHN HOLLOWAY; By MOSES PITTMAN; August 15: By JOHN YOUNG; By PATTK. COUTTS, August 16: By ISAAC CALL; By JAMES WILLIARD; By ABRAHAM MARTIN; By RICHARD CLATTERBUCK; August 18: By JOHN ASTON; By WILLIAM WATTSON SENR. By WILLIAM WATTSON JUNR., By ELIJAH WATTSON; August 21; By ROBT. WRIGHT; August 22: By JOHN PRINCE, By EDWARD DIXON, By WILLIAM MARSHALL; By MAJR. SAML. SKINKER; By WILLIAM BUTLER; By ELIZA: LEWIS; August 25: By JAMES BOWLWARE; August 26: By Majr. SAML. SKINKER. Carried to 273. 887..8..6.

(p. 211). June 26, 1749. The Debit Account of Mr. WILLIAM ELLIOTT. (one entry) To 1 pr. dble. C. pumps 13/. The Credit Account: November 6, 1749 By your accot. in L. B. 0..13..0 Curry.

(p. 211). June 26, 1749. The Debit Account of Mr. SAML. SKINKER JUNR. To 1 whole curb bridle 8/; To 1 womans whip 3/; July r: To 1 pr. mens gloves 2/; October 6: To JNO: PRINCE for a pr. pumps 9/6. The Credit Account: November 6, 1749: By your accot. in L. B. 1..2..6 Curry.

(p. 212). June 27, 1749. The Debit Account of Capt. WILLM. JOHNSTON, Caroline Court. To 1 cask Beer No. 7 Qty. 11 doz & 6 bottles @ 11/ July 19: To 1 cask do. No. 5, 12 1/2 doz. 10/6; To 1 bottle Mustard to MRS. JOHNSTON formerly; August 21: To 4 1/2 yds. S. Persian 5/9. The Credit Account: August 10, 1749: By Cash 12..9..11; By an abatement off the Beer 0..10..10; November 6, 1749: By your accot. in L. B. 1..5..10 1/2 Curry.

(p. 212). June 27, 1749. The Debit Account of Mr. JOHN BATTALEY. To 1 pr. fine single C. Boots; July 6: To 1 1/2 yds. french Ribon @ 1/4; 1 Whip 3/6; To Credit Miss DORCAS TANKERSLEY; September 13: To 1/2 yd. white buckram 10d; 2 hks. Silk 1/4. The Credit Account: November 6, 1749: By your accot. in L. B. 4..1..8 Curry.

(p. 213). June 27, 1749. The Debit Account of THOS: SHIP SENR. To 1 hatt 1/10 leghorn; check, white & brown thread; pr. fine thread hose 4/; 1 clasp knife 3d; 1 single girth 5/; 1 Shammy skin 1/4; The Credit Account: (undated: By your accot in. 219. 0..12..9 1/2.

(p. 213). July 6, 1749. The Debit Account of JAMES HURT. To 13 3/4 yds. bro. linnen 11d; 4 1/2 yds. white do. 1/10; 1/4 yd. muzlin @ 5/6 1/2; 1/2 yd. Callico 1/4; 1 snuff box 1/3; The Credit Account: November 6, 1749: By your accot. in L. B. 1..4..3 3/4 Curry.

(p. 214). July 1, 1749. The Debit Account of Mr. JOHN SNEED. 10 yds. Duck 1/2; 2 felts @ 9d; 2 fine hatts @ 6/; 1 ditto @ 4/; 1 leghorn hatt 1/4; 2 iron potts 40 lbs. 2d; 3 yds. Ermin Flannell 6/6; 1 dish cover 10d; 4 hks. silk 1/4d; To RICHD. BLANTON 221 tob: 13/; 2 Japan pints 2/; 1 fine hatt 4/; pr. mens best pumps 5/; 1 ivory comb 5d; 1 ax 1/9; 2 single girths 10d; To cash 15..5..2; September 19: To 1 cask Rum No. 4. 106 galls. 3/4. The Credit Account: June 29, 1749: By 3 hhds. tobacco on Roys 1920 @ 16/8; 1862 @ 13/; casks; July 6: By 4 Notes on Roys 273 lbs. tobo: September 2: By 1 small Note 33 lbs. tobacco; By 1 Ax return'd; September 29; By Cash. Debit paid.

(p. 215). July 1, 1749. The Debit Account of LEONARD YOUNG To 1 sett buckles 1/2; 2 1/2 yds. Serge 4/; doz. buttons; 17 yds. shalloon; thread, cotton check, oznabrig; bro. thread; 2 boys felts 1/6; 1 womans hatt 6/3; pr. mens shoes 3/; 3 yds. Ship'd holland; 3/4 1/2; 2 small knives d6 1/2; To Cash: 5..0..0. The Credit Account: July 1, 1749: By 1 hhd. tobacco on Conways 600 5..0..0; 483 @ 13/ & cask 3..4..9. Debit paid.

(p. 215). July 6, 1749. The Debit Account of GEORGE BULLARD. (one entry): To 8 lbs. shott 0..2..8; The Credit Account: November 6, 1749: By your accot. L. B. 0..2..8.

(p. 216). July 1, 1749. The Debit Account of JAMES SAMUEL. Powder and shot; paper, cloth; mans hatt 6/3; 1/2 oz. fine thread 1/8; Irish linne; pr. worsted hose 2/3; pins, pr. fine garters 6d; bro. sheeting; 4 yds. Manx Cloth 8d; 9 yds. ticking 1/4; needles; Cash 1..0..0; pr. dble. C. pumps 5/6; ivory comb 8d; The Credit Account July 1, 1749: By 1 hhd. tobacco on Occupa: 100 @ 16/8; 916 @ 13; Cask 0..3..4; November 6, 1749. By your accot. in L. B. 0..10..9 sttg.

(p. 217). July 1, 1749. The Debit Account of JOHN BOWLWARE.(one entry): To 1 pr. mens Com. Shoes 5/6. The Credit Account (undated) By 1 pr. mens shoes returnd. 5/6.

(p. 217). July 1, 1749. The Debit Account of JOHN HART. To 1 yd. Irish bro. linnen 6 1/2d; July 25: pr. mens pumps 4/; (various amounts & kinds of cloth: dimmitty; check, sacking; duck; corded dimmitty; muzlin; shalloon, fine linnen, tartan; kersey); 1 horn book; pins, powder & shott; hand saw & file 3/; claw hammer 8d; 10 lbs. sugar 3/4; 1 bowle 1/; 1 glass 4d; 2 pr. small shoes 3/4; 1 pr. do 2/4; The Credit Account November 6, 1749; By your accot: in L. B. 5..8..10 1/4; and 0..1..10 1/2.

(p. 218). June 12, 1749; The Debit Account of ROYS INSPECTORS. To sundry notes given in Nt. 1647 lbs; July 7: To ditto 1778 lbs; September 8: To Cash in full 13..5..0. The Credit Account: June 12, 1749: By 2987 lbs. tobacco and 3 casks; By Inspection of 72 hhds. p the *FRIENDSHIP;* By EDWARD DIXON for 2 do. pr. the *OLIVE BRANCH,* By prizing 3 hhds; By CUTHBERT SANDYS; By 3 hhds. pr. the *BRITTANIA*, By 2 ditto Cap: DICKINSONs; By COLLO. TURNER; By Bitto; Ballance of tobacco account 3425 lbs; By Cap. JOHN MICOU on accot. Cap. W. TALIAFERRO 420 lbs.

(p. 219). July 1, 1749. The Debit Account of THOS; SHIP SENR. To 50 needles 4d; To 1 womans hatt 6/6; 2 m. 8d. nailes 7/6; 2 m. 10d. ditto 9/6; 8 yds. cotton check 1/1 1/2; 1 yd. Callico 1/; 2 silk handkerchiefs 3/6; 1 mans saddle 25/; To your accot. in 213; July 29: To 5 mottled dishes 1/; September 4: To 3/4 Rum, 1 fine felt; October 6: To 1 lb. shoe thread; October 7: To paid ELIZA: JACKSON 5/ curry; October 21; To 1 dish & a bason 6/8; The Credit Account: July 1, 1749: By ballance brought from 86: 6..0..0.; July 9: By 4 yds 1/2 thicks return'd 1/2; 0..4..8. Account balances at 6..4..8.

(p. 219). October 27, 1749. The Debit Account of ISAAC GREEN. To 2 pr. mens best pumps 10/; 2 felts 4/8; 1 Bible 3/4; 1 Testament 1/3; 1 1/2 yds. Irish Linnen 1/6; pr. yarn hose 4d; 1/2 lb. allspice & 1 bush: salt; 1/2 gross pipes & 1/4 muzlin; pr. womans hose 2/; 1 linnen handkerchief 1/4; To Cash 0..7..6; The Credit Account: November 6, 1749: By your accot. in L. B. 1..13..5 and 0..7..6.

(p. 220). July 1, 1749. The Debit Account of JAMES STUART Recommended by THOS: SHIP. To 3 1/4 yds. fine holland 3/10; 2 1/2 yrds. collo. Check 2/4; 1 mans fine hatt 10/; pr. shoes 5/6; (other cloth: buckram, shalloon, serge); 1 hk. silk 8; 1 mans saddle &c. 35/; The Credit Account: November 6, 1749: By your accot. in L. B. 5..19..1 1/2.

(p. 220). July 10, 1749. The Debit Account of Mr. SOLO: EWELL. To paid your overseer 228 lbs. tobacco; September 19: To Cash 24..13..0. The Credit Account: July 1, 1749 By 3 hhds. tobacco on Roys 3253 lbs. @ 16/ and casks, (debit paid).

(p. 221). July 3, 1749. The Debit Account of Capt. WILLM. DICKINSON. To Cash paid the Inspecting 5hhds. tobacco; July 8: To 2 hhds. tobacco on Brays 2234 Nt., To 2 casks; To Cash 20..0..0; To Inspection of 29 hhds. tobacco; July 17: To Cash 3..18..4. The Credit Account shows the debit of 40..10..6 paid July 3, 1749 by Sundry setts as p. Invoice; By Mr. JOHN YOUNGER 1515 lbs. tobacco 10/; By Inspection of 56 hhds. tobacco; By the Ship *FRIENDSHIP,* By 25 p. cent the sttg. ballance 14/8.

(p. 221). October 19, 1749. The Debit Account of THOS: CROUCHER. (one entry): To 4 lbs. small shott 0..0..8 sttg. The Credit Account: November 6, 1749: By your accot. in L. B. 0..0..8 sttg.

(p. 222). July 3, 1749. The Debit Account of RICHARD HOLT. To ballance from 204: with additional entrys that include various kinds and amounts of cloth (callico, serge, Irish linnen; check; fine linnen; holland; kersey); 1 carpenters rule 9d; 6 small spring knives 1/6; 1 half Cirb Bridle 2/6; 1 pockett bottle 9d; 800 needs 8d; 6 m. pins 11 1/2d; 3 razors @ 6d; pr. garters 4d; 2 doz. fine thimbles @ 2/; To Cash 0..1..3; 9 felts 1/4; 1 quart mugg 9d; 6 cards buttons 4/6; 1 small bowle 6d; pr. blanketts 14/8; 3 m. 4d. nails 7/; The Credit Account shows debit of 14..5..0 and 0..1..3 balanced: August 23, 1749: By WILLIAM WATTKINS 420 lbs. tobacco; November 6; By your accot. in L. B.

(p. 223). July 4, 1749. The Debit Account of Majr. JERH: MURDOCK. To your ballance brought forward from 146; with additional entries for 1 fine horse whip 5/8; various kinds of cloth: kersey, china taffaty; camblett; ribon, 1 wash bason 4d; pr. wool cards 1/4; pr. spectacles 9d; Cash for sundries 0..11..0; gallon Rum; August 8: To EDWARD DIXON; 2 small bowles; 31 gallons Rum 3/4; To Cash Paid COLLO. TURNER 1..4..0; November 6: To ballance of Curry. acct. in L. B. The Credit Account shows Debit of 36..5..10 and 33..2..4 ballanced by: July 4, 1749: By 5 hhds. tobacco on Gibsons; By 1 ditto on Brays, 5444 lbs. 13/; casks 0..12..0; November 6: By ballance of Sterl. Accot. in L. B. By 4 hhds. tobacco on Brays & Gibsons 3902 lbs. @ 16/8; by Casks 0..12..0.

(p. 224). July 6, 1749. The Debit Account of Mr. FRAS: BALTHROP. (By various amounts and kinds of cloth: callico; irish linnen, shalloon; swanskin; narrow cloth); 4 oz. white thread 3d; 1 womans whip 1/8; 3 ditto @ 14d; To Majr. JOHN CHAMPE 22..8..0; Exchange in pumps 3/6; 3 doz. laces 1/7 1/2; 6 Hanover Necklace 7d; 2 French do. 2/8; 6 carpenters rules 4/; 1 pr. womans hose 3/8; 2 silk handkerchiefs 5/3; 4 glasses 0..2..0; August 22; 1 hhd. Rum No. 18 1099 gallons @ 3/3; 1 qt. bowle 8d; September 19: 4 ivory combs 1/4; 2 doz. mettle buttons 2 1/2; 2 prs. Childrens pumps 2/6; To Cash 7..16..0; 1 cask of Sugar No. 12 263 Nt. 1/2 doz. Ink Powder 1/6; 1 oz. nutts 6 1/2d. The Credit Account: July 6, 1749: By ballance brot. from 182: By 4 pr. Card short; September 1, 1749: By Cap. EDWARD DIXON on accot. MR. SIMPSONs Son; By Cash on accot. ditto; November 6, 1749: By your accot in L. B. 3..10..7 and 17..14..3.

(p. 225). July 6, 1749. The Debit Account of Mr. JOSEPH WOOD. To 1 yd. Flannell; To 1 pr. marking Irons; To Cash 4..4..2; July 13: To Ditto at Caroline Court 3..3..7. The Credit Account: July 6, 1749: By 1 hhd. tobacco on Roys 990 @ 16/; By 2 lbs. tobacco in ballance.

(p. 225). July 29, 1749. The Debit Account of Mr. WILLIAM MURDOCK. To 1 single loaf 9 3/4 lbs. 10d; To 1 pr. mens sheos 4/6; To 1 bridle 2/9; The Credit Account (undated in 1749): By JOHN HOLLOWAY 113 lbs. tobo: @ 13/. the debit ballance of 0..15..5.

(p. 226). July 8, 1749: The Debit Account of Doctr: JAMES DELPEACH. To your accot. brot. from 103: with additional entries for various kinds and amounts of cloth as serge & denim, shalloon; bro. linnen; jeans; chintz; check; buttons, thread, bohea Tea 5/; small sifter 8d; gallon Rum 0..3..6; 1 oz. indico 1 pr. small buckles; 9 1/2 gallons Rum; 3 felt hatts; 7/6 Curry. p. yr. Note; August 10: paid a Negro woman p. yr. Order 10/ curry; 1 mettle tankard 2/8; 1 gross corks 1/8; pr. sleeve buttons 8d; 1 key ring 2 1/2; 25 lbs. bro. sugar 0..10..0; October 25: 1 pr. best blanketts 14/; doz. shirt buttons 3d; a claw hammer 10/; a dozen pipes 0..0..2; The Credit Account July 10, 1749: By Cash 0..5..0; July 22: By GEORGE TOD 965 lbs. tobacco; By 1 womans Cloak; By 1 pr. Stays 16/; July 27: by Cash 1..15..9; November 6, 1749: By your accot. in L. B. 7..7..9; and 1..15..3.

(p. 227). July 10, 1749. The Debit Account of JAMES BOWLWARE. To 3/4 Scarlett Cloth @ 11/6, 1 hk. silk 5; 2 fine hatts 12/4; irish linnen, bro. ditto; camblett; 2 oz. thread; hank silk 5; 1/2 m. pins 5 1/2; 1/4. ct. needles 7d; 1 dridging box 4; 1 girth 10d; To cash 2..1..4; The Credit Account: July 10, 1749: By 1 hhd. tobacco on Laytons 248 @ 16/8; 732 @ 13/; Cask. for payment of debit of 4..17..1 and 2..1..4.

(p. 227). July 10, 1749. The Debit Account of WILLIAM SAMUEL. To 1 spring knife 7 1/2; 1 pr. garters; August 15: 1 yd. shalloon 1/4; yard white sheeting, 1/2 oz. thread; 1 doz. buttons; October 6: 1/4 yds. narrow cloth 3/9; 1 1/2 yds. bro: linnen, a dozen buttons; oz. of thread; The Credit Account: November 6, 1749: By your accot. in L. B. 1..2..2 sttg.

(p. 228). July 10, 1749. The Debit Account of TITUS HURT. To 1 pr. womans stays 9/; (various kinds and amounts of cloth: irish linnen, muzlin, collo. check; kersey; oznabrig; bunt, callico); 5 pr. plad. hose 5/6 1/2; 2 hand saw files 5; buttons, thread; 1 lb. ginger 1/2; 1 oz. nutts 9d; 1 Search 1/6; 1 cruett 4 1/2; 2 felts 2/8; powder & shott; To Cash 1..13..4: The Credit Account: July 10, 1749: By 1 hhd. tobacco on Ayletts. 200@ 16/8; 839 @ 13/; Cask 0..2..0; pays debit of 5..11..0 and 1..13..4.

(p. 228). July 17, 1749. The Debit Account of WILLIAM HORD. To 4 felts 1/4; 2 ditto 1/3; To 1 iron pott 3/3; September 28: To 1 mens Com: shoes 3/; October 25: To 4 yds. Kersey 1/5; The Credit Account: November 6, 1749: By your accot in L. B. 0..19..9 sttg.

(p. 229). July 10, 1749: The Debit Account of Mr. JOHN HOLLOWAY. To your debt brought from 112; with a number of additional entries through November 5, 1749; including various kinds and amount sof cloth; To Cr. WILLIAM ALCOCK 213 lbs. tobo: buttons, thread, small hose 1/2; mens hose 3/; 1 doz. Beer; nails, single girth; qt. jugg; To DANIEL BARKSDALE 5..0..0; pr. womens gloves 1/4; 2 galls. Rum 2/; 4 oz. Indico to Mr. ALLCOCK 0..1..6; The Credit Account (undated 1749): By part of yr. Cr. to ALLCOCK return'd 100 lbs. tobo: By yr. Credit brot. from 112; November 6, 1749: By sttg. ballance

(p. 230). July 12, 1749: The Debit Account of Mr. JNO: MARSHALL. includes various kinds and amounts of cloth (denim, callico, oznabrig; cotton; shalloon); 1 felt 1/2; 1 doz. table knives 8/; 1 mans fine hatt 5/; 1 ditto 6/6; 1 razor 6d; 1 broad hoe 2/10; 2 setts buckles 2/4; pr. fine knee do. 5d; pr. garters 7 1/2; The Credit Account: July 13, 1749: By 1 hhd. tobacco on Gibsons 300 @ 16/8; Transfer note; 672 @ 10/; cask.

(p. 230). October 16, 1749. The Debit Account of WILLM. DODGIN. To 1/2 lb. shoe thread 3/; 2 small felt 2/; 3 1/8 gallons rum 12/6; 1 lb. chocolate 2/6; 1 funnell 1/2; The Credit Account: November 6, 1749: By your accot. in L. B. 1..1..2 sttg. curry.

(p. 231). July 13, 1749; The Debit Account of Mr. JOHN JETT. To your debt brot. from 158; with a number of additional entries including a lb. of green tea 8/; various kinds and amounts of cloth including ticking, irish linnen, duffle, oznabrig; camb); thread, buttons, a razor strop; 2 1/2 bushel Salt; 1 1/4 gall. Rum; 25 lbs. bro. Sugar; a bowle 1/; 1 glass can 1/2; 3 tin pans 1/4; pr. mens hose 3/6; a tea Kettle 6/6; 1 lb. Bohea Tea 5/6; October 4: To ballance of sttg. accot. in L. B. The Credit Account: July 13, 1749: By your Credit brot. from 158: 34..1..1; November 6, 1749: By your curry. accot. in L. B.

(p. 232). July 13, 1749. The Debit Account of Mr. THOS: ROY. To your debt brot. from 45: with a number of additional entries including July 17: paid Negro Ben 10/; nails, various kinds of cloth; sugar, buttons; 1 qt. mugg; 1 narrow axes 11 lb. 8/3; powder & shott; The Credit Account: July 13, 1749: By your Credit brot. from 45: 308 lbs. tobo: 18..6..8 1/2; November 6, 1749: By your accot. in L. B. 22..7..6 3/4 and 5..0..1 1/2.

(p. 233). July 13, 1749: The Debit Account of Collo. WILLM. WOODFORD includes nails, thread, 3 cups and saucers 3d; 2 water glasses 9d; quart mugg 6d; pr. marking irons 6d; quart Rum; pr. knee buckles; paid yr. order to Sailor; The Credit Account: July 13, 1749: By ballance of accot. this day settled; By 2 pr. Callimanco shoes; By overcharg'd in shott; By 1 doz. buttons & 1 pr. knee buckles; November 6, 1749: By your account in L. B. 3..4..3 3/4 and 0..1..3.

(p. 234). July 13, 1749. The Debit Account of Capt. THOS: BURDON. To 1 felt 2/4; 12 lbs. bro. sugar 6/; July 17, 1749: To 1 felt 1/4; pr. gloves 6/; August 3: 7 1/2 lbs. sugar 1/10; August 8: 12 lbs. brown sugar 6/; 30 yds. brown linnen @ 1/; 6 yds. duck 1/10; August 21: 1 yd. bro: linen to DUDLEY 1/2; 1 yd. Duck 1/10. The Credit Account: August 15, 1749: By Cash 3..14..5; November 6, 1749: By Capt. EDWARD DIXON 0..3..0.

(p. 234). August 13, 1749. The Debit Account of NICHS. LONG. To 7 yds. bro. linnen 7 1/2; 1/4 white thread; 1 womans cap 7d; 1 oz. white thread; 2 prs. plad. hose, 16 yds. Cotton, 2 yds. flannel; The Credit Account: November 6, 1749: By your account in L. B.

(p. 235). July 14, 1749. The Debit Account of JAMS: BOWLWARE. Caroline, To your ballance brot. from 21; with additional entries through October 4 including To JOHN SANDERS 410 lbs. tobacco; powder & shott; bro. linnen; check, a dish 3/; doz. buttons, 1 felt 1/4; To Cash 0..3..0; The Credit Account: September 1, 1749: By 1 small Note on Roys 45 lbs. tobacco: November 6, 1749: By your accot. in L. B. 5..14..3 and 1..18..0.

(p. 236). July 14, 1749. The Debit Account of WILLM. WREN. To your accot. brot. from 89; July 22; quart Rum 1/; 32 lbs.bro. sugar 11/1; September 16: 4 yds. collo. check; 1 yd. sheeting 1/; 2 1/2 ells oznabrig; 1 dox. small gilt buttons 10d; bottle snuff 1/3; pr. rib'd hose 3/; pr. womens hose 1/8; October 24: 1 small Lock 6d; The Credit Account: (undated) By overcharg'd 1.2 gall. Rum; By 1 hhd. tobacco 1012 lbs; By JNO. WREN JUNR., 32 lbs. tobacco; Cask; By EDWARD DIXON; November 6, 1749: By your accot. in L. B.

(p. 236). October 6, 1749: The Debit Account of PETER SAMUEL. Buttons, thread, 2 yds. shalloon 1/10; doz. buttons 5d; 1 worsted cap 7d; To ballance from 79. The Credit Account: November 6, 1749: By your accot. in L. B. 0..17..0 1/2.

(p. 237). July 14, 1749. The Debit Account of EDWARD ELMES; To 1 m. large pins 10d; 2 boys felt 1/6; 1 mans felt 1/4; pr. womens shoes 3/; pr. mens shoes 4/; nails, 1 Callimanco, 1 sett buckles, 1 womans cap 7; 3 1/2 yds. check; ivory comb; 2 horn ditto 4d; To Cash 4..3..4.1 flowerd Pint 1/6; 1 oz. cloves 11d; 1 padlock 10d; 2 linen handkerchiefs 1/5; 6 Necklace 1/; 1 large rugg 18/6; The Credit Account July 14, 1749: By 1 hhd. tobacco on Gibsons; 500 @ 16/8; 507 @ 13/, Cask to ballance Debit of 3..7..10 and 4..3..4.

(p. 237). September 29, 1749. The Debit Account of CHARLES EVANS. To 1 pr. shoes 2/8; 1 yd. linen 2/; 1 ell oz; 300 8d. nails; 300 6d. nails; a pocket knife 6d; 1/2 lb. bro. thread; 1 Common Prayer & 1 him book; pr. large blanketts 14/8; 3 pecks salt; 1 lathing hammer 1/; The Credit Account November 6, 1749: By your accot. in L. B. 1..8..11 1/2 sttg.

(p. 238). July 13, 1749. The Debit Account of JOHN PRINCE. To your accot. brot. from 103: with a number of additional entries including pr. womans hose 2/; (a number of entrys, To Cash); (various kinds and amounts of cloth; 2 small ruggs, 1 large rugg; 1 quilt coat 9/; pr. mens shoes 3/; 2 felts 2/4; 1 half cirb bridle 2/2; plain hatt 4/; The Credit Account (undated 1749): By 2 hhds. tobacco, cask, By SAML. SKINKER JUNR 9/6; By GABL. LONG; By JOHN BOWTWELL; November 6, 1749: By ballance to L. B.

(p. 239). July 7, 1749. The Debit Account of GABL. LONG; To your accot. brought from 78; with a number of additional entries including To Cash paid DANIEL TRIPLETT; To quart Rum; (several entries, To Cash); To MR. GRAY for 1 pr. womens & a hatt; To JOHN PRINCE; To 1 gun hammer 8d; various kinds and amounts of cloth: The Credit account November 6, 1749: By your accot. in L. B. 11..17..1 1/2 and 55..5..1 1/2.

(p. 240). July 11, 1749. The Debit Account of Majr. SAML. SKINKER. To ballance of Curry. accot. brot. from 84; with numerous additiona entries including various kinds of cloth; thread, needles, 4 spring knives; a bed cord, 4 oz. Cloves; 4 oz. Cinamon; 1 dish cover; 1 hang lock; 1/2 doz. Delph Plates; 2 doz. dishes; hank silk; 2 thimbles, a white jugg; nails, small felt; 6 wine glasses 1/6; pr. garters 3/; To Cr. ROBT. GILCHRIST on account Lawyer fee 0..15..0; The Credit Account July 11, 1749: By Ballance of sttg. accot. brot. from 84; August 23: By 1 hhd. tobacco on Gibsons; By transfer on do; September 1; By ballance carried to 276: 29..11..1; and 0..6..0.

(p. 241). July 17, 1749. The Debit Account of MRS. WINNY BEASLEY. To cloth; ribon, 3 hanks silk 3/; 2 1/2 yds. fine linen; The Credit Account November 6, 1749: To your accot. in L. B. 0..15..0 1/2 sttg.

(p. 241). July 17, 1749. The Debit Account of Collo. MONROE. To 7 hhds. tobacco (total 7151 lbs. at 16/8. 59..11..10; The Credit Account September 4, 1749: By Collo. THOMS. TURNER 59..11..10.

(p. 242). July 22, 1749; The Debit Account of THOS: WATSON; (Various kinds and amounts of cloth: buckram, sheeting, bro. linnen, shalloon, check); a bridle 1/10; 2 linen handkerchiefs 1/2; 1 lbs. sugar 8; 1 spring Knife; mans hatt 6/; powder & shott; 1/4 Rum; 1 gall. Rum; October 4: 1 worsted Cap 9d; Cash 5/9. The Credit Account November 6, 1749: By your accot. in L. B. 3..19..8 and 1..2..6 1/2.

(p. 243). July 24, 1749; The Debit Account of WILLIAM BARKSDALE. To your accot. brought from 17; with additional entries including 3 yds. duck; 300 small nails; 1/4 yd. bro. linne; 1 qt. mugg 1/; August 10: 2 single girths; October 10: pr. mens Com. shoes 5/; The Credit Account November 6, 1749: By your accot. in L. B. 10..6..6.

(p. 243). July 25, 1749. The Debit Account of Capt. JOHN TAYLOR. (one entry); To 1 barrel sugar 242 Nt. lbs. 4..4..8. The Credit Account: November 6, 1749: By your acct. in L. B. 4..4..8 Curry.

(p. 244). July 24, 1749. The Debit Account of MARY POWELL. (Various kinds and amounts of cloth); a small comb 6d; 3 linen handkerchiefs 4/; bushel salt 1/6; 6 lbs. sugar 3/; 1/2 gallon Rum 2/3; September 22: To 1 gall. Rum; To 3 felts 1/4; powder & shot; October 27: To pr. plad. hose; pr. yarn hose 4d; 1/4 Rum. The Credit Account July 24, 1749: By ballance brought from 61; By Cash; November 6, 1749. By your accot. in L. B. 0..5..10 1.2 and 0..5..0.

(p. 244). October 16, 1749: The Debit Account of JAMS: ROBERTS. To ballance brot. from 57: and a few additional entries including pr. mens shoes 4/; bushel Salt, linen handkerchief, pr. garters; To Cash 0..0..9. The Credit Account: November 6, 1749: By your accot. in L. B. 1..0..4; and 0..9.7.

(p. 245). July 24, 1749. The Debit Account of JOHN FARRILL. By yr. accot brought from 51: with additional entries including various kinds and amounts of cloth; a skillet 1/; 2 knives 1/; 3 lbs. bro. sugar 2/; linen handkerchief 10; To Cash 1..16..0; August 21: 7 yds. irish linen; 9 yds. white ditto; qt. Rum; To ballance of Curry. Accot. as pr. Contra; To 1 pr. rib'd hose; The Credit Account (undated 1749); By Gibsons Transfer; By ballance of Curry. due.; November 6, 1749: By your accot. in L. B. 0..3..4 and 3..15..0.

(p. 246). July 25, 1749: The Debit Account of WILLIAM FURLONG. A long account including various kinds and amounts of cloth; pins, thread; 1 wrapper 4/; sugar; oz. of nutts 9d; quart Rum; 1 pr. plad. hose; powder and shott; (several entries for Cash); pr. womens hose; dozen spoons 2/5; pr. garters 4d; bushel Salt; The Credit Account November 6, 1749: By your accot. in L. B. 12..12..0 1/2; and 1..12..3.

(p. 247). July 27, 1749. The Debit Account of REVD. MR. DAWSON. To cash 4..10..0; September 16: 1/2 lb. powder; 4 1/2 gallons Rum; September 26: 2 1/4 yds. serge denim; 1 hk. silk & doz. buttons 3d; 1 oz. thread 2d; 2 1/2 yds. jeans; 1/4 canvas 4d; November 3; To Ballance to L. B. The Credit Account: July 29, 1749: By Ballance brought from 3. 2..11..2 and 4..10..0.

(p. 247). July 29, 1749. The Debit Account of GRIFFIN MORRIS. (Account has 7 entries for Rum); 2 oz. indico; 1 oz. Cinamon; 1 oz. cloves; 1 pr. boys pumps 2/4; pr. large blanketts 14/8; 2 felts 1/3; 2 lbs. sugar; 1/2 lb. shoe thread; pr. womens shoes 2/4; The Credit Account November 6, 1749: By your accot. in L. B. 2..18..1 and 2..2..9 1/2.

(p. 248). July 27, 1749. The Debit Account of THOS: SANDERS. To 1 1/2 yds. duck; 1/4 brown thread; 1 qt. Rum; September 16: 4 yds. bro. linen 2/6; 1 large blanket; yd. of linen 1/5. The Credit Account September 18, 1749: By 1 1/4 yds. duck return'd; November 6, 1749: By your accot. in L. B. 0..12..6 sttg.

(p. 248). July 29, 1749: The Debit Account of RICHD. BURISKILL. To 1 pr. dble. C. Pumps returned; To 1 oz. nutts, 1 pr. shoe buckles; The Credit Account (undated) By small debts: 0..2..6 1/2.

(p. 249). August 1, 1749. The Debit Account of GILES SAMUEL. (one entry): To 1 quart Rum. Charg'd in L. B. fo. 3; No entries in Credit Account.

(p. 249). August 15, 1749: The Debit Account of JAMS: ARNOLD. To 4 1/2 yds. scarlett shalloon; cotton check; 1/2 m. pins; September 8: 4 yds. fine shalloon; yd. fine Irish linnenn 3/8; 1 silk handkerchief; September 25: 1 bridle 2/4; yd. fine linnen 2/4; glass tumbler 4 1/2; October 6: pr. womans shoes 2/6; doz. laces 5; 6 yds. bro. linnen 3/9; yd. ribon; 3 1/4 yds. white sheeting 1/; The Credit Account November 6, 1749: By your Accot. in L. B. 3..15..11 sttg.

(p. 250). August 3, 1749. The Debit Account of Mr. WILLM. BERRYMAN. To 1 pr. sizors. doz. small buttons; 100 wt. bro. sugar 36/; To Cash 1..14..0; November 1: To 1 chafing dish damg; 1/6; 2 bushels salt 3/; 1 Cullender 1/3; bottle snuff 2/; The Credit Account August 3, 1749: By Boyds Transfer 10 @ 13/; 420 @ 16/8; November 6,1749: By your accot. in L. B. 0..11..10 1/2 sttg.

(p. 250). October 16, 1749. The Debit Account of ROBT. WRIGHT. To ballance brot. from 90; To a small sifter; 3 yds. sacking, pr. small shoes 2/4; 5 prs. plad. hose; The Credit Account: November 6, 1749: By your accot. in L. B. 1..17..9 and 9..16..8.

(p. 251). August 3, 1749. The Debit Account of HENRY TERRILL. (one entry) To 2 casks Sugar 591 lbs. 35/. The Credit Account: August 3, 1749 By 1 hhd. tobacco on Conways 1180 @ 16/8; Cask; By Cash 0..7..2. to pay debit of 10..6..10.

(p. 251). August 10, 1749. The Debit Account of THOMAS AYRES. To ballance of Curry. Accot. brot. from 50; with additional entries for various kinds and amounts of cloth; sheeting, linnen, sacking, cotton, duck, check, kersey); thread, nails, taylors thimble 10d; 5 pewter plates 5/2; 4 pr. sleeve buttons 6d; 1 Crupper 8d; powder & shott; 5 pr. yarn hose 3/4; 1 loaf dble. sugar 7 lbs. 1/2; 1 lb. shoe thread; The Credit Account: August 10: By your ballance sttg. accot. brot. from 50: November 6, 1749: By ballance 5..11..9 1/2 and 10..16..2.

(p. 252). August 5, 1749. The Debit Account of ROBERT WALKER. To your accot. brought from 22; with additional entries for 2 handkerchiefs 2/6; 2 oz. nutts 1/3; 6 yds. Kersey 14/; October 16: To 1 watch key; October 31: To 1000 lbs. tobacco & cask, The Credit Account: November 6, 1749: By your accot. in Liber B. 22..6..5 Curry.

(p. 252). September 27, 1749. The Debit Account of JOHN THORNLEY. To 25 yds. Cotton 25/; To 1 mans fine hatt 4/6; 2 snaffle bridle 2/4; doz. small buttons 4d; 1/2 oz. nutts 4 1/2d; 6 lbs. brown sugar 2/; 1 linen handkerchief 9d; 1 bushel salt 1/6; 1 Qt. Rum 10 1/2d; 3 yds. Kersey 1/4; The Credit Account: November 6, 1749: By your accot. in L. B. 154; 1..7..10 sttg.

(p. 253). August 7, 1749. The Debit Account of JOHN BODINGTON. To 1 mans fine hatt 4/6; 1 claw hammer 8d; 6 yds. cotton 6/3; brown thread, bro. linen; plad 1/; 1/2 gallon Rum 2/; November 4; pr. hand saw files; powder & shott; The Credit Account: November 6, 1749: By your accot. in L. B. 2..9..2 and 0..3..6.

(p. 253). August 7, 1749. The Debit Account of ESTHER BELL. To 1 pr. mans gloves; 10 lbs. brown sugar 0..5..0; 1/2 m. pins 2 1/2; 3 yds. Irish Linnen. The Credit Account: November 6, 1749: By your accot. in L. B. 0..11..9 1/2; and 0..5..0.

(p. 254). August 9, 1749. The Debit Account of Mr. SAML. HIPKINS. To ballance brot from 32; with additional entries for various kinds and amounts of cloth; a dozen scarlett buttons; 1 Brass Cork 3 1/2; a silk handkerchief 3/6; 1 pint oyl Terpintine 1/2; 4 pewter dishes 18 1/2 lbs. 10 1/2; a tea kettle 7/6; 2 lbs. shoe thread 0..4..0; The Credit Account: November 6, 1749: By your accot. in L. B. 7..4..4 and 0..13..4.

(p. 255). August 10, 1749. The Debit Account of JAMS: WHITE (Caroline); To Ballance brought from 108; with additional entries for various kinds and amounts of cloth, white linnen, kersey, cotton, &c. To paid MRS. LONG 10/ curry; pr. plad hose 8/; 1/4 Rum 10 1/2d; powder & shott. bushel of salt; The Credit Account: November 6, 1749; By your accot. in L. B. 3..13..6 and 1..9..11.

(p. 255). September 16, 1749. The Debit Account of JAMS: REYNOLDS. (one entry): To 1/2 m. 3d. nailes; The Cedit Account (undated) "By small Debt book 1/3"

(p. 256). August 10, 1749; The Debit Account of Mr. GEO: RIDING includes various kinds and amounts of cloth check, white linnen, druggitt, kersey, damask, swanskin; thread, 1 pr. youths Pumps 2/4; pr. womens shoes 3/; brass candlestick 1/3; 1 fine hatt 4/6; 2 quire paper 1/4; 1 lb. Bohea Tea 4/6; The Credit Account: (undated 1749): By MOSES PITTMAN 700 lbs. tobacco @ 13/ 4..11..0.

(p. 256). October 16, 1749. The Debit Account of JAMES COLQUIT. To ballance brot. from 81; with additional entires for 2 1/2 yds. rattan; shott; 2 oz. thread; yd. fine linen 4/; doz. buttons; The Credit Account November 6, 1749: By your Accot. in L. B. 3..5..0 1/4; and 3..4..2.

(p. 257). August 13, 1749. The Debit Account of MOSES PITTMAN. To 1 lb. powder 1/; September 16: To 1/2 quire paper; 1 flowered pint 1/3; 1/2 gallon Rum 0..2..0; October 31: pr. plad. hose; 1/2 oz. nutts. The Credit Account: November 6, 1749: By your accot. in L. B. 0..4..7 1/2; and 0..2..0.

(p. 257). August 16, 1749. The Debit Account of Mr. WILL: GRAY. To 1 Chair Whip 0..10..10; October 21: To 1/2 yd. China Taffety; The Credit Account: November 6, 1749: By 1 pr. womens shoes 6/; By 1 Leghorn hatt 4/11; By Sundrys for the ballance of yr. Accot. ballanced at 2..5..1.

(p. 258). August 7, 1749: CASH: To brot. from folio 26: a number of entries for Rum; a spring knife 8d; nails, sugar, check, pr. hose; bushel salt; boys felt; 1 Testament; 4 pencils; a small bowle & 2 muggs; Earthenware; 1 glass; (carried forward). The Credit Account: August 22, 1749: By Accot. from 210; August 31: By GABL. LONG; September 1: By JAMES BOWLWARE, By Capt. WILLIAM TALIAFERRO; September 2: By WILLIAM FURLONG; By JOHN HOLLOWAY, By THOMAS MASSEY; September 4: By JOSEPH REYNOLDS, By. COLLO. TURNER; By JNO: HOLLOWAY; By EDWARD DIXON; By GABL. LONG; September 5: By JEREMIAH LONG; By JOHN BOWLWARE; By ROBT. WRIGHT; September 11: By JAMES DILLIARD; September 14: By ELIJAH WATTSON; By WILLIAM WATTSON JUNR., September 16: By JAMES WILLARD; By JOSEPH REYNOLDS; September 18: By GRIFFIN MORRIS; By FRAS. BALTHROPE; By SOLOMON EWELL; September 20: By JOS: REYNOLDS; By ANN MARSHALL; September 22: By GRIFFIN MORRIS; September 26: By JOHN BALTHROPE; September 27: By WILLIAM FURLONG, By JOHN PRINCE, By PRUE BENSON (error 10/2 now); By EDWARD DIXON; By Capt. JOHN MICOU; October 4: By sundrys; By EDWARD DIXON; By JOHN BROWN, By JOS; REYNOLDS; By PROU BENSON; By THOMAS PETROSS; By WILLIAM HUDSON; By THOMAS WATTSON; By JAMES BOWLWARE. (Carried forward).

(There are no pages numbered 260-273).

(p. 274). October 26, 1749: CASH: To Transfer tobacco on Laytons 8/9; To AUGUS. WEEDEN; October 27: To LUCY DINGLE; November 6, 1749: To Cash accot. in Retail. The Credit Account: October 4: By paid for 4 plain irons; By WILLIAM JAMISON; October 7: By JOS: SHIP; By WILLIAM FURLONG; By ARCHIBALD ALLAN; October 10: By GEO: BRASFIELD JUNR., By GRIFFIN MORRIS, By JOHN RAWLINGS; By EDWARD DIXON, By ELIZA: GIBSON; October 11: By EDWARD DIXON; October 14: By ADAM LINDSEY, October 16: By JOHN COLQUIT, By WILLIAM FOX, By JAMES ROBERTS; By WILLIAM JAMISON; October 19: By JOHN PRINCE; By EDWARD DIXON; By WILLIAM FURLONG; October 20: By JOHN WREN, By JOHN BOWTWELL, By Roys Inspection, By PRUE BENSON; By WILLIAM PARKER; By GABRIEL LONG; October 25: By ROBT. CALL; By GEO: BRASFIELD, October 26: By WILLIAM JOHNSTON; October 27: By JNO: PRINCE; By EDWARD DIXON; By PRUE BENSON; October 30: By ISSAC GREEN; By JOHN YOUNG; October 31; By Majr. SAML. SKINKER; November 1; By THOMAS PETROSS; By EDWARD DIXON; By GABL. LONG; By WILLIAM FOX; By Cash on hand carr'd to L. B; By paid Inspection of 5 hhds. tobo: Conways; By ditto at Mortons 3 hhds; By ditto at FREDERICKSBURG 1 hhd. & FALMOUTH 2; By paid Capt. KELSICK for Rum; By JOHN PRINCE

(p. 275). November 23, 1748. The Debit Account of EDWARD DIXON. (numerous entries in this account for Cash); To Cr. RICHARD CLATTERBUCK; To Cr. THOMAS EVANS; To Cash paid MARMADUKE THORPE; July 3, 1749: To ditto paid Capt. BURDON; 13th: To Cr. THOMAS EVANS; August 22: To Cr. HARRY TURNER for Molasses; To Cr. Mr. JOHN YOUNGER for Cask on four setts of ( ) 515..0..0; September 1: To Cr. FRANCIS BALTHROPE on accot. of MR. SIMPSON; 8th: To Roys Inspection for 2 hhds. O. BRANCH; Ditto for 3 ditto p the *BRITTANIA;* 11th: To JOHN PROSSER for work done by his Wife for Mrs. DIXON: 16th: To WILLIAM WREN for ditto; 28th: To Gibsons Transfer for 35 hhds. pr. *The Race;* To ditto for 21 hhds. in *The Brittania;* To ditto for 6 ditto in *The Orange;* November 1: To Cr. WILLIAM PINN; To Cash to K. G. Court; 6th: To Cr. CAPT. BURDON; To Mr. GILCHRIST for a Cask Biscuit; To Collo. TURNER for H: BERRYs Accot; To Collo. CHAMPE; May 2d: To CUTHBERT SANDYS;

(p. 276). September 1, 1749: The Debit Account of Majr. SAML. SKINKER. To ballance brot. forward from 210: with additional entries for various kinds and amounts of cloth; powder & shott; lb. green tea 6/8; To 1 best lock 3/9; To 1 Bridle 2/10; To the REVD. MR. SIMPSONs Accot. The Credit Account October 17: By ARCHIBALD ALLAN 0..13..4; By 1 pr. mens gloves 0..1..0; November 6: By Ballance to L. B. 10..15..8 and 25..1..8.

(p. 277). September 4, 1749: The Debit Account of JOSEPH REYNOLDS. By your accot. brot. from 130: with additional entries for pr. kid gloves; pr. womens shoes; powder & shott; 1 felt; bushel salt; 25 ells Ozna: Cash to W. FOX; nails, 2 clasp knives, pr. small shoes; buttons, thread; pins &c. The Credit Account September 4, 1749: By our Cr. brot. from 130: By 1 housing returned; By ballance sttg. accot. due; November 6, 1749; By your accot. in L. B. 14..11..2. and 29..2..0.

(p. 278). September 16, 1749; The Debit Account of WILLM. HARRISON. (K. George) To ballance brot. from 55; with additional entries including various kinds and amounts of cloth, canvas, white linen, shalloon, bro. linnen; coat buttons, pr. mens hose 3/3; 1 oz. nutts; 1 mans fine hatt 6/6; 1 fine hatt 4/; nails, paper, thread; powder & shott &c., The Credit Account: September 12, 1749: By 1 pr. small shoes return'd; November 6, 1749: By your accot. in L. B. 167: 5..17..0 sttg.

(p. 279). September 13, 1749: The Debit Account of Mr. GEO: TANKERSLEY; To ballance brot. from 162; with additional entries for a gross of Corks, a cork screw, 1 lb. chocolate; a claw hammer, 100 20d. nails; 1 garden spade; 1/2 yd. China Taffety; To an error; November 1: Accot. given in; The Credit Account November 6, 1749: By Gibsons Transfer; By your sttg. accot. in L. B.. 1..3..7 1/2; and 23..3..0.

(p. 279). 1748/9. BRAYS INSPECTION. To Notes reced; To 56 lbs. tobacco; The Credit Account February 3, 1748/9: By EDWARD DIXON for 7 hhds. June 23, 1749: By 9 hdds. pr. *The Friendship,* By a Transfer hhd. & cask; By 1 transfer note to Capt. DICKINSON; By 2 hhds. pr. *The Friendship.*

(p. 280). September 16, 1749: The Debit Accouint of NICHOS: WILLIARD. Various kinds & amounts of cloth: oznabrig, white linnen, check, tartan, linnen; powder & shott; thread, buttons, nails, silk handkerchief 3/3; 1 gun 25/; pr. Pumps 3/6; pr. mens hose 2/6; The Credit Account November 6, 1749: By your accot. in L. B. 5..5..3 1/2 sttg.

(p. 280). September 4, 1749: The Debit Account of WILLIAM PIN; To 1/2 yds. pipes; 1 flowered Cup 1/6; 1 lb. Ginger 1/3; 50 needles 3d; 1 lb. Pimento; 1 linen handkerchief; The Credit Account November 1, 1749: By EDWARD DIXON. 0..3..0; November 6: By your accot. in L. B. 0..8..3; and 0..11..3.

(p. 281). September 18, 1749: The Debit Account of EDWARD DIXON. To your accot. brot. forward from 143: 1 oz. cinamon; 1/4 ginger, 1 oz. nutts; 1/4 lb. Pimento; powder & shott; various kinds and amounts of cloth: kersey, china taffaty, cotton, dimity, &c., 2 womens caps; ribon, thread, buttons, plad hose; womens hose; pr. blanketts 10/; 1 worsted cap 1/3; 1 felt 1/2; The Credit Account (undated 1749); By sundrys sold in the Store (viz.) 7 black wiscoasts; 3 white do; 4 coats; 1 ditto boys do; 3 prs. stays; 3 1/2 doz. mustard; 24 gross pipes; 2 casks & 2 crates; 700 darning needles; 2000 worsted ditto; 20 lbs. Green Tea; 1 Fowling piece; By Sundrays sold Mr. SANDYS for Irish Linnens.

(p. 282). September 18, 1749. The Debit Account of DANIEL WHITE. To ballance brot. from 117: with additional entries for 2 prs. yarn hose; 2 lbs. shoe thread; 1/2 m. pins; 1 oz. nutts, 1 1/2 bushel Salt; The Credit Account November 6, 1749: By your Accot. in L. B. 1..3..5 1/2; and 7..5..9.

(p. 282). September 19, 1749: The Debit Account of JOHN BURK includes nails, cloth, red thread, white thread; a fine hatt 5/6; 1/2 m. pins, 1/2 bushel Salt; powder & shott: The Credit Account November 6, 1749: By your accot. in L. B. 2..2..7 sttg.

(p. 283). September 20, 1749: The Debit Account of HENRY BURK includes cotton, a mans fine hatt 6/6; a mans fine hatt 4/6; buttons, thread, 1 oz. indico 4d; nails, linnen, muzlin, kersey. The Credit Account November 6, 1749: By your Accot. in L. B. 2..12..9 1/4

(p. 283). September 20, 1749. The Debit Account of WILLIAM COATON. To your Accompt brot. from 110: with additional entries for linnen, salt, shalloon, oznabrig; thread, rum, pr. dble. C. pumps 8/; fine linen; plad. hose 1/3; The Credit Account November 6, 1749: By your Accot. in L. B. 10..17..11 sttg.

(p. 284). September 22, 1749. The Debit Account of CATHERINE REYNOLDS includes pr. mens hose 1/3; 1/2 yd. Callico 1/3; bushel Salt; 1 1/2 yds. Kersey 1/5; 6 yds. Cotton 1/2; linnen handkerchief; shoe thread; The Credit Account November 6, 1749: By your accot in L. B. 1..3..11 1/2.

(p. 284).September 22, 1749: The Debit Account of THOS: HARRISS. To your accot. brot. from 90; with additional entries including a quart of Rum 1/; 1 mans fine hatt 7/6; 4 yds. bro. linnen 4/8; 1 horn comb 3d; 1 bason 3/1; pr. shoes 5/. The Credit Account November 6, 1749: By muzlim return'd; By your accot. in L. B. 8..3..10 Curry.

(p. 285). September 26, 1749. The Debit Account of DANIEL WHITE. To your accot. brot. from 99; with additional entries for 5 yds. Callico 2/8; pr. mens gloves 2/8; 2 combs 6d; 8 yds. serge 9d; oznabrig, check, white linnen, buttons 1/2 lb. Allspice & 1 lb. giner; The Credit Account September 26, 1749: By your Cr. brot. from 99; November 5, 1749: By your accot. in L. B. 5..17..2 1/2.. and 1..1..8.

(p. 285). September 26, 1749. The Debit Account of EDWARD WARE. To ballance brot. from 15; with additional entries including 1 1/2 gall. Rum; 7 yds. cotton; 1 pr. hose;

2 yds. serge; thread, buttons, 2 razors 1/4; The Credit Account November 6, 1749; By your accot. in L. B. 2..11..6 and 0..7..1 1/2.

(p. 286). September 26, 1749. The Debit Account of JOHN BALTHROP. To ballance of sttg. Accot; from 110; with additional entries for various kinds and amounts of cloth; shalloon, oznabrig; irish linen, check, bro. linnen, muzlim, thread, hair sifter, bushel Salt; 1/2 gall. Rum; To AUGUS: WEEDEN; pins, The Credit Account November 6, 1749: By your accot. in L. B. 9..16..2 1/2 and 2..9..11.

(p. 287). September 1, 1749. The Debit Account of Mr. LEONARD HILL. (only entry: To your ballance brot. from 59). The Credit Account September 30, 1749: By allowance of 4478 lbs. tobacco; By ditto on 1333 lbs. November 6, 1749: By your bal-lance to L. B. 8..13..2; and 4..10..6.

(p. 288). September 22, 1749. The Debit Account of Capt. JOHN MICOU. To ballance brot. from (as pr. Accot. given in) 60; with additional entries including various kinds and amounts of cloth; shalloon, cotton, buckram, china taffaty, callimanco, a skillett 6 lbs. 6/; powder & shott; nails, 1 broad ax from BOWIE; 1 claw hammer 7d; 4 hks. silk 1/; To PATT; COUTTS; 1 cask of Butter. The Credit Account November 6, 1749: By your Accot. in L. B. 19..11..4 and 4..9..11.

(p. 289). October 3, 1749. The Debit Account of JOSEPH TUTT includes pr. mens hose 5/; 1 oz. red thread 3d; 6 yds. duffle 1/3; 3 yds. cotton 5/6; 4 yds. kersey 10/; 3 yds. cotton 2/; 1/2 yds. kersey 1/3; thread, pins, 3 porringers & jugg; 5 yds. bro. linen; The Credit Account November 6, 1749: By your Accot. in L. B. 3..17..5.

(p. 289). October 3, 1749. The Debit Account of BENJA: GRUBBS. To ballance brot. from 52; with additional entries including sundrys paid your Daughter 18/; salt, rum, sugar, 2 Taylors Thimbles 4d; 100 3d. nails 2d; 2 yds. Kersey 2/10; pr. womans hose 2/; The Credit Account November 6, 1749: By your Accot. in L. B. 3...6...9 sttg.

(p. 290). October 4, 1749. The Debit Account of THOS: BUTTERY includes coat & mettle buttons; cloth; bro. sheeting; shalloon, 2 oz. color'd thread; The Credit Account November 6, 1749: By your Accot. in L. B. 2..5..4 1/2.

(p. 290). October 4, 1749. The Debit Account of WILLIAM FIDLER includes cloth, shalloon, buttons, oznabrig thread; bro. linnen; brown linnen, pr. wool cards; The Credit Account November 6, 1749; By your accot. in L. B. 1..5..4 1/2.

(p. 291). October 4, 1749: The Debit Account of FRAS: CHANDLOR includes a sett of shoe tools 10/; 1/2 m. large pins 10d; 1 horn comb 3d; pr. mens shoes 7/; 1 carpenters rule 1/6; silk handkerchief 6/; a bason 3/; 1/2 gall. Rum 2/; yd. ribbon; sugar and various kinds and amounts of cloth. The Credit Account November 6, 1749: By your accot. in L. B. 2..11..8 1/2 Curry.

(p. 291). October 4, 1749. The Debit Account of ELIZA: RANKINS includes various kinds & amount of cloth; bro. linnen, shalloon, swanskin, sacking, buckram; buttons, pr. garters, a snaffle bridle 3/; hk. silk 4 1/2; needles; sugar, a razor 5d; pr. mens worsted hose; The Credit Account November 6, 1749: By your accot. in L. B. 1..17..9 sttg.

(p. 292). October 6, 1749. The Debit Account of JOHN BOON. To 7 yds. Cotton 1/2; 5 1/2 yds. Druggitt; 3 1/2 yds. plad 2/7; thread, a dozen spoons 2.5; 1/4 Rum 10 1/2; 1 fine felt 2/4; 1 horn comb, nails, bushel Salt; the Credit Account November 6, 1749: By your accot. in L. B. 1..12..9.

(p. 292). October 6, 1749. The Debit Account of AMBROSE BULLARD. (one entry); To 1 sett of shoe tools o..6..0 sttg. The Credit Account November 6, 1749: By your accot. in L. B. 0..6..0 sttg.

(p. 293). October 6, 1749. The Debit Account of JOHN BOWTWELL. To ballance brot. from 86; with additional entries including thread, 19 galls. Rum; pr. shoes; 2 yds. duffle 2/4; To JOHN PRINCE 1..10..0; To Cash 4..4..2 1/2; To pr. mens shoes 0..3..0. The Credit Account October 20, 1749: By Roys Crop 1 hhd. viz. MB 13..1221..106..1115.. 16/8; Cask; November 6, 1749: By your accot. in L. B. 1..4..6 sttg.

(p. 293). October 6, 1749: The Debit Account of WILLIAM PARKER. To ballance brot. from 27; with additional entries including 2 m. 4d nails; 2 m. do 7/; 3 lbs. bro. sugar 1/6; Paid JNO: WREN 1/8; To gall. Rum 4/; November 1: To 1 3/4 galls. Rum 7/; 1 lathing lhammer 1/8; 1 pr. mens hose 4/; The Credit Account November 6, 1749: By your accot. in L. B. 9..18..11 sttg.

(p. 294). October 10, 1749. The Debit Account of ELIZA BARTLETT. including 2 pr. yarn hose 1/4; 2 yds. plad 1/6; thread; plad hose 2/10; 1 ell ozna;; 50 Needles; 10 lbs. Sugar 3/4; pr. mens shoes 3/; 1/4 Rum 1/3; 1 ax 2/9; November 1: To 1 pr. small shoes 1/6; 2 linen handkerchiefs 2/8; 6 yds. Plad. 4/. The Credit Account November 6, 1749: By your accompt. in L. B. 4..3..2 and 0..4..3.

(p. 294). October 26, 1749. The Debit Account of WILLIAM JOHNSTON. including cloth, thread, 1 fine hatt 5/; narrow cloth; shalloon, dozen buttons, yd. of sheeting 1/; pr. garters 6d; 2 oz. thread 4d; 2 pr. yarn hose 1/; dozen pipes & a small lock; To Cash 0..3..9. The Credit Account November 6, 1749: By your accompt. to L. B. 1..10..9 and 0..3..9.

(p. 295). October 20, 1749. The Debit Account of JERH: STEVENS. including white linen, check, kersey, duck, oznabrig, dowlass, flannell, a bottle of snuff 1/8; necklace, 1 bridle 2/6; pr. worsted hose 1/10; powder & shott; thread; The Credit Account November 6, 1749: By your accot. in L. B. 3..18..10. sttg.

(p. 295). October 20, 1749. The Debit Account of MOSES HURT including cotton, brokin, sacking, kersey, white linnen, callico, shalloon, boys fine felt 4/; thread; 1 m. pins 9d; 3/4 hund. needles 6d; 1/2 m. large pins 5; a pr. Compass 3d; 1/2 lb. ginger & 1/2 lb. Allspice 1/2; 1 whip saw 10/; The Credit Account November 6, 1749: By your accot. in L. B. 5..0..3 1/2 sttg.

(p. 296). October 20, 1749; The Debit Account of JOHN BROWN including shalloon, white linnen, manx cloth; kersey, a tobacco box 1/3; pr. garters 4 1/2d; doz. buttons 6d; The Credit Account November 6, 1749: By your accot. in L. B. 3..1..2 and 0..15..1.

(p. 296). October 21, 1749. The Debit Account of STURMAN CHILTON. To ballance brot. from 79; with additional entries for a pr. hose 1/; pr. pumps 6/6; 1 linen handkercheif 2/; 3 lbs. sugar 1/10. The Credit Account November 6, 1749: By your accot. in L. B. 6..2..3 1/2 curry.

(p. 297). October 26, 1749: The Debit Account of Collo. THOS: TURNER including 2 yds. muzlim; your whole debt brot. from 4; To HENRY JOHNSTONs Accot; 6..12..0; To ballance in L. B. 1751: To Cr. WILLIAM MARSHALL; The Credit Account November 5, 1749; To your whole Cr. brot. from 4; November 6: By 24 hhds. tobo: reced; Ballance due this day 12,350; By WM. JAMISONs 926; By JOHN BOONs 998; By 1 of R. JOHNSTONs 984; February 26, 1750/1; By JOHN RODGERS 106; April 27, 1751: By ROBERT CALL; By FRANS; WOFFENDALE, By LEWIS JONES; By CHARLES WHARTON; By an omission.

(p. 298). 1749. The Debit Account of GABL. GRIFFITH, Merchant of WHITEHAVEN; By 4 Stills ship"d to BARBADOES; By Capt. RICHD. KELSICK; 1749/50: To Cash paid Capt. ARCHER for freight of the 4 Stills to NORFOLK; 1750: To Cash pd. Capt. KELSICK for freight of 8 hhds. Rum from BARBADOES; To ditto for ditto from NORFOLK; July 4th: To 12 tons Pig Iron pr. *FRIENDSHIP,* To duties on 1083 1/2 gallons Rum @ 4d/ 18..1..2; 1751: To pd. Capt. KELSICK for 2 hhds. Rum from BARBADOES; May 24th: To 12 hhds. tobacco ship'd you p *DUKE of CUMBERLAND,* nett 11310 lbs; To 12 casks 30 lbs. each; To 8 hhds. tobacco ship'd you pr. *The How,* July 10, 1752: To 5 hhds. Tobo. shipt. you in *The How,* Capt. WALTERS nett 5018; 5 casks @ 30 each; The Credit Account: 1749: By 1 Copper Still 3..0..17; 17d; 1 Pewter worm 1..1..1 1/; By 1 ditto 2.2.20 1/5; 1 pewter worm 1..0..0 1/5; By ditto 2..2..17 1/5; 1750: By 8 hhds. Rum reced of Capt. RICHARD KELSICK; By Sundry goods pr. *The Peace ;* July 14th: By a sett of Excha: payable to JOHN SPOTSWOOD Esqr., for 56..15..11 Sterling; By 2 hhds. Rum of Capt. RICHARD KELSICK; By balla. of the Stills as pr. Accot. Currt. from BARBADOES; (See Ledger G., folio 219).

(pp. 299-309 are blank.)

(p. 310). (undated 1748). The Debit Account of Mr. JOSEPH BARWISE. To 20 m. Needles returned; To loss in 5 crates of pipes one fourth; To 4 hhds. tobacco ship'd you in *The Brittania,* To 8 ditto in *The Orange.* Inspection of 12 hdds. tobacco at 3/. curry. 20 pr. ct. ded.d, Jun 11, 1750: To 1 box of shoes on hand; July 10: to 10 hhds. tobacco ship'd you pr *The Blackwell,* nett 10322; Inspecting of 10 hhds. Commisson 162..10..0 at 15 pr. cent; July 25, 1750: To ballance as per contra. The Credit Account 1749: By sundry goods as pr. Invoice; By diito P. NELSON; By ditto pr. *The Friendship,* July 25, 1750: By ballance due EDWD. DIXON; July 25, 1750: By a box of shoes when sold (See Ledger H. folio 176). Total Credit 175..5..10 1/2.

(p. 311). (undated 1748). The Debit Account of Collo. THOS; TURNER. To sundry good of Mr. TIMOTHY NICHOLSONs accot. as pr. Invoice; To part of BARWISEs goods amotg. to 79..12..10. The Credit Account (undated 1748). By 63 hhds. tobacco ship'd in *The Peace,* nett weight 62572; By 20 ditto pr. *The Brittania,* By 83 casks; By r hhds. pr. *The Brittania;* By 8 ditto pr. *The Orange;* By 12 casks;

(p. 312). (undated 1749). The Debit Account of Mr. TIMOTHY NICHOLSON. To 63 hhds. tobacco ship'd you in *The Peace* nett weight 62372; To 20 ditto in *The Brittania,* nett 19667; Inspection of 83 hhds. tobo; at 3/ Curry. Commission on 428..17..1 2/4 at 5 pr. cent; The Credit Account: By sundry goods sold Collo. THOMAS TURNER amotg. to 418..17..10 3/4; To ballance as pr. account currt. sent. 31.. 8..4. 1749: By a Sett of Excha: favor Collo. JNO. CHAMPE 31..8..4.

(Unnumbered page) 1749. DR. Mr. JOHN YOUNGER Commissions. To the Ship *FRIENDSHIP* Disbursements; 1750 To ditto for ditto; To sundry freights in the River & other charges; To paid for a Flat; To duty on 20 hhds. Rum; To Inspection of 595 hhds. tobo. @ 3/; To pd. for 300 bushels of Salt 50..0..0; To 500 hhds. Staves; Tobacco shipt. in ye *FRIENDSHIP*, 248 hhds. 153776; Ditto in *BETTY & JENNY*, 50 hhds 49760; 1750: ditto in *FRIENDSHIP* 247 hhds. 247963; Ditto in *NORFOLK*, 50 hhds. 50001; 595 hhds. @ 30 each; To my Commisson on 130472 tobo: @ 3/

(The Commission Account of Mr. JOHN YOUNGER extend through 1771. These accounts and several other merchants with commission accounts will appear in subsequent books in the appropriate time periods.)

www.ingramcontent.com/pod-product-compliance
Lightning Source LLC
LaVergne TN
LVHW061251100826
845148LV00008B/1097
9781680341102